"I relate to Rubén Funkahuatl Gueva~~~ ~~~ ~~~~~~ ~~ spent his early youth in Santa Monica like me, not because we went through the '60s side by side on the Sunset Strip, but because he is obsessed with the creative process. It's in his blood. He gets sidetracked by constantly, impulsively, being caught under the spell of the Goddess, but art is his lifeline as it is mine. Respect."

—JOHN DENSMORE, author of *Riders on the Storm: My Life with Jim Morrison and the Doors*

"Rubén Funkahuatl Guevara, L.A.'s irrepressible impresario and 'culture sculptor,' is a generous mentor and consummate collaborator. In these pages, he takes us on a candid tour of the steps and missteps that have shaped his outlook, creativity, and public productions. Part confessional, part manifesto, these writings map his evolution, through family migrations, rock 'n' roll highs, personal lows, and collaborations with diverse activists and artists. With a keen sense of history, and mining his compulsions and desires with candor, Guevara has penned a powerful love letter to his greatest muse of all, his 'beloved, unpredictable city of multihued angels.'

—SOJIN KIM, CURATOR, Smithsonian Center for Folklife and Cultural Heritage

"Hilarious and heartbreaking, Guevara's memoir chronicles decades of artistic and spiritual fire. I cannot recommend this work highly enough as a wonderful and wonder-filled resource for students of multicultural Los Angeles, Chicano masculinities and identities, the music industry, performance art, and spiritual seekers in the Southwest. Since it is a treat to read and a joy to teach, I urge my colleagues to share *Confessions of a Radical Chicano Doo-Wop Singer* with their students."

—JACQUELINE M. HIDALGO, author of *Revelation in Aztlán: Scriptures, Utopias, and the Chicano Movement*

"With provocative observations and original insights, this illuminating musical history also incorporates poetry, performance, and education. Guevara engagingly chronicles a lifetime of financial and emotional ups and downs with honesty and vulnerability. As a meditative 'funk monk,' Guevara treats art as a political-spiritual calling."

—ANTHONY MACÍAS, author of *Mexican American Mojo: Popular Music, Dance, and Urban Culture in Los Angeles, 1935–1968*

"A man sings and in his singing he carries the grace, pains, missteps, and triumphs of his life. Guevara's memoir is such a song—*de aquellas y* beyond. A *con safos* defiance against systemic injustices and erasures of Chicanos and all oppressed people, Guevara's book is also flesh and bone, blood and brains, beauty and truth. Sing on, brother, sing on."

—LUIS J. RODRIGUEZ, author of *Always Running: La Vida Loca—Gang Days in L.A.*

"Guevara utilizes intimate vignettes and inspiring poetry to chart his personal and artistic evolution into an 'artivist,' a socially committed artist. His memoir is also an invaluable academic resource, documenting an extensive yet long-ignored history of L.A.'s cross-cultural artistic hybridity and the sociopolitical contributions exemplified by Guevara's fifty-year career."

—TEREZITA ROMO, author of *Malaquias Montoya*

"Rubén Funkahuatl Guevara, polymath Azteca warrior and Chicano superhero—it is difficult to imagine that there was ever a Los Angeles without him. It was as if he rose with the first East Los Aztlán sun that gave creative light to the barrio. In this book, Guevara gives us the opportunity to grab hold of his belt loop and walk with him through his sometimes glad and sometimes sad but always inspiring life. Hang on tight."

—LOUIE PÉREZ, musician, songwriter with Los Lobos

"Rock's greatest untold story is Chicano rock, and doo-wop is its bedrock. Guevara, with his long experience and deep commitment to both the sound and the Chicano community, is the perfect writer to tell the tale. He's one hell of a storyteller, too, and this is one hell of a story."

—DAVE MARSH, veteran of *Creem Magazine* and *Rolling Stone* and biographer of Bruce Springsteen

SIMPSON

The publisher and the University of California Press Foundation gratefully acknowledge the generous support of the Simpson Imprint in Humanities.

Confessions of a Radical Chicano Doo-Wop Singer

AMERICAN CROSSROADS

Edited by Earl Lewis, George Lipsitz, George Sánchez, Dana Takagi, Laura Briggs, and Nikhil Pal Singh

Confessions of a Radical Chicano Doo-Wop Singer

Rubén Funkahuatl Guevara

With an introduction by
George Lipsitz and Josh Kun

UNIVERSITY OF CALIFORNIA PRESS

University of California Press, one of the most distinguished university presses in the United States, enriches lives around the world by advancing scholarship in the humanities, social sciences, and natural sciences. Its activities are supported by the UC Press Foundation and by philanthropic contributions from individuals and institutions. For more information, visit www.ucpress.edu.

University of California Press
Oakland, California

Library of Congress Cataloging-in-Publication Data

Names: Guevara, Ruben, author.
Title: Confessions of a radical Chicano doo-wop singer / Rubén Funkahuatl Guevara ; with an introduction by George Lipsitz and Josh Kun.
Description: Oakland, California : University of California Press, [2018] | Includes bibliographical references and index. |
Identifiers: LCCN 2017049896 (print) | LCCN 2017054483 (ebook) | ISBN 9780520969667 (Epub) | ISBN 9780520297227 (cloth : alk. paper) | ISBN 9780520297234 (pbk. : alk. paper)
Subjects: LCSH: Guevara, Ruben. | Rock musicians—United States—Biography. | Mexican American musicians—California, Southern—Biography.
Classification: LCC ML420.G925 (ebook) | LCC ML420.G925 A3 2018 (print) | DDC 782.42166092 [s B]—dc23
LC record available at https://lccn.loc.gov/2017049896

Manufactured in the United States of America

26 25 24 23 22 21 20 19 18
10 9 8 7 6 5 4 3 2 1

Dedicated to my family

The memory of my beloved parents:
Sara Casillas-Gutiérrez Guevara and
Rubén Ladrón de Guevara Sr.

Sisters: Linda Marie Guevara-Reid,
Bonita Sara Guevara-Mavros,
Loretta Vickie Guevara-Vanni, and their families

Brothers: Mariano, Miguel, and Rafael Ladrón de Guevara,
and their families

Sons: Ben L. Guevara and family, Rubén G. Guevara III
and family

Daughter: G. B. G.

Cousin: Doña Marie Guevara-Hill and family

Cristina, Adriana, and Gabriel Shallcross and family;
Bob and "Chata" Manley and family; tía Hortencia, Adriana,
and Blanca Rivera and family

The Casillas, Gutiérrez, Becerra, Primo,
and Galván families,
from barrio La Veinte, Ese Eme, Santa Monica

c/s

What matters most is how well you walk through the fire.

There is always something left to love.

CONTENTS

ACKNOWLEDGMENTS

The genesis of this book came when Josh Kun introduced me to George Lipsitz at the "disChord: One Nation Under a Groove" conference at UCLA in 1997. George suggested that I write my memoir, but my crazy life and lack of writing confidence got in the way. Then, in 2012, approaching my seventieth birthday, I was sitting behind them at the Johnny Otis memorial, and after the inspiring service and George's stirring testimonial, I turned to them and said, "Well, I guess it's time to write the book while I'm still kicking." Three years later, with their rock-steady commitment and brotherly mentorship, I finished it. Thank you, George, Josh, and UC Press for finding value in my life and work. Forever grateful to the UC Press staff, Niels Hooper, Bradley Depew, Dore Brown, Claudia Smelser, Jolene Torr, Peter Perez, and my exceptional copy editor Anne Canright, as well as the original reviewers of the manuscript. A special thank you to my devoted friend, assistant, and *curandera* Eréndira Bernal.

Thanks to the following for opening and strengthening my heart with the inspiration that shaped my life and this book:

Music: My father, Rafael Méndez, Johnny Ace, Johnny Otis, the Penguins, the Flamingos, the Jaguars, Jesse Belvin, Don & Dewey, Little Richard, Ritchie Valens, Lil' Julian Herrera, Carlos Brothers, Bo Diddley, James Brown, Bobby "Blue" Bland, Aretha Franklin, Tina Turner, Frank Zappa, Gil Scott-Heron, Béla Bartók, Igor Stravinsky, Los Lobos, the Eastside Luvers, Quetzal, Roco/Maldita Vecindad, "Atomic" Nancy Matoba

Literature: Oscar Zeta Acosta, Rodolfo "Rudy" Acuña, Carlos Castañeda, Charles Bukowski, Wanda Coleman, Pablo Neruda, John Steinbeck, John Fante *(Ask the Dust),* Charles Mingus (memoir), Don Snowden,

Gloria Anzaldúa, Cherríe Moraga, Gloria Enedina Álvarez, Patti Smith, Joy Harjo, John Trudell, Luis Javier Rodriguez, Luis Alberto Urrea, José Montoya, Rubén Martínez, Kamau Daáood, Carey McWilliams, Eckhart Tolle, Craig Werner, Ann Powers

Activism: Lucio Cabañas, Dolores Huerta, César Chávez, Kathy Masaoka (NCRR), Mo Nishida (Manzanar Pilgrimage), traci kato-kiriyama, David Monkawa, Victor Shibata (Ministers and Yellow Brotherhood, Manzanar Pilgrimage), NCRR 9/11 Planning Committee, Karen Ishizuka, Robert Nakamura, Craig and Gayle Wong, Suzy Katsuda, Fr. Greg Boyle, Carrie Morita, Mike Murase, Jim "The General" Matsuoka (Black Juans from J-Flats), June Hibino, Evelyn Yoshimura, Jenni Kuida, Tony Osumi and Maiya

Visual art: Salvador Dalí, Los Tres Grandes (Diego Rivera, José Orozco, Davíd Siqueiros), John Altoon, Los Four (Carlos Almaraz, Gilbert "Magu" Luján, Frank Romero, Beto de la Rocha), John Valadez, Francesco X. Siqueiros, Judithe Hernández, Yreina Cervántez, Margaret Garcia, Barbara Carrasco, East Los Streetscapers (Wayne Alaniz Healy and David Botello), Paul Botello, Chaz Bojórquez, Arturo Urista, Ofelia Esparza. Photography: Manuel Álvarez Bravo, Loomis Dean, Annie Leibovitz, George Rodriguez

Theater/performance art: Eugene Ionesco, Jerzy Grotowski, Sam Shepard, Luis Valdez, Peter Sellars, Guillermo Gómez-Peña, Hanay Geiogamah, Harry Gamboa Jr., Nobuko Miyamoto (Great Leap), Dan Kwong, Kristina Wong, Casa 0101 Theater, Culture Clash, Susan Tanner (TheaterWorkers Project), Oliver Mayer, Sankai Juko, Asco

Film: Federico Fellini, Ingmar Bergman, Stanley Kubrick, Andrei Tarkovsky, Carlos Reygadas Barguín, Akira Kurusawa, Alejandro Jorodowsky, Charles Laughton (*Night of the Hunter*), John Huston (*Duel in the Sun*), Cheech Marín (*Born in East L.A.*)

Firme friends: Rodolfo "Rudy" Acuña, Lou Adler, Steve Alaniz, Martin Albornoz, Elsa Flores Almaraz, Pablo and Yvonne Amarillas, Mario Araujo, Lucero Arellano, Nico Avina, Lee Ballinger, Ramón Banda, Aurelio José Barrera, Max Benavidez, Pepper Black, David and Lupe Botello, Denny Bruce, Rude Calderon, Rafael Cárdenas, John Cantú, Jill Carol, Juan Carrillo, Michael Centeno, Theresa Chavez, Tommy Chong, Jeff Chop, Christopher Dean, Emmanuel Deleage, John Densmore, Pamela Des Barres, Yvette Doss, Shannon Dudley, Armando Durón, Ofelia Esparza y *familia*, Quetzal Flores, Richard and Shari Foos, Sesshu Foster, Helen Funai, Harry Gamboa Jr. Joel

García, Oscar Garza, Ana Maria Garcia-Gomez, Hanay Geiogamah, Martha Gonzalez, Jeanie Greenman, Sergio Ladrón de Guevara, Clement Hanami, Wayne and Romelia Alaniz Healy, Beverly Helm, Barbra Hernandez, Maceo Hernandez, Willie Herrón III, Jacqueline M. Hidalgo, Leslie Ito, Falling James, Gaye Theresa Johnson, Renée Karst, Elaine Katzenberger Sojin Kim, Tarabu Betesari Kirkland, Dan Kwong, Gary Leonard, Walter Little, Josefina López, Willie Loya, Steve Loza, *Familia* Luján, Christine Ma, Anthony Macías, María Madrigal, Cheech Marín, Jacqueline Martinez, Dave Marsh, Emiliano Meno Martinez, John Martinez, "Atomic" Nancy Matoba, Yaotl Mazahua, Rubén Martínez, Rubén Mendoza, Marisol Berríos-Miranda, Kathleen Mitchell, Judy Mitoma, Nobuko Miyamoto and family, Shin Miyata, Adrian Monge, Carol Montgomery, Moses Mora, Emilio Morales, Chris Morris, Brendan Mullen, Ricardo F. Muñoz, Mike Murase, Steve and Patty Nagano, Al Nodal, Rick Noguchi, Marisela Norte, Victor Ochoa, Rick Ortega, Michelle Habell-Pallan, Miguel Paredes, Louie Pérez, Stella Pérez, María Ramos, Eddie Resto, Bob Robles, George Rodriguez, Reyes Rodriguez, Rudy Rodriguez, Silvia Rodriguez, Luis J. and Trini Rodríguez, Terezita Romo, Jennifer Sánchez, Melissa Sanvicente, Peter Sellars, Francesco X. Siqueiros, Don Snowden, Mike Sonksen, Jackie Stains, Gary Stewart, Lorraine Suzuki, Binnie Sykes, Josie Talamantez, Michelle Tellez, Jesús Treviño, Guillermo Uribe, John M. Valadez, Kathleen Vickroy, Victor Hugo Viesca, Katie Volk, Tommy "Flash" Volk, Bill Watanabe, Jonny Whiteside, Isabel Rojas-Williams, Kristina Wong, Michael and Lilly Yanagita, Alliance for California Traditional Arts, Eastside Arts Initiative, Apollos, 1958.

Introduction

THE FIRE AND FLAMES OF FUNKAHUATL

Josh Kun and George Lipsitz

HENRY DAVID THOREAU CONTENDED THAT the great majority of people live lives of quiet desperation. Rubén Funkahuatl Guevara has known despair in his life, but he has never been quiet about it, or complicit with it. In *Confessions of a Radical Chicano Doo-Wop Singer* he looks back on more than seventy years of a life filled with struggle to act joyfully, to create boldly, to love freely, and to live fully. The colorful and chaotic sprawling succession of experiences, identities, and achievements that appear on these pages might seem to exceed what a single life can contain. If *Confessions of a Radical Chicano Doo-Wop Singer* appeared as a work of fiction, it might seem improbable, even implausible. But history is not bound by the logic or reason of fiction. It creates unpredictable people who do unexpected things. Rubén Funkahuatl Guevara is one of them.

How you see the history of popular music in post-WWII Los Angeles has always depended on where you're standing. Viewed from Sunset Boulevard, you might be blinded by star-dusted names like the Doors and Buffalo Springfield. From the beaches, you might be staring into the sun of the Beach Boys. But if, like Rubén Funkahuatl Guevara, your favorite view is from the Sixth Street bridge, the one that straddles the L.A. River and connects downtown to East Los Angeles, then the city you hear sounds a little different: Chicano doo-wop, blues, and funk, rock *en español* soaked in ska blasting from backyard parties, Japanese *taiko* drums pounding in parking lots down the street from a mariachi plaza and a Jewish synagogue. If the beach and the

Sunset Strip are your centers, then Guevara is a marginal figure. But if the bridge is your center, if your west is east, if your north is south, if the river that fed the founding plaza of this global pueblo is your point of reference, then Guevara is a rainmaker, one of L.A.'s greatest musical heroes, who has never stopped believing in the redemption and deliverance that thrive in the city's underground networks of community, culture, and change.

Guevara is best known to the general public as a musician—as the "Ruben" of the 1970s popular music group Ruben And The Jets, as an influential architect of Chicano R & B, as the producer of landmark compilations of Chicano music, as a key spokesman for Latin American rock *en español* in L.A., and as of this writing, still a working solo artist honing his craft in the bars of Boyle Heights. As he delineates on these pages, however, he has had many other musical identities and personas, performing at different times as one of the Apollo Brothers, as Jay P. Mobey, as Aztec Watts, and as Lord Funkahuatl.

Moreover, music has only been one facet of his creative life. *Confessions of a Radical Chicano Doo-Wop Singer* reveals Guevara's restless and relentless creativity across different art forms as a playwright, poet, performance artist, activist, author, music critic, actor, and arts institution programmer. For Guevara, to be an artist is not to "make art" in any conventional aesthetic or market-driven sense, but to live life as art, to approach life as an experiment with—and a struggle over—the politics of form, style, and imagination. His creations resonate within the spaces of political and cultural activism where music is community glue, within the classrooms and community centers where he works with disadvantaged youth, all informed by his experiences as a working-class Chicano who has witnessed firsthand the hardships of labor and cultural exploitation in his own life and in the lives of those around him.

In this memoir, Guevara recalls his youthful experiences in the La Veinte barrio of Santa Monica in the 1940s, with subsequent moves by his family to a variety of neighborhoods throughout California and Nevada. These prepared him for early success in music as a teenage member of the Apollo Brothers rhythm and blues group. He explains how a career in music led to the exhilaration of performing side by side with Frank Zappa, Tina Turner, and Celia Cruz; appearing in films with Cheech and Chong; opening for Deodato in New York's Central Park and for the Doobie Brothers at the San Diego Sports Arena; performing in chic nightclubs like Max's Kansas City one week after Bob Marley and one week before Bruce Springsteen; and leading his band on a stadium tour with Marc Bolan and T-Rex, Mitch Ryder, and Three Dog Night. The life of a touring musician made it easy for him to indulge in the pleasures of alcohol, marijuana, and LSD. He relates how the rowdy behavior of Ruben And The Jets once got them banned from every Holiday Inn in the nation.

Part of this saga also includes that other part of the "sex, drugs, and rock and roll" cliché, but here sex—and love, and lust—take on a charge that produces particular results with Guevara. He relates how his onstage charisma and seemingly insatiable erotic drives and desires opened the door to a long, lover-man chain of sexual and romantic adventures (often with Tantric and shamanistic inflections). His narrative reveals an oft-remarked truism of music's relationship with desire, that performing music in public can be a sexually charged activity: a way to be noticed, admired, and coveted, a path toward interpersonal passion and pleasure. At moments in this book, Guevara's openness about intimacy resembles the seemingly endless, and mythic, romantic and sexual encounters and assignations that jazz musician Charles Mingus deployed in his book *Beneath the Underdog* to demonstrate the centrality of erotic desire to his personal and artistic life, and its complicated and often violent and destructive role in the shaping of his racial and gender identity.[1] Yet as other parts of the book show, a plenitude of sexual partners is not sufficient to fend off loneliness and isolation; these sections parallel the discussions in *Divided Soul* by David Ritz that contrast Marvin Gaye's popularity as a sex symbol and the singer's inability to establish reciprocal, mutually respectful relationships with actual women.[2] As for so many other straight male entertainers of his era, the chronic attempt to conquer female fans had become part of the power dynamics of the male-dominated music industry, where misogyny and male sexual power were (and continue to be) common features of touring life. Frank Sinatra boasted that all men were animals, and so as a man "I'm just looking to make it with as many women as I can."[3] Sam Cooke's widow recalled that her husband had an "insatiable" need for attention from women.[4] Johnny Otis noted in his memoir that life as a working musician in the 1940s and 1950s was like "swimming

1. Charles Mingus, *Beneath the Underdog: His World as Composed by Mingus* (New York: Vintage, 1991).

2. David Ritz, *Divided Soul: The Life of Martin Gaye* (Cambridge, Mass.: Da Capo Press, [1985] 1991).

3. Quoted in Anthony Summer and Robbyn Swan, *Sinatra: The Life* (New York: Vintage, 2006), 52.

4. Edward J. Boyer, "The Soulful Legacy of Sam Cooke," *Los Angeles Times,* December 23, 1994 (http://articles.latimes.com/1994–12–23/news/mn-12372_1_sam-cooke/2; accessed February 4, 2017).

in a sea of beautiful women."[5] For Guevara, erotic desire fueled creativity and served as motivation and reparation for the hardships of life on the road and the economic uncertainty of work in the music industry, where more performers lose money than make money.

To be sure, there are moments in *Confessions* when Guevara—like Mingus before him—may be a little too frank about his macho womanizing, and overly indulges his sexual and romantic appetite on the pages of this written memoir. He delineates in fine detail the exact physical features of the many women who entranced him and describes carefully his own approaches and techniques of making love to them. Yet for all their focus on visual stimuli, these accounts are concerned with more than the purely physical. His *desire for desire* fuels expectations of mystical connections and romantic fulfillments so intense that very few real relationships could fulfill them. Time and time again, when reality fails to conform to the intensity of the dream, when ordinary and everyday worries, tensions, and frustrations reemerge, the relationships dissolve, sometimes amicably and sometimes angrily, but always awkwardly.

The artistic and erotic aspects of Guevara's life story emanate from the same place. He sees the flaws in the "what is" and desires the "what can be." Creative artistry and erotic adventures promise connection to others; they require cooperation, trust, reciprocity, attention, affection, and intimacy. Both artistry and eroticism channel bodily hunger and pain, nervous energy, and alienation into moments of triumphant passion and pleasure. Yet Guevara also recognizes the costs of his sexual fixations, which he continually reassesses, critiques, and attempts to conquer. At a crucial moment in the memoir, Guevara, realizing that he has attached too much of his self-worth to his sexuality, creates the "Tao of Funkahuatl," a philosophy designed to move sex from the center of his psyche in the hopes of helping himself and other men to become "less dogs and better lovers. Better husbands. Better fathers. Better men."

Part of the motive behind Guevara's extended discussions of sexuality in this book is to diagnose his struggles with what Audre Lorde famously called—in an influential 1978 essay about the historically denigrated power of the erotic within women—the inherent link between eros and chaos. "The erotic," she writes, "is a measure between our sense of self and the chaos of our strongest feelings." Guevara's early fascination with the erotic power of

5. Johnny Otis, *Upside Your Head! Rhythm and Blues on Central Avenue* (Hanover, N.H.: Wesleyan/University Press of New England, 1991), 89.

women shows up in these pages, as does his fear of the chaos that his own eros brings. He is likewise frank about the consequences of making erotic desire a primary motivation for his work: emptiness, solitude, depression, and the destruction of some of his most important personal relationships. Writing from a queer-of-color standpoint very different from Guevara's cis-gendered heteronormative masculinity, Lorde explains that women like her have been taught to distrust the erotic, while heterosexual men have been taught to embrace and manipulate it, at women's expense. Because the erotic is a source of power, she explains, every form of oppression has a stake in corrupting or distorting it. While women learn to fear the erotic, men are socialized to demean and trivialize it, to reduce it to sensation, to use the feelings of others rather than share their own. "Use without the consent of the used," she writes, "is abuse." If used properly, however, the erotic can be a source of liberation. When in touch with the erotic, Lorde maintains, "I become less willing to accept powerlessness, or those other supplied states of being which are not native to me, such as resignation, despair, self-effacement, depression, self-denial."[6] For Guevara, male desire can be like a knife: a productive tool if grabbed by the handle but a source of self-destruction if grasped by the blade. In these pages, Guevara crafts a unique meditation on Chicano hetero-masculinity, writing about the cage of his masculinity and opening up about a decade of sexual abstinence.

Toward the end of his narrative Guevara presents a rare glimpse into the sex life of an older adult. Now in his seventies, he recognizes that he still longs for sexual pleasure and personal connection, but also that what he refers to as "the dog" in him needs to be contained and controlled. Motivated in part by the long period of abstinence, and marked as well by the sad recognition that the personal attractiveness he could always count on in his youth to smooth the path toward sexual and romantic connections works differently in his senior years, he is forced to concede that the younger women he still desires no longer view him in the ways to which he had become accustomed. Yet this realization also frees him in a certain way. The unasked-for celibacy motivates him "to sculpt my spirit, sex, funk, and soul onto the path of the Beloved while living my life as a work of art." He writes lyric verses and songs

6. Audre Lorde, "The Uses of the Erotic: The Erotic as Power," in *Sexualities and Communication in Everyday Life: A Reader,* edited by Karen E. Lovaas and Mercilee M. Jenkins (Thousand Oaks, Calif.: Sage, 2007); available at https://uk.sagepub.com/sites/default/files/upm-binaries/11881_Chapter_5.pdf.

expressing his new beliefs, and forges them into a song cycle that he records as *The Tao of Funkahuatl*.

These are not the only struggles he shares. The numerous sexual escapades recounted in this narrative—often with a sense of joy, often with clear desperation—take place in the context of a long and repeatedly frustrated search for romantic fulfillment, lasting relationships, spiritual connection, and an ever-elusive knowledge of self. They also reverberate with the arduous tasks of making a living. The same person who stayed in luxury hotels while on tour was also the man who found himself at times functionally homeless, living out of his car and plugging away at low-wage jobs in order to survive. Guevara's seductive brushes with stardom were accompanied by crushing disappointments caused by unpaid fees and royalties, by recordings that were insufficiently promoted or not even released, and by disastrous live performances undermined by the egos of other musicians or the incompetence and bad faith of promoters.

Guevara punctures the sensational myths that many fans have about the music business. This is not an ode to celebrity stardom and financial success. He gives us the music industry as work, as a grind, as a constant battle to create in the face of the demands and limits of commerce. To be sure, there are many triumphant moments on stage, stories about magnificent recording sessions, and the pride of accomplishment that comes from favorable reviews and adulation from fans. Yet Guevara also demonstrates in excruciating detail that a career in music requires attention to many different kinds of nettling, petty, and onerous tasks: putting bands together, supervising practice sessions, writing arrangements, designing sets, creating choreography, choosing costumes, setting up equipment, arranging travel, and generating publicity. In this book, "show business" is as much about the inner workings of the business as it is about the spectacle of the show. "Playing" music turns out to be a lot more work than play.

Confessions of a Radical Chicano Doo-Wop Singer is not a conventional musician's biography: it concerns itself with more than a linear musical career. Guevara recounts how his seeking spirit, unquenchable curiosity, and irrepressible artistic imagination led him to studies in the World Arts and Cultures Department at UCLA. His senior thesis advisors there were the renowned opera and theater director Peter Sellars and founder of the American Indian Dance Theater Hanay Geiogamah (Kiowa). For his senior project Guevara created the kind of cross-cultural mixed media work that has characterized his oeuvre ever since, fusing East L.A. rhythm and blues with

Native American ritual shamanism and Japanese butoh dance theater to tell an unconventional history of Los Angeles. A stand-alone performance piece, *Funkahuatl Speaks,* emerged from that project. In it, Guevara poured water over his head as he emerged from a large plastic bag, mimicking the experience of birth. After reciting the spoken-word prose poem and song "C/S," his powerful counterhistory of Los Angeles, he and his young son, Rubén III, threw pieces of candy from around the world to audience members, who spontaneously jumped up and danced to the sounds of Al Green's "Love and Happiness."

It should not be a surprise that Guevara found his way to theatrical writing, performing, directing, and producing. The entire narrative he presents here is replete with a ferocious theatricality where appearance and drama matter. He dresses himself for one performance by donning Tibetan quilt pants, a vintage Chaz Bojórquez Graff t-shirt, a coat from Bali, Brazilian canvas leopard-skin shoes, a rust-colored Panama straw hat, a faux leopard floor-length bathrobe, and shades. "Superman and Funkahuatl never looked so good!" he exclaims. On another occasion, an effort to go backstage with his then love interest without an appropriate pass is magically facilitated by her attire in a midnight blue chiffon miniskirt and electric blue suede heels, while Guevara accompanies her in a brown suede flat-brimmed hat à la Clint Eastwood in *A Fistful of Dollars,* a brown leather coat, black shirt with a mariachi bow tie, custom-made leather pants, and custom-made green suede knee boots. The security guards do not even ask to see a pass; they take one look at the couple and open the doors. "I guess we looked like movie stars," Guevara recalls.

The plays, mixed-media productions, and performances that Guevara has crafted over the years, blending speech, song, dance, and visual imagery, have posed bold challenges to the conventions of spectatorship. These endeavors entailed collaborations with visual artists John Valadez, Patssi Valdez, Chaz Bojórquez, Leo Limón, Gilbert "Magu" Luján, and multimedia artist Harry Gamboa Jr.; with actors and performance artists Marisela Norte, Guillermo Gómez-Peña, John Trudell, and Kristina Wong; with writers Rubén Martínez, Dave Marsh, and Luis Rodriguez; and with Guevara's fellow art activists *(artivistas)* Quetzal Flores, Martha Gonzalez, and Nobuko Miyamoto. In addition to creating his own works, Guevara has also been involved in arts administration and programming. He served as director of Latino and Asian Pacific Islander audience development for Hollywood's Ford Amphitheatre, creating events that greatly expanded the cultural

diversity of that institution's offerings. Guevara has also labored to incorpo-
rate music into the exhibits and activities of art museums. Drawing on his
work in both music and theater, he staged *Surcos Alternativos / Alternative
Grooves from Mexamérica,* a site-specific performance concert, for the inauguration of the Getty Museum's 2002 summer concert series. He created
music-listening stations for the Japanese American National Museum's 2002
exhibit on the history of Boyle Heights, as well as for the 2011 landmark exhibition at the Museum of Latin American Art *MEX/LA: "Mexican"
Modernism(s) in Los Angeles, 1930–1985.*

Although the arts have been at the core of Guevara's life, they have rarely
provided him with an adequate livelihood. In this memoir he relates stories
about wage labor, cooking and delivering chicken dinners for a franchise
chain restaurant, moving heavy barrels of sulfuric acid in a warehouse, and
stacking other artists' albums (and sometimes his own) in a record wholesale
distributorship. Yet he has also carried his art into new realms of instruction
and apprenticeship through employment as a teacher, tutor, and mentor to
disadvantaged youths. Through over two decades of work with Arts 4 City
Youth, which he founded in 1993, he has supervised instruction of more than
nine thousand young people in schools, housing projects, and parks as they
learned to write, paint, film, dance, and make photographs. He taught poetry
to fifth-grade students in Trinity Elementary School in South Central Los
Angeles, to older students in Metropolitan State Hospital (a facility for the
mentally and emotionally challenged), and to young people in detention
centers and other carceral institutions. He has also worked as a substitute
teacher in the Los Angeles Unified School District. In each of these settings,
he felt compelled to devise new pedagogical techniques geared to the particular needs and experiences of his students. This work takes place without the
public visibility and (sometimes) acclaim that characterizes his professional
performing life, but it has planted seeds of inspiration and hope in the lives
of students who might otherwise not have encountered the arts.

Guevara's memoir is as unusual in the realm of race as it is on the subject
of sex. *Confessions of a Radical Chicano Doo-Wop Singer* presents a unique
cartography of the U.S. racial order as seen through Guevara's life experiences, identifications, and affiliations. He delineates with care and precision
how a Mexican American with both Iberian and indigenous ancestry became
immersed in Black music, how he forged lifelong connections to Japanese
American culture, and how this history led him to see Frank Zappa as a
kindred soul and to collaborate productively with him. Zappa, who described

himself as Sicilian, Greek, Arab, and French, shared many of Guevara's eclectic interests and tastes. The two forged a close and deep connection in the course of a conversation in which they discovered their mutual admiration for the Western art music of Igor Stravinsky and Béla Bartók. Guevara approached Ruben And The Jets (which started as a novelty conception of Zappa's and later became an actual group headed by Guevara) as a vehicle for incorporating the "ethnic folk music" of East L.A. into new musical and theatrical forms, just as Stravinsky and Bartók had done with the folk arts of their nations.

In his life and his art, Guevara came to view racial identity as composite, contested, and complex, as something that could neither be fully embraced nor completely evaded. His first girlfriend was a Filipina. He lived near and played music with Asian Americans and Blacks. In college, he studied under the supervision of a Kiowa mentor. Late in life he discovered that he has three half-brothers from the Okanagan reserve in British Columbia, Canada. Yet for all of these multicultural meetings, mixtures, encounters, and engagements, discovering the significance of being Chicano remained at the center of his consciousness.

Growing up in a family headed by a Mexican immigrant father and a Chicana mother, Guevara learned early in life about the complicated contradictions of Mexican American identity. His father boasted about his family's distant relation to ninth-century Spanish royalty but said less about the ancestry they inherited from Rubén's indigenous grandmother. Rubén's mother's side of the family claimed indigenous Tecuexe ancestors from Jalisco on one side, and on the other, a prominent Spanish-Mexican family that included the architect who designed the Guadalajara Cathedral, built in 1618. Hearing his father's stories at home and being surrounded by members of his mother's extended family in Santa Monica's La Veinte barrio instilled in Guevara a strong sense of his identity as a Mexican American. At the same time, this identity seemed always under assault. The anti-Mexican racism that he experienced from white classmates in school and that he discerned in many forms of popular culture alienated him from the U.S. part of his identity. Yet he could not feel completely at home in Mexico either, as he realized on a trip to Guadalajara in 1974. Asking directions from a man on the street in his rudimentary Spanish provoked a torrent of contemptuous abuse from the stranger, who proclaimed that *pochos* (a common slur by Mexican nationals about Mexicans living in the United States) were mongrels who had no culture of their own.

Later on that trip, Guevara experienced what he describes as "a soft epiphany." The feeling of being betwixt and between, at home neither *aquí* nor *allá* (here nor there), that is so common to the Chicano experience filled Guevara with determination to create an art that expressed the vitality, dynamism, and knowledge of the intersections he inhabited. He embraced a Chicano identity of his own design, one that was neither separatist nor assimilationist but instead a collaged stance made possible because of—rather than despite— its contradictions. He began to call himself a Chicano Culture Sculptor, an artist working in many different media to transform the aspirations, alienations, indignities, and impulses of an aggrieved people into aesthetic experiences that could point the way toward liberation. In music, plays, performance art, theater, and fiction he worked to turn the poison of negative ascription into the medicine of positive affirmation, to embrace, exaggerate, and invert demeaning stereotypes, to uncrown power with laughter, to challenge the humiliating and subordinating signs and symbols of the dominant culture by staging counterspectacles that called new communities into being through performance. He reports that he could not sleep the night that this soft epiphany came to him, because his head was filled with "millions of ideas, dreams, songs, and poetry."

In fashioning himself as a Chicano Culture Sculptor, Guevara both conformed to tradition and broke with it. Both sides of his family had long histories of migration, adaptation, and transformation. The family of his mother moved to Santa Monica in the midst of the turmoil that eventually came to a climax in the Mexican Revolution of 1910. Some of his earliest lessons about how culture could be sculpted came from the irrepressible theatricality and joyful festivity of his mother and her relatives. He savored listening to family stories of the strolling musicians playing traditional Mexican music in *Fiestas Patrias* Day (September 16) parades. He learned to play the maracas and sing *boleros* at family gatherings. Yet his uncles also introduced him to radio broadcasts of Black big band swing orchestras and taught him to dance the boogie-woogie. One of his uncles later became a singer and conga player in a Latin jazz band. In this memoir, Guevara relates the exhilaration he felt one night as a child when his mother took him to a neighborhood dance. He was entranced: the sweet smoky smell of *carne asada* on the grill, his mother's beautiful bright red lipstick and flowing black hair as she displayed her prize-winning abilities as a dancer, and the steady rhythms and beautiful harmonies of the music.

Guevara's paternal grandfather was a classical violinist from a prominent family. After he married an indigenous woman, he was disinherited and reduced to an impoverished existence. When his wife died, he drank himself to death, leaving Rubén's father—Rubén Ladrón de Guevara Sr.—an orphan who was forced to fend for himself at the age of eleven. The youth played music on the banjo, guitar, and drums on the streets for tips, sang for customers in houses of prostitution, and served as an army bugler during the Mexican Revolution. He became a bullfighter, a boxer, and a jockey before re-forming Trio Los Porteños (they became Los Porteños) when Miguel Aceves Mejía left the group in the early 1940s. Rubén Sr. settled in Los Angeles, where his group enjoyed success as a Spanish-language recording and stage act. He met Sara Gutiérrez at a show and decided to stay in the United States to marry her and start a family. Finding work as a musician in Hollywood film studios, he befriended the Mexican American actor Anthony Quinn. Later he moved the family to Las Vegas, where he performed in most of the major lounges; Frank Sinatra and Ava Gardner liked the music he made.

Eleven-year-old Rubén Jr. liked to go the lounges where his father performed, standing outside rooms that he was too young to enter, listening to the sounds of forbidden worlds. The music he heard was in the middle of a large cultural transition and transformation. It was an era when big band jazz was giving way to rhythm and blues and rock 'n' roll, and when segregated venues in Las Vegas were just beginning to allow Black artists to perform. One special night, he recalls seeing Louis Prima and Keely Smith put on an unforgettable show accompanied by Sam Butera and the Witnesses. Prima had Italian ancestry and Smith was of Irish and Cherokee descent, but because of the way they played and sang, some listeners thought both of them were Black. On other nights in Las Vegas, young Rubén savored the sounds of Black acts like the Treniers and white acts like Freddy Bell and the Bellhops and Vido Musso.

Guevara's first public appearance as a musician came when he was in the fifth grade, playing the trumpet in the school band as they paraded through the downtown streets of Palm Springs. A few years later, he played first trumpet, second chair, with the California All-Youth Symphony Orchestra, appearing with them in a televised broadcast on Easter Sunday in 1957. He received another kind of musical education, however, in middle school from the school janitor Henry Williams. An accomplished pianist steeped in African American performance styles, Williams tutored Guevara and another student who played drums to perform popular hits like Louis Jordan's "Caldonia" and the Johnny Otis Orchestra's rendition of "Harlem Nocturne." Within a year Rubén was playing those songs and others he had learned from his father in a band that played school dances and performed at a graduation concert.

After moving back to Los Angeles, Guevara joined the Apollos car club. One night he and his fellow club members were walking in Hollywood and they stumbled on Perry's Rehearsal Studios. Drawn to the music inside, they entered timidly, then watched as the Vibrations, the Olympics, and the Carlos Brothers rehearsed their hit songs for an upcoming concert. The musicians were friendly and invited them to attend the show, which inspired the car club members to imagine themselves as a musical act. Guevara quickly became as interested in the way band members moved on the stage and the costumes they wore as he was in the music. When later in life he turned to writing and performing theatrical pieces that included music, he was not so much moving away from rock 'n' roll as bringing its performance techniques and visual vocabularies to new venues. He never forgot the impression that stage performers made on him when he was young, and he continued to embrace their sense of theater as he aged.

Guevara's lifelong quest to create art with social influence resonates with the aspirations that author, filmmaker, and social activist Toni Cade Bambara once described as the desire "to walk upright and see clearly, breathe easily, think better than was taught, be better than one was programmed to believe."[7] Yet these lofty ideals emerged from social conditions that were far from ideal. Guevara has been a participant in, and a product of, the politics and passions of the era in which he has lived. His artistic expressions and appeals for a kind of politicized love have been crafted as instruments of self-defense against what he sees as clear political evil. Guevara was an eyewitness to the emergence of the youth counterculture in Los Angeles, and he joined the protests against police repression when officers rounded up young people loitering harmlessly along the Sunset Strip in 1966. Guevara created and staged the gospel rock cantata *Who Are the People?* as a protest against the Vietnam War. From the fires that consumed large swaths of Watts in the 1965 riots to the killing of journalist Rubén Salazar by a sheriff's deputy at the Chicano Moratorium in 1970, he has been close to the flashpoints of racial, class, and state violence. He recounts in this memoir a perpetual effort to use his art to respond responsibly and honorably to systemic subordination and violence. In his sixties, he worked tirelessly to stage numerous interfaith

7. Toni Cade Bambara, *The Salt Eaters* (New York: Vintage, 1992), 107.

and interracial cultural collaborations as counters to the Iraq war and its promotion of a climate of hate directed against followers of Islam.

Throughout this memoir Guevara portrays his life "as a steady series of burnings," with both literal and figurative references to fire appearing throughout the text. He suffered second-degree burns as a five-day-old infant left out in the sun too long by a well-meaning relative who worried that the baby looked too pale. As an adult, a sulfuric acid drum exploded and scarred his face in an industrial accident. The Peppermint Lounge West nightclub caught fire and burned to the ground the week before the Apollo Brothers were slated to perform there. A fire in Nayarit, Mexico, incinerated his father's birth certificate. During his performance of a piece protesting the 500th anniversary of Columbus's arrival in the Americas, Guevara lit an incense burner and accidentally set fire to the *piñata* headdress that he was wearing.

Other burnings held symbolic significance and more figurative implications for him. As a soon-to-be lover entered his apartment, he discerned an ominous portent when all the bulbs in a lamp burned out at the same time. In crafting a performance piece about the Spanish conquest of Mexico, he returned again and again to the punitive burnings of Mexico City and of indigenous libraries by the conquering Spaniards, leading him to title the production *La Quemada*— The Burning. When he encountered a group of young immigrant Algerian graffiti writers in a city in France, it seemed fitting to him that the meeting took place in a burned-out building. Moreover, throughout the text Guevara punctuates his narrative with wordplay that evokes fire, referring to burning questions, feelings of burnout, accounts of being burned in business deals, images burned into his brain, and confessions of firing up more than a few joints and contending with what he describes as the two fires that he felt burning constantly throughout his life, one in his heart and the other in his pants.

The burnings that Guevara describes as the recurrent symbols of his life have been accompanied by similarly perilous flights, falls, crashes, and cuts. As a young boy he joined his cousins in Tijuana as they stuffed themselves into large truck tires and rolled down hills, flying along the steep mountain canyons in tires that they pretended were space ships. Another kind of flight and fall took place on the Santa Monica Pier at the age of four or five, when a group of aunts and cousins tossed him into the ocean in the belief that this would teach him to swim. He remembers having no fear of the water, just as he had no fear of the steep hillsides in Tijuana, surmising that he must have seen himself as invincible. When walking home from kindergarten one day, he was thrown to the pavement when a car hit him, the tires screeching to a halt right beside his head. An ambulance arrived and drove him home, where the medics who attended to him assured his mother and grandmother that the boy was well. The two women were greatly shaken by the experience, but Rubén merely decided that he *was* invincible. He grabbed a towel, wrapped it around his neck, and ran down a brick walkway with his arms stretched out straight before him, pretending to be Superman. He crashed headfirst though the glass front door and landed in the living room with cuts all over his arms. Twenty-six stitches were needed to repair his arm, leaving a seven-inch scar that he carries today as reminder of what he describes as "my life-long quest and desire to go beyond this world."

Follow the flames long enough and *Confessions of a Radical Chicano Doo-Wop Singer* leads you right into the heart of the Los Angeles that has been Guevara's quaking spiritual center, his tumultuous artistic stage, and his vibrant social laboratory. More than four decades ago he wrote "C/S," a magisterial spoken-word prose poem put to a rock 'n' roll world beat accompaniment that stands as a great distillation of the historical violence perpetrated against indigenous and Mexican people in Los Angeles. He concludes this memoir with a similar lyrical and poetic rumination, "Take Me Higher, *Mi Reina.*" Drawing on decades of experience with the city, especially its most desperate precincts, Guevara reads the built environment of Los Angeles as an archive of histories of exploitation, suppression, and repression. Seen through his eyes, the lake in Westlake Park is a site of "penny wishes and drowning tears," and Union Station is a "grand cathedral of trapped ghosts of ripped hearts and laughter, where the *pinche* Manifest Destiny Railroad connected east and west over the blistered, busted backs of human beasts of burden." The corner of 8th and Alameda appears to him as the place where "Tongva and other Indigenous men, women, and children were corralled like cattle, left to howl and pray to the moon in honor and in shame." Everywhere Guevara looks in the glamor capital of the world, he sees evidence of oppression and exploitation, ruin and decay. The San Fernando Valley's orchards have been transformed into "a spiritual wasteland by toxic film studios," and "the smoldering embers from the 1965 Watts riots still threaten to ignite as Brown and Black people continue to experience police brutality."

He describes the concrete banks of the Los Angeles River that divides downtown from East L.A. as "cemented with Angelino apartheid." Even though murals on Eastside streets still sing "*corrido*–doo-wop–hip hop epiphanies," the tacos sold by vendors filled with "tongues, ears, brains, and intestines" only fuel "a better dream for a better death" among the people whose tongues, ears, brains, and intestines are wasted every day in jobs that pay too little to support lives of decency and dignity. Guevara takes aim at the mythmakers of Los Angeles, even the hard-boiled noir writers like John Fante, who professed to be truth tellers but who in Rubén's eyes colluded to occlude the racism in the city that oppresses dreams and kills hopes.

Declaring, "I know you, L.A., and I know you know me," Guevara seeks refuge in the "satin wings of fallen angels, broken promises, unanswered prayers, songs never heard, and the tortured hearts of poets, priests, pimps, and prostitutes." Merging his own identity with that of the city, he closes with a plea that encapsulates his life and art. "Sculpt me," he commands, "into a lusty funk of fire, rhythm, and blues." The sculptor has become the sculpted, the Chicano Culture Sculptor now a living sculpture who asks that his "perfect tears and songs of dust caress, and cover, your, our, sinful sacred streets." He invites his beloved and brutal city to "watch me burn, *mi reina de los ángeles.* . . . Watch me burn. Stoke the fire. Kiss the flames." This is a remarkable conclusion to a remarkable book, an expression of poetry and prophecy from an artist who refuses to succumb to despair quietly and who invites us to follow him into the flames, to transform our lives into creative works of living sculpture.

Prologue

I CAME INTO THIS WORLD ON FIRE.

My *tío* Xavier thought I looked too pale when I came home from the hospital, so he put me out in the sun to get some color. He never came back.

I suffered second-degree burns on my newborn face, arms, and hands. I was tightly wrapped in sheets so I wouldn't scratch myself. I was taken to several doctors, but they couldn't heal the burns. I'm sure I flipped out a little. I cried nonstop. I was only five days old.

Finally, my dear great-aunt, *tía* Victoria, cured me by giving me a Mexican potion of goat's milk and indigenous herbs. Miraculously, I recovered.

That's the way my life started out, and that's pretty much the way it's been: a steady series of burnings and a steady series of miracles that kept saving my mind, my face, and my life. A long, absurd, hilarious, surreal serenade of being pushed to the edge of my singed psyche, but through leaps of good faith and good karma I've managed to dive off that cliff into the forging heat and pulse of the heartbeat, the crucible of the soul, and live to tell about it.

I'm past seventy now. I might only have a couple hundred bucks in the bank and might not know when the next gig will come along to pay the rent. But my life has never been about playing it safe in the cool shade anyway or about becoming rich and famous. It's been about making music and making love, rockin' and rollin' with the punches, and letting life keep the beat.

La Veinte: A Santa Monica Barrio

I ARRIVED ON THE PLANET in the barrio of Boyle Heights on the East Side of Los Angeles, on Saturday, October 17, 1942, at 12:27 P.M. My parents lived in Laurel Canyon, where I was christened to a crisp shortly after my birth. We moved to Echo Park for a while, then briefly lived at the fashionable Saint James Hotel on the Sunset Strip. The following year we moved to La Veinte (by Olympic and 20th Street), a smart, poor, working-class Mexican neighborhood in Santa Monica, roughly a half square mile with a population of around two hundred. I lived there with my grandparents, *nana* Victorina Casillas-Gutiérrez and *tata* Rito Gutiérrez Sr.; my mom; and my younger sisters, Linda and Bonita. My musician dad was usually on the road.

There is both Spanish aristocracy and indigenous blood on my mother's side—a double irony. Her mother and the Casillas clan of La Veinte were descendants of the indigenous Tecuexe people of Jalisco *and* the Spanish-Mexican architect don Martín "El Alarife" Casillas (1556–1618), who designed the main cathedral in Guadalajara. His descendants grew up on his hacienda in El Valle de Guadalupe. Members of the Casillas clan emigrated from there to La Veinte around the turn of the twentieth century, before, during, and after the Mexican Revolution.

The barrio of La Veinte was composed mostly of two *familias:* the Casillas and the Gutiérrez. The two families intermarried and were successful entrepreneurs, starting with my great-grandfather Ruperto Casillas, who recruited laborers from El Valle to work in the brickyards and clear the land for subdivisions in Santa Monica. He also rented them rooms at his boardinghouse located in the neighborhood. My mother, Sara Casillas-Gutiérrez Guevara, was born in Santa Monica in 1923. My mother's many aunts, uncles, and cousins all lived within blocks of my grandparents' home. No one ever went hungry, because you could always go to a relative's house to eat. There was a certain pride my *tías* took in competing to be the best cook, so the food was always the very best.

The neighborhood would put on 16th of September Mexican Independence Day parades, traveling down Olympic from 20th Street to 14th. These included colorful floats and strolling musicians. The fun times were over-shadowed, however, by "repatriation" raids, in which several relatives were rounded up and sent back to Mexico.

The only non-Mexican in the neighborhood was Mr. Jackson, an African American man who lived a couple of houses over from my grandparents. He was very friendly, always waving to us from his front porch with a big grin on his face as we walked or drove by. He reminded me of Uncle Remus from the controversial Disney cartoon *Song of the South,* which was where I first saw an African American. I'm sure he had many stories to tell.

There was a neighboring barrio to the east called Sotel, which was adjacent to a sizable Japanese American community that unfortunately I never got to know.

The beach wasn't far, and that was one of the best parts about living there. The beach, the pier, and the grand carousel were like a live musical fairy tale, a gateway into my hungry imagination.

My first five years living in La Veinte were formative for me musically. My father taught me how to sing *boleros* and play the maracas. He taught me the song *"Amor"* (Love), which would become my life mantra. I sang and played at family get-togethers and holidays. I loved the attention that performing brought me, especially from the beautiful women who were always around. I became kind of a musical novelty.

My *tíos,* Teodoro "Lolo" and Rito Jr.—my mom's brothers—were major influences. Rito Jr. was my first cool role model. He was a very handsome and stylish cat. He taught me how to dance the boogie-woogie while listening to the big bands on the radio in the mid-forties. His younger brother, Lolo, was the lover-boy of the family. He had a beautiful girlfriend named Margie. I loved singing to her and looking up her mile-high legs. Lolo would later become a fine ballad singer à la Frank Sinatra and a *conguero* with the Estrada Brothers Latin jazz band from Oxnard. He passed away in 2004 from brain cancer. I'd never witnessed watching a loved one shrivel up like burning paper, then die. I wrote this poem for him and read it to him on his last birthday, his seventy-fourth. It was Christmas Eve.

The Song of Life
(For my *tío* Teodoro "Lolo" Gutiérrez)

Music is the heart of the soul
Its song is heard through rock and steel
It caresses the wind

It embraces a kiss
It lights the sun
It soothes God's heart

Songs always keep singing
Even after they are sung
They stay in the heart's memory
Like your first kiss
Like your first love

The life of a singer can be rough
Can be glorious
Can be tough

But the singer needs to sing
Like the sun and stars need to shine
Like the wind needs to blow
Like a lover needs to love

Singers are the voice
The breath of God
Messengers of the heart

A Hindu writing says,
"God respects me when I work,
But He loves me when I
Sing"

Music is the air we breathe
Songs are medicine
They keep the world alive
Because we listen with our heart

There will always be singers
Some sing with their voice
Some with their eyes
Some with their smile

I loved hearing you sing, *tío*
It reminded me of my childhood
When I learned *rancheras* and *boleros* from my father

He taught you like he taught me
To sing from a deep place
To watch the flow of the breath
To let it carry the words
To let it carry the song
The song
The bittersweet song of Life

We come from the music of God
We return to that music
To sing
To sing
To sing

And I breathe your song, Lolo
The world breathes your song
God breathes your song
Thank you for singing

He smiled, thanked me, and shook my hand real hard. Then he squeezed it again, saying, "I don't wanna die." Shortly thereafter, he went into a coma; he died a few weeks later.

Rubén Ladrón de Guevara Sr., 1914–2006

"HEY, DAD, WHAT'S WITH OUR MIDDLE NAME? Doesn't *ladrón* mean 'thief' in Spanish?"

"*Sí, m'hijo, pero no te preocupes*. Yeah, but don't worry about it, son. *Somos miembros de la familia real*. We are members of the Spanish royal family."

"Yeah, right, Dad."

Although he was one hell of a storyteller, he never made things up. So I did. I imagined there was some knight *vato* dude back in the day that stole the hearts of wives and girlfriends, kind of a rogue Don Juan. Turns out, that pretty much could describe my dad.

Rubén Ladrón de Guevara Sr. was born in Compostela, Nayarit, Mexico, on February 23, 1914. At least, that's the town and the year he gave me, explaining, "All records were burned in a fire."

His father, Mariano Ladrón de Guevara, was a classical violinist who came to Mexico from Madrid on a concert tour around 1900. He met and married Dad's mother, María Espino, an indigenous woman, and was disowned from the family for doing so. It was a scandalous taboo for someone of aristocratic Spanish background to marry an indigenous person.

They moved to Guadalajara with Dad's older brother, Xavier, where my grandfather Mariano gave violin lessons. My father was born soon after. My grandmother tragically died giving birth to a third son when Dad was eight months old. Mariano took up drinking and died a few years later, some say of a broken heart.

Dad and his brother were sent to live with relatives in La Colonia Ladrón de Guevara, a wealthy neighborhood in Guadalajara, but were badly

My father, Rubén Ladrón de Guevara Sr., at twenty-eight years of age, 1942. He sang with the reformed Los Porteños. My mother, Sara Casillas-Gutiérrez Guevara, at nineteen, La Veinte, Santa Monica, 1942. Photos courtesy of the Funkahuatl family archive.

mistreated for being mestizos, of mixed blood. And so they hit the road, becoming street musicians at barely eleven and thirteen years of age. Dad sang, played guitar, banjo, and drums, and performed in the grand brothels of Mexico City. He was also a child bugler during the Mexican Revolution. Later he had a short career as a young *torero,* dubbed *El Niño Prodigio,* the Prodigal Son, and he became a boxer and a jockey to make ends meet as well. Talk about paying dues.

Sometime around 1939, my dad re-formed Trio Los Porteños (they became Los Porteños) after two members left the group along with future Mexican film and singing icon Miguel Aceves Mejía. The new trio came to Los Angeles in 1941 on a tour promoting two of the group's former hits, "Blanca" and "Solo para ti."

My father was a very handsome "ladies' man." It was rumored that he and the Mexican movie stars Dolores del Río and María Félix were once lovers. My mother was once compared to both. So I can only imagine what it was like when they first met.

Tía Victoria, a fan of Los Porteños, chaperoned my mom and a group of her cousins to a concert at the Million Dollar Theatre downtown. After the show, *Tía* took my shy eighteen-year-old mother by the hand and led her backstage to meet the dashing singer. There must have been intense sparks, because shortly thereafter they eloped and were married. I was born the following year. Talk about romantic.

My mother didn't want to move to Mexico, so Dad quit the trio to pursue his career in L.A. One other possible reason for dad's quick action may have been that he wanted to marry a citizen to become one himself. He was a hustler that way. He worked as a studio musician in the film industry, where he befriended Mexican/Irish American actor Anthony Quinn and many other film stars. (Quinn owned a bar in Echo Park on Echo Park Boulevard and Sunset that was a favorite hangout for actors and musicians in the 1950s.)

Dad recorded an album of traditional *boleros* and original compositions on Coast Records in the early '50s, and released a single, *Quiet Village,* on Kent Records in the mid-'50s. In the sixties he recorded two albums of mainly *boleros,* Mexican standards, and his originals, *Viva!* and *T-Town.* The Coast recordings were marketed to Mexican audiences in the United States and Mexico. I'm not sure who the later recordings were aimed at, but I don't think he ever saw any royalties. I know my mother didn't.

When I was fifteen, my parents broke up. After the marriage ended, he did a ten-year stint in Vegas playing the major lounges on the Strip, disappeared, then resurfaced. He moved to Panama in the early '80s, remarried, and gave occasional singing and guitar lessons. He returned in the mid-'80s to Inglewood with his Panamanian wife, Nelly, and pursued recording projects before moving back to Panama again. He returned to L.A. in 1998 to receive medical attention for his recurring asthma.

Sometime around then, I saw an announcement for an art exhibit by Mexican painter Sergio Ladrón de Guevara. I was intrigued. This must be a relative. If so, maybe he could enlighten me about our name.

When I introduced myself, he said I "had the eyes of a Ladrón de Guevara," whatever that meant. "So, Sergio," I asked, "how *did* we get that crazy name that means thief?" So began the saga of sagas, more epic and mythic than anything my dad could've ever come up with.

THE LADRÓN DE GUEVARA STORY

"Sometime in the late 800s in the Vasco region of northern Spain," Sergio began, "the invading Arabs attacked and ransacked the main castle in Aragón,

My ancestor Sancho Guillermo Nuñez de Guevara performing a C-section on Queen Urruca Jimínez, ca. late 800s in northern Spain. Detail © The British Library/The Image Works.

killing the king of Navarre, don Ignacio Íñiguez, who left his pregnant queen, *la reina* Urraca Jiménez, to die in a fierce battle." A soldier, he went on, noticed a tiny hand sticking out of the queen's slit stomach, lifted her onto his horse, and rode out of the battle scene into a safe secluded glen. There, he removed the infant by cesarean section as the queen died. He took the infant to live with him in the mountains, where he maintained a herd of goats and sheep. When the child, Sancho Garcés I de Navarre, turned eighteen, the soldier, Sancho Guillermo Nuñez de Guevara (who was from the town of Guevara, or Gebara, in Vasco), returned the boy to the royal court to assume his role as king. In gratitude, the new monarch knighted his adoptive father Sancho Guillermo Ladrón del Rey Niño de Guevara—Sancho Guillermo Thief of the Baby King from Guevara. Sancho Guillermo was given land and a castle in Portúa, northern Spain, where sections of the castle remain.

So Dad was right, I am royalty after all, and best of all, not by blood—by deed. Paradoxically, I had become a fierce anticolonialist in the '80s and '90s.

I despised the Spanish invasion of Mexico and used that theme in later theater pieces, *La Quemada* and the adaptation, *Aztlán, Babylon, Rhythm & Blues.*

Sergio's wife, Karen, later sent me a scanned page from *Renaissance Painting in Manuscripts—Treasures from the British Library,* the catalogue of an exhibit at the Getty Art Museum in 1983–84. It is a painting of Sancho performing the C-section, proving the legend was true.

When I told Dad about the legend by phone, he just laughed. He had a great laugh. How sad that he didn't believe me. Then I asked him to sing the first song he taught me, "Amor." He did and he sounded better than ever.

Amazingly for a musician, he never missed a day's work, never had a cold, didn't drink, only smoked for a short while, then quit. I never saw him depressed, and he never complained. He was an affectionate father to me and to my sisters, Linda, Bonita, and Loretta. He never said a mean word to my mother, at least not in front of us. Yet he was a chronic twister of the truth and a secret womanizer. It might have come from his hustling days as a kid on the streets of Mexico, a survival skill that became a habit.

The last time I saw him was at LAX airport in 1999. He was in a wheel-chair holding his beloved guitar on his lap, looking sharp and dapper with his black fedora tilted to one side, very Sinatra-like, as Nelly wheeled him away. He turned back, smiled, and waved goodbye.

He peacefully passed away in his sleep on Sunday, March 19, 2006, in David Chiriquí, Panama, at 6:10 P.M. from complications due to asthma and bronchial pneumonia caused by a lifetime of singing in nightclub smoke. He was buried in Dolega, Chiriquí, Panama, on Tuesday, March 21, 2006. He was ninety-two. May he rest eternally in song.

Superman in Ese Eme

MY GRANDPARENTS' HUMBLE TWO-BEDROOM HOME at 1742 22nd Street in *Ese Eme* (Santa Monica) had a large front yard that stretched to the street with a rainbow of fruit trees and flowers planted by my dear *tata* (grandfather). Those trees gave us avocados, oranges, lemons, figs, peaches, and plums. It was my Enchanted Garden. There was also a big cactus patch, a *nopalera,* and my dear *nana* (grandmother) would harvest the prickly pears, then cut and remove the cactus spines, dice, and boil them. There's nothing like fresh *nopales* fried in butter and onions, then wrapped in a tortilla freshly handmade by your *nana.*

A long narrow brick walkway laid by my *tata* led from the sidewalk to the front door. He worked in the local brickyard, and he tended a rose garden in a nursery where the roses were specifically raised for the annual Pasadena Rose Parade. He later opened a small neighborhood market on Olympic by 20th Street. My grandparents, along with my mother, her siblings, and cousins, also worked the agricultural fields in Oxnard to help make ends meet.

I was very close to my grandfather, *mi tata,* Rito Gutiérrez. When I was four I helped him prepare the ground in a large section of the front yard so we could plant a vegetable garden. It was my first lesson in gardening, my first lesson in the miracle of nature. We turned the rich, damp, Tongva soil, and dug the long rows. *Tata* handed me the magical seeds, and I pressed them into the soil and covered them. He taught me the names of the seeds while I buried them: *zanahoria* (carrot), *apio* (celery), *calabasa* (squash), *sandía* (watermelon), *melón* (cantaloupe), *tomate* (tomato), *rábano* (radish), and *nabo* (turnip). We also planted herbs that all households had, including the minty *yerba buena* and *epazote* for Mexican tea.

"Ahora, m'hijo, tenemos que dar una oración para que broten las semillas. Now, my dear son, we need to pray for the seeds to grow." I didn't know what he was talking about, but I went along with it. It sounded important. As I finally saw them start to sprout, it blew my mind. The earth was alive! When it was time, I pulled up a carrot and ate it. I could smell the damp earth on it. Man, it was so sweet, cool, and juicy. The *maíz* (corn) grew tall like bamboo trees, and watching their silky, golden fur darken was a trip. I loved running through the giant stalks, chasing my cousins and friends. The garden was a wonderland, a safe haven. It was home.

We had many Casillas relatives in Tijuana, and we would go visit them often. I loved the long rides down Highway 1 in *tata's* old green Ford pickup truck, passing miles and miles of orange orchards and flower farms. I was five and we only spoke Spanish. In Tijuana, *tata* took me to bullfights at the old bull ring on Agua Caliente. I loved the roar of the crowd with every pass the *torero* took, the brass band blasting through to punctuate the drama. It was a kind of brutal, yet heroic, circus-ballet ritual, and my introduction into the world of theater. *Mi tata* proudly told me of the time he saw the famous matador Manolete fight his only fight in Tijuana, in that same bull ring. Later on, there was a time I too, wanted to be a *torero*. In a way, maybe I did become one, with my many future brushes with death.

We often visited an uncle of my mother's, Crispín Casillas, who lived in a shack with his beautiful young wife and several kids on the outskirts of town in the canyons by Rosarito Beach. My cousins and I would stuff ourselves into huge truck tires and roll down the steep mountain canyons, yelling and flying through the air. I had no fear of flying or of dying inside those truck-tire spaceships. I didn't know that people could kill themselves until Crispín committed suicide a few years later from the pressure of keeping his large family fed. We also took drives up Highway 1 along the coast to visit Casillas relatives in Oxnard. I loved those rides too, the emerald green ocean roaring down below, the old Ford truck chugging along while *mi tata* told stories of his youth. He was a great storyteller, with a wonderful sense of humor.

He suddenly passed away from cancer when I was seven. It was my second funeral after that of my mother's cousin, Velia Casillas-Becerra, not long before, and it was very confusing and very sad. He was a father to me in many ways, since my dad was always on tour. I loved him very much.

My dear *nana* Victorina Casillas-Gutiérrez used to work making tortillas by hand at the Gallegos Brothers *tortillería* and at the Casillas Market. She made the best *frijoles de la olla*—fresh bean soup—on the planet. I loved watching her make *gorditas,* fat little tortillas, and the way her hands would go slap, pat, slap, pat, slap to the *masa* cornmeal to shape them. Once they were cooked she'd pinch up the top edge of the *gordita* to make a ridge so the butter wouldn't run off. Then she'd slice the cooked *gordita* and stuff it with the fresh cooked beans. Let me tell you, the smell of fresh *masa* in the air, beans boiling, eating one of my *nana's* killer butter-and-bean *gordita*—with another one browning on the *comal* (griddle): that was pure love, my *nana's* love. The gentlest, sweetest, and most generous woman I have ever known. She was always cooking for us, taking good care of us. She was a mother to me in many ways. I still sleep with a wild-colored handwoven wool blanket she knitted for me right before she passed away. It's been a warm shelter from many storms.

My mom's cousin Carmen "Topsy" Casillas owned a hot dog stand on the corner of Olympic and 20th. He was always the life of a party with his sharp suits and fancy footwork. Topsy also had a barbershop next to the hot dog stand. Yeah, he was one very enterprising cat. My great-aunt *tía* Virginia Gutiérrez-Casillas, *tata's* sister, co-owned the landmark Casillas Market with her husband, Esperidión Casillas, my grandmother's brother. It was on Olympic by 20th, the hub of the neighborhood until the mid-1990s. Another cousin, Ben Casillas, owned a barbershop on 14th by Olympic. One day someone there taught me to read the headline "War Ends." Those were the first words I read in English. I was three.

My great-aunt *tía* Victoria Casillas-Becerra was the rebel of the Casillas women, a feminist actually. None of the men ever messed with her. She was very outspoken yet gentle and kind, like her twin sister, my *nana.* She bought me a guitar and a little chair from Tijuana when I was three. She encouraged my singing, and I loved her very much for that, as well as for her magical potions.

Her daughter, Clara Casillas-Becerra Primo, lived with us for a while. She had a rich, low voice and the greatest laugh of all my relatives. I loved her voice, and I loved her. Her brother Tyvy was also a hip influence. My mother's sister Anita gave me the nickname of "Sluggo" based on the *Nancy* comic strip.[1] I'm still known as "Sluggo" to the older Casillas clan.

1. Here is the way Sluggo is described in an online advertisement for a comic book and a button featuring Sluggo. Was this prophetic? "Nancy's 'boyfriend' Sluggo was a character of some mystery. Cartoonist Ernie Bushmiller depicted Sluggo, a young boy, as living alone in a ramshackle house with no adult supervision. He wore clothes with patches. He had no visible means of support. His 'house' was furnished with only the barest necessities. Holes in his walls revealed plaster and lath work. All of which begged a question which became

Me standing my ground and ready for the world at my grandparents' home in La Veinte, Santa Monica (*Ese Eme:* SM), 1945, age three. Courtesy of the Funkahuatl family archive.

My mother once took me to a *Jamaica,* as the neighborhood dances organized by my *tía* Victoria were called. I was four and it was right after World War II. I was dressed nice and my hair was neatly combed. It felt like I was going someplace special. She took me by the hand as we walked up the alley off Olympic by 20th, right across from the Casillas Market. She was wearing

---

the title of the book promoted: *How Sluggo Survives,* the second in a series of 'theme' collections based on Nancy & Sluggo newspaper comic strips. To make matters worse, Sluggo was a lazy boy, summarized by his sleeping pose ('sawing wood'). . . . Today *somebody* would call social services, but for decades no one in the neighborhood intervened. The mystery persists" (www.deniskitchen.com/mm5/merchant.mvc?Store_Code=sk&Screen=PROD&Product_Code=BP_KSP.129).

a bright red dress, red lipstick, with her long black hair flowing, and she looked every bit a movie star, though I didn't yet know what that was. All I knew was that I felt proud to be with her. Like I was with a goddess, though I didn't know what that was either. When we walked in, everyone turned, and the men practically fell to their knees. That was my first lesson in the power of women. I didn't feel jealous, just curious. She was twenty-three, gorgeous, and a star in the neighborhood. The memory makes me think of the song by Ben E. King, "There is a rose in Spanish Harlem . . . "

The band was playing traditional Mexican party music and everyone was dancing and having a ball. The air was filled with the sweet smoky scent of *carne asada* (grilled beef), rice and beans, and fresh tortillas. My mother loved to dance. She once won a jitterbug contest at the Hollywood Palladium when she was sixteen. That moment—that red dress, that candy-apple lipstick, that long swaying shimmering black hair as she danced so free—is etched deep into my bones, a template of love. It was the beginning of my fascination with beautiful women and music, and the beginning of my love for both.

My *tío* Raúl Sánchez, from the nearby barrio of Sotel, married my mother's sister Marina. He was the designated master storyteller of the family. All my cousins, including three of their sons, Danny, Desi, and David, would gather at *nana's* house on Sundays and holidays, and he would tell us the scariest stories I'd ever heard. They were terrifying and inspiring. He was another influence on me besides my father and grandfather regarding my love of stories. He was our Uncle Remus. I also loved listening to the radio dramas of the late '40s, like *Gang Busters* and *The Shadow Knows*. Then, when television came along, I loved *Space Patrol* and *Flash Gordon*. I was fascinated with urban reality and the mystery of outer space. I still am.

Trauma seemed to follow me like a shadow, starting with the burning of my face at birth. When I was four or five, some of my aunts and cousins threw me off the Santa Monica Pier into the ocean. They thought it was the best way for me to learn how to swim. I was thrown into the water where a circle of cousins were waiting for me. After I hit the water I thought I'd never come up. But I wasn't frightened. I had a sense of invincibility. Maybe that crazy courage came from being a big fan of Superman comics. (Which, by the way, is how I learned to read in English.)

The happiest birthday party I ever had was my fifth. Mom and dad, my sisters Linda and Bonita (we called her "Baby"), my cousins, relatives, and all my friends from the neighborhood were there. Crepe paper was taped across the living room and there was a beautiful cake with five candles. Everyone sang "Happy Birthday" and I felt like a star. It wouldn't be until my sixty-seventh birthday party–concert that I would have a party like that and feel that happy again.

TIRE ON MY HEAD, SUPERMAN

One day as I was walking home from kindergarten at McKinley Elementary School on Santa Monica Boulevard I was struck by a car while crossing the street. I was thrown to the ground, my head on the pavement as the front tire screeched to a halt right up against it. It happened so fast it didn't register what a dangerous moment had just occurred, and that I could have been killed instantly. Surprisingly, I didn't feel any fear. It felt like I was in a movie and I was the star-hero that never dies . . . again, like Superman.

The ambulance came and the paramedics checked me out. To everyone's amazement, I was okay. Then they drove me to my *nana's* house only a few blocks away. My mother and *nana* were home and freaked out as the paramedics walked me down the long brick walkway. They told them what happened and that it was a miracle I was alive. My mother and *nana* broke out in tears and hugged me. I felt powerful.

As a fan of Superman, I was convinced that I too could fly. Why not? I knew I was already a superhero, having survived several brushes with death. So I went outside and tied a towel around my neck and, with arms outstretched, started running up the brick walkway toward the house with all my might: I had no doubt that I could fly right over it. No doubt at all. I had defied the L.A. sun, the canyons of Tijuana, the Pacific Ocean, and just now the car tire that almost crushed my head. I was indestructible, immortal. All I had to do was lift off when I got to the end of the brick walkway.

Running full tilt, I reached the end of the walkway and confidently reached up to the sky, ready to fly—and promptly crashed through the glass window of the front door and onto the living room floor. My mom and *nana* jumped and screamed again. I was cut all over my arms and bleeding all over the floor. Miraculously, my face was spared. I was rushed to the hospital and received twenty-six stitches on my left arm. The scar is seven inches long and has remained to this day as a reminder of my innocence and of my lifelong quest and desire to go beyond this world. Maybe my subconscious made a pact with my psyche that I would never feel the fear of dying. Or maybe I was just one crazy kid.

Music and Movie Moments

WE MOVED TO CATHEDRAL CITY in 1947. Dad got a gig at the nearby Chi Chi nightclub in Palm Springs, a favorite watering hole for the Hollywood movie star set. I made my nightclub debut there one Sunday afternoon for a special party. I sang "Amor" with dad's band, the Caballeros, with his brother, Xavier, on piano and Charlie Cota on upright bass. A gorgeous blonde wearing a black gown covered with sparkling sequins complimented me. I can still see her otherworldly face, her movie star smile, her perfect teeth and platinum hair. Her perfume made me feel strange. It was my first rock 'n' roll moment. I was five. (Maybe this was when my attraction to white women began. I had only known them from the movies, and they seemed like they were from another planet—mysterious and untouchable.)

I started playing the trumpet in the fifth grade. Dad had an album of 78s of the Mexican classical trumpet virtuoso Rafael Méndez. They were friends back in Mexico City when they were both kids hustling to make a living. His playing set an unattainable standard, but I was determined to try. I developed a nice tone but not much fingering technique. Still, Dad would tell me that that tone was the heart of my soul. I didn't understand what he meant at the time. It was probably the deepest thing he ever said to me.

I used to take hikes into the desert and build little altars of flowers, stones, and sticks. No one taught me how to do that and I'd never seen anybody do it, I just did it because it felt natural and I needed to get away and pray in my own way. The desert had a calming effect on me: the wind songs, the animals screeching or skirting across my feet, the vultures circling above, the air, clean as a dried bone. The desert and death seemed serene, holy, a friend.

My first gig as a trumpet player was in the fifth grade, marching with the school band for a parade in downtown Palm Springs. I spotted Mom and

Dad together cheering me on. That was the only time they would ever see me perform together. It was one of the happiest and proudest moments of my life. My father, sadly, would never see another performance, although he did come to several of my private lessons that he set up with James Stamp, who was jazz trumpeter Shorty Rogers's teacher. My mother managed to come to a concert at the Wilshire Ebell Theatre in 1957 when I played first trumpet, second chair, with the California All-Youth Symphony Orchestra. That was the last time she saw me perform live. Later that same year I made my TV debut on NBC with the orchestra on Easter Sunday, but unfortunately my parents missed the show.

While gigging at the Chi Chi, Dad became close friends with Frank Sinatra and his then wife, Ava Gardner. According to Dad, Frank would come to the club and sit in with his trio, then would proceed to get plastered. This was during Sinatra's descent into alcohol and a busted movie and singing career, right before his famous comeback in 1952. Dad would invariably drive him home afterward, where they sometimes had wild after-hours parties. Ava loved to dance flamenco, and Dad was the designated guitarist. She loved his playing so much that she wanted to take him to Spain as her "personal guitarist" when she was heading off to film *The Barefoot Contessa,* costarring Humphrey Bogart. Dad declined because of his loyal friendship with Frank. That same year, Sinatra set up an audition for Dad's new band, the Guadalupe Boys, at his new nightclub, the Sands Hotel in Las Vegas. Dad got the gig. We later moved there in the summer of '54.

First, though, in that winter of '54, we moved to L.A. from Cathedral City. I joined a YMCA after-school baseball team in the sixth grade while attending Hoover Street Elementary. We practiced on Berendo Junior High's asphalt field on Friday nights. One such evening, above the field in the gym, a dance was going on full-tilt boogie on the second-floor. Some of the windows were open; people were looking out, and I could see the crepe-paper streamers strung across the ceiling. I was transfixed. I had never seen a school dance before. A tune with a tenor sax solo was blazing away. I'm not sure what record it was, but I'm guessing it could have been Joe Houston, Big Jay McNeely, or Chuck Higgins. After the song, people were cheering and clapping. Then some slow music played with smooth, sweet harmonies. My imagination was flipping out because I couldn't see the people dancing, only those that were looking out the window. That memory is as clear as a doo-wop falsetto. I couldn't wait to start school there in the fall, but we moved away because of Dad's gig at the Sands in Vegas.

Las Vegas in the mid-fifties was a small, segregated, Mormon desert town (African Americans had to live on the Westside) with only a few casino hotels on the Strip. The first one was the Flamingo Hotel on the right side of the highway as you came into town from L.A. It was opened in 1947 by the legendary gangster Benjamin "Bugsy" Siegel, a founder of Murder, Inc. Las Vegas was destined to become the ultimate adult playground, inspired by the excess of a playboy mobster. It seemed appropriate. And here I was, twelve years old, in this contradictory world combining sin and Mormon piety.

Another defining rock 'n' roll moment occurred when I saw the movie *Blackboard Jungle*. The movie starred Glen Ford and introduced Sidney Poitier, Vic Morrow, and a Puerto Rican kid, Rafael Campos. I thought Rafael was Mexican and strongly identified with his role, and I was also inspired by his great acting. Although Bill Haley and the Comets were closer to rockabilly than to rhythm and blues, the juxtaposition of a juvenile-delinquent drama with a hard backbeat was pretty impressive and liberating back then, especially for a budding teenager. Dang! I think we even vandalized some cars on the way home!

Since my parents weren't book readers, I learned about life lessons and building character by watching movies. I learned about integrity and how to be tough yet gentle with love in *On the Waterfront* through Marlon Brando's passionate performance with Eva Marie Saint, and about the anguish of being a misunderstood teenager in *Rebel without a Cause* with James Dean. Through the stark, poetic cinematography of *Night of the Hunter* with Robert Mitchum I learned about the psychosis of religious people. Films were also instrumental as I began to develop my core aesthetic: bold, tender, uncompromising truth and love.

One of the few times I saw a movie with mom and dad as a teenager was when we watched *Duel in the Sun* with Jennifer Jones and Gregory Peck. Jones played a tough, fiery *mestiza,* a half-white indigenous woman (Pearl Chávez), who falls in love with Peck, a ladies' man. Now *that* was a cool first for a Hollywood "cowboys and Indians" movie.

The ending blew my mind: Peck and Jones engage in a jealous shootout in the mountains. Then, realizing that death is imminent, they crawl toward each other on their wounded, bleeding legs and arms while crying out their love for each other. Finally at the end, they die in each other's arms. Suddenly, love took on a deeper, darker dimension for me.

One other movie we saw together was *Guys and Dolls* with Marlon Brando and Frank Sinatra. I never heard my mother laugh so hard before or since.

With one of the scenes, she continued laughing uncontrollably even after it was over. The audience turned to look at her. I was amused, a little embarrassed, but proud. That would be the only time I would ever share her unbridled laughter with my dad.

Movies turned me on. They were liberating, heartbreaking, and transformative. The best school I ever attended. The best books I never read.

I used to hang out around the entrances to the lounges where Dad played and luckily heard some of the musical giants of the day. Louie Prima and Keely Smith backed by monster tenor sax player Sam Butera and the Witnesses rocked the Sahara Hotel into smithereens. Freddy Bell and the Bell Hops, the Treniers, and another tenor sax great, Vido Musso, were also powerful inspirations with their high-octane showmanship. The music and the scene were a wild mix of jumping zany fun and romance, a party-*Jamaica* to the max. Hooked and shaped between movies and music, I began my life-long journey into the crazy world of rock 'n' roll—and life—at heartbreaking speed. There was no turning back.

Miss Las Vegas

MY FIRST GIRLFRIEND WAS BINNIE, a jazz dancer and a Filipina beauty. We were both thirteen. I loved the way she moved. She floated. Her mother was a cocktail waitress on the Strip and turned me on to jazz trumpeter Bobby Hackett and the album *For Lovers Only* with the Jackie Gleason Orchestra. I loved the standard ballads and the tone of his trumpet. I would later emulate his sound and style.

Binnie and I would meet at the local movie house for Saturday matinees. It was a kick making out with her while the movie played. I had two fires burning, one in my heart and one in my pants. But all we did was kiss, and I perfected it. I didn't try to touch her body, although I wanted to, because there was the stigma of a girl being thought of as a slut if you did, and I didn't want to disrespect her.

One night I asked her to go to one of my dad's gigs, a grand opening for an exclusive men's clothing store on the Strip. Mom drove us there. It was a trip sitting in the back seat with Binnie and having Mom be our chauffeur, all dressed up and looking beautiful as usual.

We watched Dad play, and she seemed to enjoy it, although it was basically traditional Mexican *bolero* ballads. I had a sport coat on with a white shirt and tie, and she was wearing a kind of prom dress, low cut, bare shoulders, red lipstick, and long black hair. She looked like my first Christmas present, and I was proud to introduce her to my dad. He smiled at her, then at me, and I felt good. I looked around the store, thinking to maybe buy something with money from my paper route. I spotted a brown cashmere overcoat, but damn! It was almost a thousand bucks! So if I wanted to dress sharp for my lady, I'd have to make a *lot* of money as a musician. That was life and reality lesson number one. More than fifty years later, I still can't afford a coat like that.

After the gig, Mom took us to a drive-in hamburger stand, the kind where the waitresses come to your car. We all had burgers, fries, and malts. I watched Mom and Binnie enjoying the food, and for a moment I felt like a man.

A while later, Dad got a gig at the Ambassador Hotel in L.A., so we moved back in '55. I completely believed that I would see Binnie again, and I promised to come back. After all, she was my girl. We kissed for a long time, we hugged for a long time, we cried for a long time, then we said goodbye. Sadly, I never saw her again. First rule of being a musician: You have to go where the gigs are, no matter what. The gig is your meal ticket. It is how you survive.

La Gatita

LA GATITA WAS KNOWN AS the "bad girl" from Berendo Junior High—and Berendo had a bad reputation. She ran with Las Gatas, a gang of *pachukas,* which included Mexicans and one fine Japanese American girl. I hadn't heard the word *pachuko* since my early days in La Veinte. I knew *pachukos,* but I never saw or knew any *pachukas.*[1] I was intrigued and fascinated by this "Gatita" chick, especially since she wasn't Mexican. She was white.

I started Berendo in the eighth grade in '55, when we lived near Olympic and Normandie, which included a large Japanese American community. We weren't called "Mexican Americans"—we were just Mexicans, or Japanese, or Chinese, or Negroes. I guess we weren't considered Americans yet. I sold newspapers on the corner of Olympic and Normandie, right up the street from the Japanese American–owned Uptown Nursery. I would bring the owner the paper every day, and he would always give me a little tip for doing so. Those were my first tips. I thought he was so generous for doing that. The tip was always good for a cold bottle of soda and a bag of peanuts. This was the beginning of my lifelong friendship with and respect for Japanese Americans.

It was during the time of the McCarthy hearings, which dominated the headlines for months. My interest in journalism began while selling those papers on the streets. I learned about world affairs and local news by reading the headlines as I called out, "Extra, extra, read all about it! Joe McCarthy censured!" That's when I learned about communists. The way McCarthy told

1. *Pachuko/Pachuka* was commonly spelled with a *k* within the Los Angeles Mexican American community as a rebellious act of identity.

it, they were "un-American traitors." I later learned that they were freedom fighters fighting against the tyranny of capitalism.

I also cleaned offices and polished floors in buildings on Wilshire and Vermont to earn more money to go to the movies. One was *The Seven Year Itch,* with Marilyn Monroe. Now, that flick turned me on. (I had to sneak in because I was under age.) This memory evolved into me looking at Marilyn like she was an ethereal cartoony sex kitten, part blonde Betty Boop and part Jennifer Jones. I thought, hell, I can seduce this chick. Why is that Tom Ewell character having such a hard time getting down with her? Shit, *I* could! Or so I thought. That's how sure of myself I was becoming. Then I saw *The Barefoot Contessa* with Ava Gardner and that was it. I'd met my match, and I've been looking for her ever since. I didn't know at the time that my dad knew her. It must have really been tough turning down her invitation to go to Spain as her personal guitarist, probably the noblest act of his life.

The first time I learned about white racism toward Mexicans was in '56 watching *Giant,* starring James Dean and Elizabeth Taylor. The scene where a Mexican family was refused service in a Texas diner struck a raw nerve. What the fuck was that about? That scene burned into my brain as a constant reminder that this land of the free isn't that free, that there's a price to pay to get service at the American counter of life, the price of humiliation and disrespect. It was a history lesson I never learned in school.

Every year there was a gathering of mostly JA's—Japanese Americans—at the annual Saint Mary's Bazaar, a carnival fundraiser for the Episcopalian church on Mariposa by Olympic, not too far from where I lived. That was where I saw my first JA *pachuko* gang, the Black Juans from J Flats (Virgil district). According to former member Jim "The General" Matsuoka, naming their turf "J Flats" was inspired by the First Street and Fourth Street Flats gangs from Boyle Heights. One of the gangs, not sure where they were from, had black knee-length club jackets with an embossed head of a JA dude on the back with a mile-high pompadour, Fu Manchu moustache, and shades. Damn, Japanese American *pachukos* were fuckin' cool, and I wanted to become their friend. And I did, with Kembo Shimizu (his favorite greeting was "ah so, muthafuckuh") and Ronnie Hamamoto.

I guess I still had Binnie the dancer from Vegas on my mind when I first saw the JA beauty Helen Funai walk across campus. She also floated when she walked. Her poise, grace, and elegant beauty later landed her a role—after she graduated from Berendo—as a featured dancer in the Broadway and movie versions of *Flower Drum Song.* Nobuko Miyamoto, another beautiful and famous Berendo alumna, danced in *West Side Story,* cast as a Puerto Rican. We would later become great friends and collaborate on several theater projects in the 2000s.

Helen only seemed interested in her schoolwork and dancing career. So I turned my attention to Gatita, even though she seemed a little too hot to handle. She had a body that would have made even Ava Gardner jealous. She was the hottest chick in school, bar none. One Friday night at a dance in the boy's gym, I spotted her wearing a short tight black skirt, tight black sweater, big earrings, and white Bunny shoes that were real popular with the *pachukas* at the time. She had all the moves, slow *and* fast, and all the guys were asking her to dance. I didn't have the guts, though, so I just checked her out. I decided to wait until the last dance of the night, when they always played a slow R & B doo-wop ballad. "Earth Angel" by the Penguins came on. Since it was slow, I knew I could handle it, but I still wasn't sure if I could handle her. La Gatita was most definitely thee *pachuka* Queen of the Hop.

Teenage dances were the way a young man learned how to move his body next to a woman, how to handle his emerging manhood, his sexuality. My hip *tío* "Lolo" had taught me all about that. "You don't hold her too loose or too tight," he told me. "You move in rhythm and imagine you're making love. You gotta show confidence in how you hold yourself—and her—and how you move her to the beat. It's all about smooth, sincere seduction."

When that last dance came on, the lights were turned down and I finally walked up to her, offering my hand. "Can we dance?" She turned, and man, she had the most beautiful piercing emerald green eyes I'd ever seen. No wonder she was called "La Gatita," with those cat eyes. She checked me out, smiled, and took my hand. I slowly put my right arm around her waist, not too loose, not too tight, just right. Gradually, I pulled her a little closer to me, but not too close, just enough for us to lightly brush against each other. I waited to see if she was okay with it. She was, and she took it further. She held me tighter. We locked in sync, in the heart of the beat, the pulse, in the pocket. Now was the time to bring her closer, cheek resting on cheek, locked in perfect rhythm. I tried with all my might not to kiss her neck: I didn't want to push my luck. I loved the feel of her breath, feeling it get louder against the side of my face. That's when I put both my arms around her waist and waited to see if she would follow. She did. Our bodies once again brushed against each other. We were in teen-lust heaven. The song ended and we held each other close for a few more beats. I pulled away and we looked into each other's eyes for a few seconds in silence. "Hi, I'm 'Chico.'" "Hi, I'm 'Gatita.'" Then she turned and slowly walked away.

I started hanging out with some young 'chukos who were in the neighborhood Pico-Union gang, Los Gavilanes, an offshoot of the Eastside Zapeta Flips, a younger division of the Primera Flats gang from Boyle Heights. Primera Flats had expanded to what was then called the "Westside," which meant west of downtown, including the Pico-Union district. I was initiated into the gang, or "jumped in," by staying on my feet for five minutes with only a belt as a weapon to fight off the members. I held my ground. I decided to get "jumped in" because that's what we thought we had to do in the barrio. Looking back, I realize I subconsciously did it to prove I was bad enough to get Berendo's bad girl, La Gatita.

Her mother was a cocktail waitress at a bowling alley in Culver City. She had a boyfriend who was a cool Filipino 'chuko cat known as "Johnny Midnite," with the baddest, tallest pompadour and shiniest ducktail around. I felt proud when he would pick us up after school and drive us home in his lowered '49 midnight blue Merc' just like the one James Dean drove in *Rebel without a Cause*. Everybody would check us out. We were quite a sight together—La Gatita, bad little punk 'chuko me, and Johnny Midnite. It was too much. I wanted to train my hair like Johnny's, but it was too curly. But I tried anyway. I had to use a lot of Royal Crown pomade to straighten it and keep it down.

I formed a duo with me on trumpet and my friend Frankie on drums. We were mentored in the fine art of boogie-woogie and jump blues by Mr. Henry Williams, the school custodian and master piano player. He'd open up the auditorium during lunchtime and we'd jam up a storm. He taught us "Caldonia" by Louis Jordan and "Harlem Nocturne" by Johnny Otis, the closing theme song on his KTLA TV show. We later played those tunes, plus Glenn Miller's "Little Brown Jug" that my dad taught me, at the next Friday night dance. It was my first rock 'n' roll gig, 1956, and we rocked the joint. Las Gatas were all into it, dancing along, with La Gatita leading the pack. She was so impressed with my music that she wanted to join the band as our singer. For the big graduation concert we worked up the Latin jazz hit "Begin the Beguine," and she nailed it. Man, that girl could move *and* sing! As we walked off the stage she threw her arms around me and said, "Hey, Chico, that was too much, *ese!* I felt like a star. Thanks for giving me a chance. Let's go get something to eat, baby." I finally had her, and it blew my mind. That's when I learned that music meant beautiful women. It was a powerful lesson . . . and a dangerous one too.

One Saturday Dad drove us to the movies at the Boulevard Theatre on Washington by Vermont. She was wearing her usual tight clothes and had to really wiggle and squeeze to get into the front seat of the car. As she slid in between us, I saw his eyes bulge out. I couldn't blame him. It cracked me up a little, even made me feel proud.

Our formative teenage soundtrack was R & B/doo-wop music. We'd listen to Art Laboe and Dick Hugg "Huggy Boy" on KPOP and Hunter Hancock on KGFJ while cruising with Johnny Midnite. Our song was "Why Do Fools Fall in Love" by Frankie Lymon and the Teenagers. We looked good dancing the "Pachuko Hop" to it. We looked good in everything we did. She was La Gatita, the queen of my heart, and I was her king *vato*.

Graduation finally came and Johnny Midnite and La Gatita's mom threw a party for us at his pad in Echo Park. I had a little half-pint of I. W. Harper bourbon that I'd gotten a taste for at Gatita's house. It was her grandmother's favorite. Finally the night had arrived for the smooth moves into her sweet luscious body. We were alone in a dark bedroom that had a tall window that opened onto a balcony overlooking a patio below with palm trees and a fountain in the middle. It looked like Mexico. We started kissing like crazy, my hands moving all over her body. I was on top of her, kissing and rubbing her, when suddenly her mother walked in and screamed at us to stop. Fuck! We had no choice but to stop. Next thing I knew, Johnny was driving me home. He said, "Don't worry, *ese*. Try it again. She's yours."

We moved before I could try it again. Dad got another gig in Vegas. It tore me up. She promised to save herself for me. "Chico, you know I'm yours *por vida*." "Gatita, I'll be back, I promise!" But it didn't happen. I had no control over abandoning my girlfriends, and it made me angry.

Aside from rock 'n' roll, chicks, and gangs, I developed a strong interest in American history in school, especially World War II. I got straight A's in that course. I discovered large photography books in the library showing the crazy shit committed against Jewish people in the German concentration camps. My interest in cultural genocide began there. It would impact my poetry, starting in 1975 with "C/S" describing the unjust imprisonment of thousands of innocent Japanese Americans during the war. Later, my theater performance piece *La Quemada* focused on the invasion of Mexico. History became the greatest movie of all, and I could be in it. I had a good history teacher who encouraged my studies. She was also very sexy, sitting on a stool in front of me with her legs crossed. I was a very attentive student to what she said and how she moved. What an education!

Las Vegas and the Breakup of Our Family

AFTER I GRADUATED FROM BERENDO we moved back to Vegas, where I started at Las Vegas High. I looked for Binnie, but no luck. After a couple of months, though, my mom, sisters, and I were on the road again, on our way back to L.A. It was a sudden and unsettling move. The night before, I'd heard my mom and dad having a long, serious conversation. I couldn't hear what they were talking about, only the sobs of my father. I'd never heard him cry before, and I never would again. Something heavy was up. As we drove across the barren desert I looked down at my sweet baby sister Loretta who was peacefully sleeping on my lap and remembered the altars I used to build in Cathedral City to help me find peace and to pray. I felt like I needed to do that now. I looked over at Mom and asked her why we were going back to L.A. "Your father and I have decided to buy a house," she said. "We'll finally have a place to settle down. I'll look for one, then he'll come and be with us later. Don't worry. It's going to be alright." I didn't ask why dad was crying the night before. I was too embarrassed to ask and too afraid to know.

We stayed with my *tía* Marina and *tío* Raúl and their kids for a few weeks in Sun Valley, then moved into a tiny motel room in North Hollywood. We waited and waited. Dad never came. My mom would tell me that my dad never sent child support like he'd promised. It turned out there was another woman. We were shattered when we learned the truth—we hadn't seen it coming. Out of desperation, Mom started working as a dance instructor for the Arthur Murray dance studios. Later she set off on an acting career in television and the movies. What a trip, watching your own mom becoming a Hollywood starlet. It was surreal and scary because I was attracted to

Hollywood starlets, and now my mom was transforming into one in front of my eyes.

I felt deep anger and humiliation walking to school every morning, feeling like a lost, displaced wanderer. As an act of rebellion and a way to get back at my dad, I quit playing the trumpet. I even changed my name to Ben to distance myself from him. So instead of music, I excelled in track and field, reaching City Preliminaries in the 120-yard high hurdles in my senior year. I tied the school record at 10.1 seconds (wind aided) and was the high point man on the Varsity track team. Sports became a way to get a somewhat secure handle on my life. Music was just too dangerous.

I made friends with Ron Mercado, a Mexican cat who was an artist and a football player. He invited me to join the Apollos, a combination athletic and car club sponsored by the YMCA. There were a few working-class white cats in the club, but mostly they were Mexican and Japanese American bad boys who had been kicked out of San Fernando High and Polytechnic High. Most of them had been on the football team. They were the baddest cats around.

Me, I was just a tall skinny *vato* kid trying to find my way. The school I attended was made up mostly of white middle- and upper-class kids whose parents worked in the local film studios. I'd never been in that kind of school environment before: Berendo had had only a few white kids. At my new school, I soon picked up on the racial vibe in the air. The white kids didn't like the Apollos since we were a mixed bunch of colored misfits. Except for the athletes—they got some respect. That was my introduction to racism as well as my challenge to fit in. I eventually attacked both racism and fitting in through music.

Part of my initiation into the car club was to walk up to random white "socialite" girls and croon to them in what is now called a doo-wop style. A club brother, Ronnie Rosati, understood the racism and made up the lyrics for me: "My name is Benny the Beaner from San Fernando and how the chicks dig my grease. Say hey little girl, would you like to go ridin' in my '49 Chevy with the Power Glide?" He was an Italian cat with a crazy and wise sense of humor. He gave me my nickname, "Little Julian," after the first Chicano rock star, "Little" Julian Herrera. But the song that really got the girls squirming was "Teardrops" by Lee Andrews and the Hearts. The effect it had on them was seductive in many ways. It smashed the racial divide and gave me a new sense of control, a new sense of worth. It taught me that rock 'n' roll music was powerful, and it was ours. It didn't belong to my father. I could be in charge of it. I owned it like I had at the dance at Berendo. Suddenly music wasn't my enemy anymore.

One night my Apollo club brothers "Flash," Pablo, "Rat," and I were walking down an alley past Perry's Rehearsal Studios on Highland in Hollywood on the way to see the Christmas Parade. It was Thanksgiving 1959. Suddenly we heard some singers, saxophones, and a band wailing away. We thought it was a party and decided to crash it. "Hey man, you go in first." "No man. You go in first." "Uh uh. You go in first." "Awright, let's all walk in together, like we're somebody, like we're a band, gotdammit!" We slowly crept in, looked around, and then our eyes and heads exploded. Working on their choreography were the Vibrations, going through "Hang On Sloopy"! Then came the Olympics hully-gullying to their hit of the same name, followed by two knockout-gorgeous dancers going through their moves backed by the monster Masked Phantom Band. Good God-a-mighty! What was this?! Then a duo of Mexican cats, the Carlos Brothers, walked up to the mic and launched into their current hit, "Tonight, Tonight." We had fallen into a freaking Alice and rock 'n' roll Wonderland!

It turned out to be a rehearsal for an upcoming concert at the Long Beach Municipal Auditorium. We struck up a conversation with the Carlos Brothers, telling them we wanted to learn how to get started as a group. They were friendly and invited us to the show. They were on Del-Fi Records, the same label that our Valley homeboy and inspiration Ritchie Valens was on. His death a few months earlier in a fiery plane crash had sent a chill up my spine, reminding me again of the dangers of music. But this was different. This was rock 'n' roll—*my* music—and this time I wasn't afraid of the fire.

The concert was a stone revelation, a psychedelic circus-hallucination, a New Year's Eve Halloween rock 'n' roll *Jamaica* all wrapped up in Crazy! The Masked Phantom Band, including Chicano tenor sax giant "Little" Bobby Rey and "Handsome" Jim Balcom on bass, walked out dressed in purple wrestling tights and black hoods with holes cut out for the eyes, nose, and mouth, like the cartoon-strip hero, the Phantom. Following them were the two knockout dancers, the Phantomettes, wearing black leotards, high spiked heels, fishnet stockings, stacked *pachuka* hair, and black Lone Ranger masks. Then the band tore into their local hit "Corrido Rock" and immediately turned the dance floor into a blur of flying bodies.

There was a popular dance at the time that went with the "Corrido Rock" song. Imagine a Mexican *norteño* tune cranked up on speed. Two long lines of couples facing each other with interlocked arms would take four steps toward each other, almost crashing into each other, then four steps back, along with the beat. Then both lines would make a quarter turn and do the four steps forward, four steps back again. When they would make that quarter turn, the last ones on the ends of each line would get whipped around off their feet.

Then out came our boys the Carlos Brothers, the Vibrations, and the headliners, the Olympics. Too much! This was rock and fucking roll, and I wanted to be in the heart-of-the-heat-of-it. We talked to the Carlos Brothers again after the show and reminded them that we were starting up a vocal group. They invited us to more of their shows, where we learned the fine art of soul showmanship—how to dance and work with the mic, and most importantly: if you can't make the audience go crazy, you're not doing your job.

THE APOLLO BROTHERS, 1960S

I met Tommy "Flash" Volk when the two of us were getting initiated into the Apollos car club. We had to do some crazy shit that wound up bonding us as brothers for life. One night at a party, Tommy cut loose on the piano and he rocked the house down. He played in a mean barrelhouse boogie-woogie style that I hadn't heard since my Berendo days during the jams in the auditorium with the school custodian, Mr. Williams. Tommy was also a star athlete on the Varsity gymnastic team, eventually winning first place All-City in tumbling. So we had a strong connection through both music and sports.

Pablo was from the South Central Adams district and grew up in African American culture, music, and slang. He sang in a doo-wop group called the Van Teers. We met one day in the boys' bathroom while I was combing my hair. He was looking at me in the mirror and said, "Hey, can I borrow your comb, *ese?*" I checked out his pressed khakis, pompadour, French-toed shoes, and Sir Guy shirt, looking every bit like the *'chukos* I hung with at Berendo, and said, "*Órale,* sure." To ask somebody to borrow their comb was an act of trust and brotherhood, *carnalismo.* He started singing some lick from an R & B ballad as he combed his hair, and I joined in. There's nothing like a little doo-wop in the echo of a school bathroom. Our voices blended perfectly. I later got him into the Apollos.

We formed a vocal trio keeping the Van Teers name, with Pablo, me, and Robbie "Rodent" Warren singing and Tommy on piano. We were quite the hit on campus. Nobody else was cool enough to be doing R & B ballads like

"We Belong Together" and crazy rock 'n' roll like Don and Dewey's "Justine!" We tore it up at school assemblies and talent shows and at all the Apollos parties. Tommy would steal the show with his risqué rhythm and blues versions of "Big Ten Inch" by Bull Moose Jackson and "Baby Let Me Bang Your Box" by the Toppers. He had the hippest record collection on the planet. We were bad and we were cool. We were Apollos.

After barely graduating from high school in 1960, Pablo, Tommy, and I met Bobby Sanders, a manager-producer-singer at a coffeehouse talent show in Van Nuys. He took one look at Tommy and nicknamed him "Flash" after the science fiction super hero, Flash Gordon. There was a resemblance. Sanders later introduced us to record producer Mabel Lafferty, which surprisingly led to an audition and then a recording contract. We recorded two of our tunes: a ballad, "My Beloved One," based on an old girlfriend, and an up-tempo rocker, "Riot (In the Quad)," about lunchtime food fights at school. Veteran producer Scotty Turnbull produced and conducted the session, with Flash (then only nineteen) playing along with studio session pros without making any mistakes. After only two takes we'd nailed both tunes.

We decided to name ourselves the Apollo Brothers after our car club and brotherly bond, and also because of the Innocents, a rival car club. Three members from that club had formed the Innocents trio and were riding high with their hits "Honest I Do" and "Gee Whiz." They were great, and they were our competition.

Our record promoter was a colorful character: Al Husky, cousin or brother of country singer Ferlin Husky. One of the many highlights for us was appearing at the Long Beach Municipal Auditorium, where we'd gotten our first taste of rock 'n' roll a few years earlier. The headliner was Paul Anka, promoting his hit single "Diana." We were backed by Mike Adams and the Red Jackets, a smoking kick-ass band, with Flash joining us on piano. He'd never played with a pro rock band before. Now he was a pro. We all were.

Then we played the Mecca of rock, the El Monte American Legion Stadium, with our heroes Richard Berry and the Pharaohs, and the Olympics. Man, that was too much! Nothing like walking out on stage with no one knowing who you are and getting to blow their brains out with your music, and walking off with them screaming for more. We also got to sing with our idols Don and Juan of "What's Your Name" fame on Wink Martindale's TV show, first at P.O.P. (Pacific Ocean Park), an amusement park in Santa Monica, and then at the show's Hollywood studios. We were on a hot roll.

Alan Freed was out here in Los Angeles after being kicked out of New York because of the payola scandals, and he picked up on our record and played it on his show. I remember the first time I heard it on the radio, on KDAY: he started the record and said, "And now here are the Apollo Brothers . . . *and* they are handsome girls." We eventually met him and his "beautiful wife, Inga," as he would say on the air. He was cordial and very nice to us, contrary to his media reputation.

We were set to do some more shows, but they didn't happen. Still, we felt that we were launched and the sky was the limit.

Sue Dean

I WAS ENGAGED TO MY high school sweetheart, Sue Dean, during the time my music career was taking off. The first time I saw her I was walking across campus. She stopped and dropped me dead in my tracks. She was tall, wore a beehive-backcombed hairdo à la Ronnie Spector, heavy Cleopatra eyeliner and mascara, a bulky orange turtleneck sweater, short plaid skirt, thick orange-and-black striped stockings, and short, orange heels. "Phew!" You could say very Amy Winehouse of her day and very *Vogue* and very radical and stylish for a late-1950s white high school girl. I didn't dig the chicks in *Playboy*. They were too safe, too predictable. High fashion models were more mysterious, more intriguing. Sue was one of a kind, a star on campus— a work of art—and I fell crazy in love with her.

She was the daughter of Loomis Dean, a highly respected photographer for *Life* magazine. His iconic images of playwright Noel Coward and Spanish *torero* El Cordobés, among many others, have become part of photojournalism lore. On July 26, 1956, he and his wife, Mary Sue, and their three kids, Sue, Chris, and Debbie, were on the ocean liner *Île de France* returning to the U.S. from Paris (where he was stationed with the magazine) when they sailed close by the sinking *SS Andrea Doria*. Loomis managed to get the first photos of the sinking ship, which later appeared on the cover of *Life* magazine. He was a Southerner, a gregarious, outspoken, *bon vivant* kind of guy, but he didn't approve of my relationship with his daughter. He didn't dig non-whites. Luckily, he went back to Paris to live. And his wife, Mary Sue, was cool with me.

Sue and I once went to Catalina Island on a seaplane for a weekend with her mom and siblings. We hiked to the Wrigley mausoleum, where I carved our names on the marble wall: Ben & Sue, P/V—meaning *por vida,* for life. We were so in love with each other. We felt so right for each other. Our song was "We Belong Together" by Robert and Johnny, which became part of the Apollo Brothers set list.

It all felt like a Hollywood movie. The future looked bright, what with gigs and the record getting steady local air play on KDAY by Alan Freed, on KGFJ by Herman Griffith (who called it a VIP—Very Important Platter, a first by a Mexican act), and on the Dick Hugg "Huggy Boy" radio show. With all this action supporting us, we got married. I was nineteen, she was seventeen. Our son, Ben, was born the following year. "Do you promise to take care of us?" she asked. "Oh yes! I promise!"

One day as I was driving home, I was sideswiped and my car rolled over three times. It was a little Renault that her father had sent us from Paris as a wedding gift. I stiffened and straightened my arms, gripping the steering wheel with all my might, determined not to die. The sunroof was open, and during one of the rolls I felt my head scrape the pavement as I heard the sound of wings flapping. Angel wings? I walked away from the totaled car pulling sand from my scalp. I had dodged another bullet. I still had Superman in my corner.

Unfortunately, the gigs became fewer and a follow-up release didn't happen. So I went to work as a house cleaner to keep the marriage from falling apart. But the strain of struggling to make ends meet trying to support a wife and child finally took its toll and we split up after a couple years. Her father had warned her not to marry me, saying I suffered from "delusions of grandeur." Maybe he was right.

While I was sitting in a court cafeteria waiting for the child support hearing, the news came on the TV that John F. Kennedy had just been shot. I thought for sure he would be okay. Everybody did. He was a bigger-than-life hero for the country, with all that Camelot shit. When the news came on that he'd died, I surprisingly felt a sickening sense of panic and abandonment. Like the time my mother didn't come to pick me up from school in the second grade. Like my dad dropping the family. Like my *tata* dying. It was strange. I had never felt that kind of sorrow and loss over a non–family member. Lonely, scared, and desperate, I tried to reconcile with Sue to keep a sense of soul safety and sanity, but she turned me down. My world collapsed like the house of cards that it was. I was shattered, just like my *nana's* glass front door that I crashed through as a kid.

We finally divorced, and Sue went on to become a successful high fashion model in L.A., New York, and in Paris with the house of Chanel. My history with raising our son wasn't always the best. I tried to see him as often as possible and contribute financial support, but it was never enough. It was my first failure as a husband and a father.

Miss Hollywood

I PURSUED MY SEDUCTIVE MUSICAL MUSE even though she was a dangerous siren. The Apollo Brothers finally got a steady gig at Pandora's Box, a hip coffeehouse on the Sunset Strip. We were backed by the Du-Vals with Bill Wild on bass, who later played in Ruben And The Jets.[1] "Flash" had quit the group. We opened several times for the mighty O'Jays and smooth soul pop singer Dobie Gray. We were lucky to be getting R & B gigs, since the bubblegum British Invasion had just struck.

The Hollywood music scene in the early '60s mostly involved discotheques, which had started in Paris then moved to New York's Peppermint Lounge. Chubby Checker helped it along with his dance hit "The Twist," a cover of an earlier hit by Hank Ballad and the Midnighters. There were still the old glamor spots from the '40s and '50s like Ciro's, the Mocambo, and the Crescendo that featured jazz, but by the mid-sixties even these establishments were booking rock 'n' roll bands. So Pandora's Box was one of the last joints on the Strip, along with Gazzari's on La Cienega and a few others, that still featured R & B.

Pandora's Box was a cool place to gig at, even though the pay sucked, but there were perks: namely, the waitresses. One who had my undivided dog attention was Melissa, a stunning lesbian beauty with Sophia Loren cheekbones and green eyes. There was going to be an after-hours house party at her girlfriend's apartment after a gig one night, and she invited me. I got there

---

1. Ruben And The Jets was spelled out, with each word capitalized, to differentiate between this later band and the fictitious Frank Zappa band on his album *Cruising with Ruben & the Jets*.

and watched her dance with her lover and wondered what the hell that was all about. Lesbianism was new to me, and I found it fascinating: Why would she prefer a woman instead of a man? Then they disappeared into her bedroom and my mind went wild.

I poured myself another scotch, lit a joint, and watched my first lesson in hedonism unfold, Hollywood Babylon style. I was diggin' it to the max, high as a satellite, when bam! In walked a tall, gorgeous blonde. I wasn't into blondes, but she was different in a freaky high fashion kind of way. She was wearing shiny brown leather knee boots, beige wool culottes, a tight brown leather bolero jacket, and brown turtleneck sweater; her hair was in a pixie cut, and she had the bluest green eyes I'd ever seen. I swear she looked like Kim Novak. I intently watched her walk across the room with the confidence and poise of a prima ballerina and the swagger of Jane Russell. She smiled and said, "Hi, I'm Beverly," and offered me a joint. Later on I wound up in her bedroom and everything fit and clicked.

As the sun was rising Melissa and her girlfriend walked into the bedroom and regarded us in disbelief. Then Beverly said, "Good morning ladies, meet 'Little Pedro,'" referring to the likable cartoon character in the comic strip by William de la Torre. Probably the only reference she had to a Mexican, since she was from a farm in Illinois. Funny, it didn't offend me; it only cracked me up. It was all too crazy.

Beverly made me breakfast. I asked to see her again and she said, "Sure, I can do that. I'm in an open relationship." "What's that?" "Well, my girl-friend and I have an agreement to sleep with whomever we want." "Girlfriend?" I asked. "Yeah, Jasmine." "Oh, outta sight." I was momentarily dumbstruck, bewildered, yet fascinated. For the next couple of days I fanta-sized crazy shit. The situation was offering an opportunity to broaden my sexual repertoire. I had to call her. She agreed to another rendezvous, and we took it to a higher frequency talking about life, love, and future dreams in a deep, serious way. She said she never had that kind of intimacy with her girl-friend. We fell in lust, then in love. She broke off with her lover and she later asked me to move in.

After Pandora's we were booked into the famous discotheque Peppermint Lounge West, the hippest club in town. It was named after the one in New York. Man, we were tripping out! It would have been our biggest break, but the joint burned down a week before the gig. Burned again! Why does fire follow me like a shadow? Discouraged and once again broke, I took a day gig in a chemical warehouse in southeast L.A., on Bandini and Atlantic. Beverly worked at a wig shop on Hollywood Boulevard, where her clients included Little Richard and Sam Cooke's manager.

One day I was dumping old sulphuric acid out of fifty-gallon drums into a ditch that emptied into a street gutter. As I turned the key on the small vent cap, the built-up pressure inside blew off my facemask. The right side of my face caught on fire. The intense heat from the acid momentarily blinded me. I only saw white space, then I surreally saw my name in lights go out on a marquee. Another fiery trauma.

There was an outside shower for accidents like this, but I couldn't see it because of the pain. I kept my cool in spite of the fact that my face might be disfigured for life. The movie *Beauty and The Beast* flashed across my mind. My career was likely over. My hustling good looks were over. But I still had that crazy sense of being Superman. By sheer instinct and blind will, I staggered with outstretched zombie-like antennae-arms searching for the outside shower stall, and miraculously, I found it. By this time my supervisor had arrived, and he rushed me to the hospital. The pain lingered like a hot branding iron stuck on my face. The doctor said he didn't know how bad the burns were, but they looked like third-degree burns. He prescribed some ointment, wrapped my face in bandages, and sent me out the door. "*Tía* Victoria, where are you!" I cried, remembering when she healed my burns as an infant with her magical potion.

When I took the bus from Hollywood to work, people would cringe and look away. They could see some of my black charred skin at the outer edges of the bandages. It was horrible. I went into a deep depression. I felt like the character in the 1980s flick *The Elephant Man,* like a monster. Then another miracle happened: my face started to heal. The doctors were amazed. They had been talking skin graft operations. But after four months my face was very close to healed, although it was badly scarred. But over time, I recovered. Somebody up there actually does like me, and maybe I am invincible after all.

After that fuckin' nightmare I decided to quit the gig and go back to music as a solo artist. I'd rather face the dangerous life of a musician than get killed working as a slave. I started singing again, slowly getting my voice and confidence back. I sang in after-hours bars as Aztec Watts, a nickname given to me by tenor saxophonist "Scooby." This was in 1964. I'd also hang out at an after-hours bar in Hawthorne with Pablo and Flash where Richard Berry led the house band. It was inspiring to hear him sing and play like he did back at the Legion the night we were all on the same bill. Pablo and Flash weren't into continuing with music, but I had to come back.

Beverly got an offer to open her own wig shop on Sunset and Poinsettia, so we moved back to Hollywood, finding a place on Hayworth up the street from Greenblatt's Deli on the Strip. It was a very fancy apartment. I felt rich, strong, and ready to finally conquer Babylon.

Shindig! *with Tina Turner and Bo Diddley*

IN 1965 MY MOTHER, who was still working as an actress to make ends meet raising my three sisters, set up an audition for me on *Shindig!*, a popular national TV rock 'n' roll variety show. The Du-Vals, with Bill Wild on bass, backed me up for the audition on Bobby "Blue" Bland's "Turn on Your Love Light." I gave it everything I had, from the bottom of my funky feet to the top of my greasy head. I knocked it out of the park. Thanks to my dear mother, I was about to finally make the Big Time.

"You were great! Fantastic! You're on! You've got the gig! Hope you don't mind changing your name?" "Huh?" "We'd like you to change your name to J. P. Moby." "J. P. Moby? That sounds a lot like P. J. Proby," I said, puzzled as a motherfucker. *Shindig!* had had a blue-eyed soul singer from Texas named P. J. Proby. He left the show on bad terms, and the producers weren't too happy about it. So they wanted to get back at him through me: "J. P. Moby." I didn't know what to say. I remembered Ritchie Valens went through that. He followed orders. Chubby Checker's stage name was another version of Fats Domino. Actually, it was kind of a twisted compliment. The name was later modified to Jay P. Mobey at my request. So what's the big deal, changing your name? Who cares?

I was about to learn that in mainstream rock 'n' roll you're a product, not a person. I wasn't into ethnic identity yet. It was my pre-Chicano period. So I didn't see it as a cultural misstep then. But I sure do now. Still, I was being offered a potentially recurring role as a "regular" on a nationally televised TV show. That meant decent steady money for a change, independence, a car, being able to pay the rent and buy food, and some badly needed self-respect as a man.

Another reason I wanted to do the show was because Miss Hot Thing Tina Turner was going to be on *and* so was my rock 'n' roll hero Bo Diddley. One of the first rock 'n' roll records I bought, in 1955, was "Bo Diddley/I'm a Man," and here I was on the same bill and even sharing my dressing room with him. For the taping of the show, I sang live to a prerecorded track and got it in one take. I was on fire. It turned out that Tina was to follow me in the order of the show. She came on. She missed a cue. Then she nailed it.

After the taping I spotted her sitting alone in the empty auditorium. I didn't see Ike around, so I made my move. "Hi," my name is Jay." "Hi, I'm Tina. Where did you learn to sing like that?" she asked, not quite sure what I was, since there weren't many Mexican soul singers around at the time. "I grew up in L.A. listening to R & B. The tune I just did was Bobby 'Blue' Bland's 'Don't Cry No More,'" I said, all confident. "Oh, wow, yeah, I recognized it." She smiled at me with her perfect bright shiny teeth. She was probably around twenty-five; I was twenty-two. And oh yeah, her legs. They were fine, fine, *super*-fine, and like the cocky kid that I was, I wanted them.

Bo was very gracious and cool with me. He didn't complain about having to share his dressing room. Before the broadcast in front of a live audience, we talked about life as a musician over his bottle of gin. He said it was tough but worth it. I said I was never going to give up and passed him the bottle. Then we went out and rocked the show. The lineup also included Jackie De Shannon, Billy Preston on Hammond B-3 with the Shindogs house band, and the vocal group the Blossoms. I was in a tribute medley for Bo, singing "Bo Diddley," a surf medley, my solo spot, and the closing finale with Bo and Tina and cast on "Can Your Monkey Do the Dog?" I was launched. I was on my way. I was in Rock 'n' Roll Heaven, and Tina was on my radar.

After my smashing debut I got the offer to be a regular on the show. Finally, I was going to make a living from this crazy fuckin' business. But for some stupid reason the format was changed to two thirty-minute shows airing twice a week. The audience didn't tune in and the show got canceled before I could shing-a-ling into a mansion in the Hollywood Hills. There went my dreams. There went Tina, all up in smoke.

I left Beverly before the show aired, foolishly confident that I could get something going with Tina. Instead I wound up living in my car broke and

Singing with my idol Bo Diddley on *Shindig!* ABC studios, Los Angeles, 1965. Photo courtesy of Rhino Records.

starving, and had to get a job right away. Gotta eat, gotta work. I started working at Chicken Delight on Sunset and Fuller delivering chicken up and down the Strip and the Hollywood Hills. "Hey, didn't I see you on *Shindig!* last month?" another driver asked. "Yeah," I said. "Well, what are you doing here?" "What does it look like, man? I'm delivering fuckin' chicken!"

To keep my sanity, I put an R & B band together, the Bag, with a Hammond B-3 (with bass pedals), guitar, and drums. I sang and played trumpet. We were the house band for a while at the Kabuki Lounge in the Japanese American and predominantly African American Crenshaw district. The VIPs (pre El Chicano) were also playing there on alternate weekends. It was a very trippy place, a Japanese bar that specialized in R & B and jazz. The waitresses were Japanese American and *fine*. They reminded me of some of the *pachuka* JA girls at Berendo. Crenshaw was a trip: Japanese American kids who grew up and lived there spoke, dressed, and acted like Blacks. Man, how cool was that? Evidently, both groups felt an affinity and a bond based on being targets of historical white racism.

Before gigging at the Kabuki Lounge I would often go to the Whisky on the Strip where I saw Otis Redding, the Young Rascals, Gladys Knight and the Pips, Mitch Ryder and the Detroit Wheels, among others. One night after I got off at Chicken Delight I went into the London Fog, a funky little bar next to Sneaky Pete's and the Whisky. The lead singer of the band was a trip. He reminded me of James Dean, all deep into his own world. The band was the Doors.

Somebody set up an appointment to meet idol maker Bob Marcucci, who was Frankie Avalon and Fabian's manager. We talked, he pitched; nothing happened. Then I hooked up with Helen Noga, who managed Johnny Mathis. That was a real mismatch. The most she did for me personally was book me into a talent night at the Action on Santa Monica. I lost. It was humiliating. Then she booked the Bag into a bowling alley in Bakersfield and a dive bar in Lancaster, Big Daddy's Lounge, where we followed Captain Beefheart. Yeah, man, I was in the Big Time. One night at the Bakersfield gig the drummer took off into a solo and wouldn't stop playing. I kept yelling at him to stop, but he ignored me. He was stoned out of his mind. I had to finally grab him and pull him off his kit. We got into a fight on stage, sticks and drums flying through the air. We were fired on the spot. At the bar in Lancaster a fight broke out in the audience and the band broke into the Gillette fight song: another highlight. But still, it was better than delivering chicken.

I did some gigs at the Hullabaloo—the old Moulin Rouge, where my dad gigged for a while in the '50s. Now I called myself Jay Mobey. After being introduced as America's answer to Tom Jones, I came out with my guns blazing and did my best "Please, Please, Please" and "Got My Mojo Working," but it didn't work on the audience. I got booed off the stage. I couldn't compete with that British bubblegum shit. And what really blew my mind was that teenagers were saying that rock 'n' roll was invented in England! It took the Rolling Stones years to say who their inspirations were, like Howlin' Wolf and Muddy Waters. The whole British scene made me sick in many ways. I felt displaced, irrelevant, and washed up.

Later I hooked up with Jack Spina, Pat Boone's manager, also a mismatch. But at least he managed to set up a recording session with David Gates of the hit pop group Bread as producer. We recorded "Turn on Your Love Light" and "On Broadway," with Bruce Botnick engineering. I was floored because Bruce had produced the Doors. David suggested I change my name to Montezuma. I dug the idea. An associate of Jack's, Henry Hurt, took the record to the just-founded UNI Records (Universal Records). Russ Reagan, head of A&R (Artists and Repertoire), loved it, but a deal couldn't get struck.

The record remains in their vaults. Montezuma could have been a cool contender.

After *Shindig!*, the Bag, and the whole comeback fiasco, I hit another deep, raw emotional low. The gut-wrenching blow of being abandoned by my rock 'n' roll dreams kicked me in the nuts and I went down hard. Out of desperation and stoned-out panic, I asked Beverly to take me back. She did.

Her wig client Little Richard invited us to his concert at Ciro's (Le Crazy Horse) on the Strip. The guitar player in the band was too much. I couldn't believe my eyes or ears. He tore into a solo playing his guitar on his shoulder and plucking out the notes with his teeth. It was Jimi Hendrix. Little Richard looked over at him pissed off with his eyes bugged out as the crowd roared. It was hilarious. I bet that was the last gig Jimi played with Mr. Richard.

Beverly was friends with Pat and Lolly Vegas (né Vázquez) and took me to see them at the original Gazzari's on La Cienega. They were basically a guitarist-singer, bass, and drum trio and the best band in Hollywood as far as I was concerned. They played R & B, rock 'n' roll, blues, and sang their asses off. They could do it all. No one knew they were Mexican Indians. They would later take the name Redbone in honor of their Mexican Yaqui roots. They remain unknown as the best Mexican American rock band ever.

The clothes designer of a new duo called Sonny and Cher was also friends with Beverly. She invited us to a party in Laurel Canyon where there was a musical revolution going on with residents Frank Zappa, Jim Morrison, and Joni Mitchell. Ironically, this was the same canyon where my face was barbequed as an infant. The place brought back dark memories.

The legendary freaky hippie bohemian Vito Paulekas, his wild child bride, Szou, and crazy Carl Franzoni were at the party, tripping out on some Ravi Shankar. There were a couple of guys with Beatle haircuts. One was "Beetle" Bob, who later became "Buffalo," the wild tenor sax player with Ruben And The Jets, which I would later cofound with Frank Zappa. The other guy was in a new band called the Byrds.

Although I was back living with Beverly and she was turning me on to new inspiring music, I wanted to get closer to my son, and Sue was still the queen of my hop. When I started dating Sue again, I realized I was still in love with her. Feeling twisted by torn emotions, I decided to break it off with Beverly. But sadly, Sue and I could never get back on track, so I returned to Beverly once more.

Beverly was still connected to the gay community and introduced me to one of her close gay friends, Bobby, who had a great gospel record collection. He turned me on to singers Brother Joe May, Sister Rosetta Tharpe, and Shirley Caesar, among others. One night he took us to Grace Memorial Church of God in Christ in South Central, where Little Richard sang early on in his career. My first up-close gospel experience was a stone treat and revelation. I was in the cradle of rock, and bam! I was reborn.

The Sunset Strip Riots and
My Second Marriage

MY FIRST FORAY INTO SOCIAL PROTEST and activism was during what became known as the Sunset Strip Riots of 1966, although they were merely demonstrations. No one was killed and no buildings were burned down, aside from a police car that somebody allegedly torched. Young people forging a new counterculture habitually congregated on the Strip, drawn to the scene in and around clubs featuring psychedelic music and recreational drug use. Local officials imposed a 10 P.M. curfew on the area, attempted to close the businesses that attracted crowds, and sent in police officers to clear the streets. I got involved when Larry, an ex-con and manager of Chicken Delight, organized some of the drivers for a demonstration to preserve Pandora's Box nightclub/coffeehouse at the corner of Sunset and Crescent Heights Boulevards. County officials attempted to close the club after police efforts failed to drive away the teenagers who hung out around there. Larry and I created my first placard, which read, "Give me liberty or give me Debs." Ernest E. Debs was the L.A. County supervisor behind the move to tear down the club. I was crossing the street in front of the other marchers, proudly waving my sign and shouting "Save Pandora's Box," when a cop came up to me, pulled me aside, and gave me a jaywalking ticket. It was an interesting moment, facing off with helmeted police officers with face guards in riot gear all around me. It reminded me of the TV footage of the Black civil rights marches in the south. I felt I was doing something important yet dangerous. What was important about the so-called riots was that it was the first time that predominantly white L.A. youths came together to protest police brutality. This was the beginning of my activism, and it reminded me of my commitment to music.

A little later I met film composer Lalo Schifrin. I'd been recommended to sing on his new soundtrack for a Clint Eastwood film, *Coogan's Bluff*. It was Lalo's first rock score and I was to sing on one track. We met to sketch out the song and elaborate on how to turn it into rock 'n' roll. He was very easy to work with and accepted all my comments and suggestions, a real gentleman, a real pro. When the day of the session arrived, I was buzzing on rock adrenalin. We were in one of the huge Universal Studios sound stages, where a lone mic on a stand was waiting for me in front of a full orchestra and a giant screen. I didn't feel intimidated. The strength and confidence I had on the *Shindig!* show three years earlier was still burning inside me.

Lalo walked in confidently, took off his jacket at the podium, and lifted his baton as the screen came alive and the music began. I started singing like I was on *Shindig!*, dancing around like a fool when I should've been focused on singing into the mic. I think I stunned the orchestra and Lalo. I don't think any session singer had ever recorded like that. You're not supposed to dance and sing. You're supposed to stand still and sing into the microphone consistently. Luckily, I kept in vocal range to the mic and wasn't told to stop dancing. After a couple of takes I was ready to nail the tune and nail it hard. I did. We recorded "Pigeon-Toed Orange Peel" and Lalo thanked me for a good job. I hoped it would lead to more sessions, but it didn't. And why would it? I was lucky I wasn't fired on the spot.

After two years of getting closer with Beverly, I decided it was time to settle down. So I asked her to marry me. The ceremony took place downtown at the L.A. County Courthouse. We had dinner later with a few friends. Our relationship was solid, or so it seemed. She had a very steady temperament and never yelled during our arguments. Also, her wig shop was doing well, I thought that could serve as a good safety net. I did some gigs with the Right Direction, a band that included the Doors' Ray Manzarek's younger brothers Jim and Rick, but those gigs, too, stopped coming. Disgusted, I left music again for a steady job refinishing antique furniture on Melrose in West Hollywood.

Beverly started working as a high fashion runway and print model and wound up at the same agency as Sue. They became good friends. How crazy is that? One night we double dated, taking conventional social male-female decorum to a new high. I couldn't believe we all got along so well.

And then, along came the Southern Belle.

The Southern Belle

I MET HER AT A JAM SESSION in Beverly Glen Canyon in 1968, at the house of Jules Buccieri, who owned the antique store where I worked. He invited me to stop by, said he was starting to manage a rock band called the Bourgeoisie Looney, and there was a rumor that John Lennon wanted to produce them. His assistant was a cat I called the Wizard. He had a full-on Afro and a mustache that turned up at the tips like Salvador Dalí's. On top of that, he drove a brand-new black Porsche convertible. The band and the Wizard were a colorful bunch of loonies all right, and I thought it would be fun to hang with them.

She was eighteen, a poet and a folksinger-guitarist à la Joni Mitchell, born in Roanoke, Virginia, who had recently graduated from Beverly Hills High School. She was the first poet I'd ever known, and that fascinated me. Her beauty and her voice shimmered. She was tall, shapely, with long, flowing tawny hair, a voice that could seduce a saint, and a smile that could've melted the Devil's heart. I felt an uncontrollable urge to have her. The dog had to be fed.

Beverly was with me, and I tried with all my might not to lose it and give myself away. But I couldn't take my eyes off of this glorious gift. Somehow we all wound up in the same car going home, and I wound up sitting in the back seat between the Belle and Beverly. If that wasn't difficult enough, Beverly mentioned that she used to model for the same agency that the Belle said her mother was with. Turned out the Belle's mother and Sue Dean were best friends(!) And I'm sitting between both of them high as a satellite.

I offered to give the Belle some vocal coaching as a ruse to seduce her. She gave me her number. I called the following day. We agreed to meet at my place while Beverly was at work. She arrived looking like a celestial being, wrapped in long flowing scarves. When I opened the door I just stared, stunned into silence. As she glided into the living room, a lamp we had on a table suddenly turned off, all the bulbs burning out at once. We talked about music and her career. Then she sang. I was bewitched and enchanted by her voice, soft and sure with an inner power and sincerity that gently grabbed and held my heart. I flat out fell in love with this angel-goddess-siren-muse, even though her presence portended danger.

After agonizing for weeks over how I was going to tell Beverly, I finally just said I felt the marriage was over and told her the truth, that I no longer was in love with her. She surprisingly responded with no drama, no questions, only acceptance. Did she know and didn't want to say it, because it hurt too much? Whatever it was, she hid it. A few weeks later, as I was leaving the apartment after packing everything up, I went to say goodbye to the two pet dogs we had and saw her fuzzy slippers thrown in the trash can. Those tattered slippers were trashed just like I was trashing the marriage. I felt my heart snap and was overcome with deep guilt and shame. I suddenly felt a deep love for her—but it was too late.

I moved into an old Howard Hughes mansion on the Strip sharing a three-bedroom suite with Jeff Woodruff, a music composition major at USC and former Chicken Delight delivery brother. He had a state-of-the-art sound system and a classical music library that covered everybody, as well as a library of books on painters, musicians, and poets. A new chapter in my life had begun. I'd always been interested in art but never pursued it. I used to hang out at Barney's Beanery on Santa Monica after high school with Ron Mercado, the artist cat that got me into the Apollos. The Beanery was a local bar where the painters from the La Cienega gallery art scene would hang out. One night we met John Altoon, who was known as a part of the "Ferus Group." He graciously invited us to his drawing class at the Chouinard Art Institute in the Westlake district, which was held outside the day we went. I tripped out on the students and their work. They were serious as a heart attack about what they were doing, unlike many rock musicians I'd known. These were dedicated artists, and I respected that, just as I respected the discipline that I'd had as a classical trumpet player as a kid.

I started studying the work of the surrealists in Jeff's library, especially Dalí, tripping out on his dreamy psychedelic stretched-out take on reality. The colors and the images, all perfectly drawn and twisted into otherworldly dreamscapes, took a deep hold on me. Painting opened up a new world for me, a world of unlimited imagination, mind travel, and expansion. It was better than acid. Then one night Jeff played *Music for Strings, Percussion, and*

Celesta by the Hungarian composer Béla Bartók on his killer sound system and I became one with the powerful sonic rush like a hurricane. I'd never been transported to another dimension before, aside from acid. I'd never heard music that complex and powerful, and was amazed that it was made by humans. Suddenly I had an epiphany: you could paint with sound! I decided to become a composer.

The Belle started to visit, and we became lovers on the night that it started to rain nonstop for several weeks. The L.A. River almost crested. I wondered if it was some kind of omen. There were many far-out extrasensory-perception moments with her. There was always something in the air and in our skin pushing us to new heights, sexual and spiritual. I'd never been there before. Yeah, it was like cosmic, man . . . for reals. Once, Jim Morrison opened the doors for us at a BBQ place on Crescent Heights below Sunset. He had a beard and smiled at us. Doors would often open for us.

One day in '69, the Belle excitedly handed me an album, *Cruising with Ruben & the Jets* by Frank Zappa and the Mothers of Invention. She said it reminded her of me since I told her I used to sing doo-wop back in the day, and of course because my name was also Rubén. I listened to the album, and at first I didn't get it. It sounded like a sarcastic joke. But still, we decided to go check them out live at their upcoming album release concert. I was curious to see what this Zappa cat had up his sleeve. I remembered hearing his first double album, *Freak Out!*, back in '66 and being impressed by his bizarre avant–rock 'n' roll. And the inscription *"The present-day Pachuco refuses to die!"* on the *Cruising* album also got my attention. How could this freaky dude know anything about *pachukos?* Who and what was this cat all about?

The Shrine Exposition Hall was a cavernous space with high ceilings. The music boomed out, reminding me of the time I played at the El Monte American Legion stadium. Maybe that was the reason for him playing there. The audience was a weird and wild mix of hippies and a few Mexican kids sprinkled in. Maybe they thought Ruben & the Jets was a real band and came to hear them play R & B oldies-but-goodies. The show started with a group of girls singing some old doo-wop standard. They were young and unpolished, but their hearts were into it. Then the band started to play tunes from the album. The lead singer, Ray Collins, used to sing with "Little" Julian Herrera's backup group, the Tigers. He was great. Then I got it! They were doing a parody of a doo-wop garage band. I dug the boldness of that, playing R & B in the middle of the psychedelic rock scene. At intermission, I suggested we try to go backstage and tell Zappa what a trip the set was.

The Belle, being a high fashion model, could dress like nobody's business. That night she was wearing a midnight blue sheer chiffon mini-skirt and electric blue suede high heels. I was wearing a brown Clint Eastwood *Fistful of Dollars* suede flat-brimmed hat, brown leather coat, black shirt with a mariachi bow tie, custom-made rust leather pants, and the custom-made green suede knee boots I'd worn on *Shindig!* As we approached the burly security guards, they just nodded and swung the doors open for us and we walked straight on in. No questions. No badges. The Southern Belle and I looked good together. I guess we looked like movie stars.

We made our way to Frank's dressing room and walked into a room full of hippies with their kids. I think his son, Dweezil, and daughter, Moon Unit, were among them. I went up to Frank and told him how much I'd dug his set and especially that he was bringing back R & B doo-wop vocal harmonies. Then I said, "I used to sing a little. I had a record out in the early sixties with the Apollo Brothers. And by the way, my name is Rubén." He took a long look at me with his dark steely eyes, then said, "Hmm, that's a grand name." Then after another long pause and stare, "Are you still singing?" I didn't know what to say at first, since I had no interest in getting back into rock. But then, out of courtesy, I said I had some demos I was working on. He took another long look, then said, "Why don't you drop them off at my office on Sunset. I'll take a listen." "Okay. Sure. Thanks." But I never did.

My plan was to enroll in the music composition program at L.A. City College in the fall. My goal: to learn how to write scores for movies and TV. Shortly thereafter the Belle and I got an apartment together.

The Belle's stepdad was a TV producer and writer at Universal Studios and had offered to find me work if I got some training first. One of his shows was *Star Trek*. One night we went to the home of the show's creator, Gene Roddenberry, to shoot some pool. He was a very gracious and down-to-earth cat. We got along well and he wished me luck in school. That was a big push to succeed.

Unfortunately, the pressure from my classes—and from life generally— put a painful strain on the Belle's and my relationship, and we parted shortly after I started back at school. Maybe it was the ten-year age difference and my total commitment to become a composer.

LACC and the New Revelations Gospel Choir

ONE DAY IN '69 AS I was walking down the hall at L.A. City College between classes, I heard a gospel choir singing. I was reminded of the night Beverly and her friend Bobby took me to my first gospel experience. It was over-the-top glorious. I walked in, sat, and listened and was once again transported. The group was the New Revelations Gospel Choir, featuring the mighty Michael Grey, who later sang in the musical *The Wiz*. After stopping by a few more times I got up the courage to ask if I could sing with them. They graciously said yes. I sang second tenor, and it seemed like I held my own. Then, the ultimate honor, they gave me a song to learn, the gospel classic "My Father's House." The next thing I knew I was singing in a little storefront church on Western in South Central. I was the only non-Black in the twenty-voice choir except for a bright-red-haired hippie chick.

We started the performance and ceremony by walking in from the sidewalk door singing a slow marching chant—everyone in gowns and keeping step along with the tambourines keeping time. It sounded like some kind of gospel Vodou dirge. It was the coolest entrance I've ever made: hipper than opening an Apollo Brothers set with "Money" by Barrett Strong and our slick Motown choreography. Even hipper than blowing the lights out on *Shindig!* No, this was deep, soul deep, down to the core of the primal bloody guts and roots of rock 'n' roll.

LACC opened up new cultural worlds for me, allowing me to journey into new creative experiences and possibilities, from gospel to modern music to experimental theater. I was slowly becoming an artist through exposure and osmosis. One of the turning points was experiencing ballet-theater for the first

My dear sister Bonita ("Bonnie" a.k.a. "Baby") at my grandparents' home in La Veinte, Santa Monica, age three. Courtesy of the Funkahuatl family archive.

time at the Dorothy Chandler Pavilion in downtown L.A. *Swan Lake* showed me the magic of telling a story through precise movement in sync with music. While taking theater courses I discovered the absurdists Becket, Ionesco, and Pirandello, and was reminded of the bullfights in Tijuana with my *tata:* the bizarre juxtaposition of man against beast in a ballet-like ritual of life and death. Consequently, an experimental theater piece was being forged in my head.

Then tragedy struck.

My younger sister Bonita, whom I adored, was tragically killed in a car accident. She was only twenty-two and a mom to two young boys, my nephews Tony and Sammy. Not only was it a devastating emotional shock to me and the family, but what hurt even more was that my father didn't come to the funeral. He was living in Seattle at the time with a new family. He later said he had a nervous breakdown after I told him the news. Still, I never forgave him for that.

I went to the CHP office in Buellton to see the accident report and bring home whatever property of my sister's was picked up at the scene. I then searched and found the exact spot where the accident occurred. I found some purple yarn that I recognized as hers. I picked it up and walked into the woods by the highway. I wanted to pray to the one we called "Baby," after my *nana* the sweetest and kindest person I've ever known. We loved her very, very much.

As I sat in a beautiful green secluded meadow building a little altar of twigs, flowers, and stones, I remembered the family move to Vegas in '54. The caravan of cars belonging to the musicians in my dad's band had stopped for gas in the middle of the Nevada desert at dawn. I walked over to the car she was in to check on her. She was around five or six at the time. When I opened the door, she was sitting in the passenger seat in her pajamas and blue terry-cloth bathrobe with her favorite doll on her lap. She looked so sweet, beautiful, and serene as she smiled up at me. She had the smile of a Buddha.

The sun's rays were shining through the tree branches as I stared into the sun. With tears burning my eyes I cried out, repeating as in a chant, "I love you, I love you, I love you," over and over again. "If there is a God, show your face now! Show me my sister, now! Baby, Baby!" I shouted repetitively, as in a mantra. Then silence. Exhausted and still sobbing, I slowly looked up again, and suddenly—she appeared. Her beautiful face and serene smile shone through the branches along with the sun's rays. I fell to my knees still crying and thanked God, promising I would dedicate my life to educating and enlightening through art in her honor. Then, after all the drama, I looked around, and all was quiet. There were no cars on the highway, just a few birds were chirping. I took a few deep breaths and knelt again in prayer and gratitude. A fundamental shift in my mind and heart had occurred. Art had suddenly taken on a deeper meaning and purpose.

As a way to console my shattered spirit and to reach my goals, for the next two years I immersed myself in school as if on a fanatical mission. I received Honors every semester. For my composition final, I analyzed the score of Bartók's *Music for Strings, Percussion, and Celesta,* the same piece that had turned my head and life around at the Hughes mansion two years earlier. With renewed confidence and new knowledge, I decided to enter the annual composition contest. I wanted to leave school with a bang.

Before starting on the piece, I went to Manhattan Beach for spring break. I picked up the clap and the flu during a drug-crazed weekend hangin' with my homies Pablo and "Flash." I got home and collapsed. With no car, I had to drag myself to the local Silver Lake Free Clinic to get a shot of penicillin and antibiotics. I needed a blood test, but there were no doctors available. I was too delirious to notice that it was the janitor who pulled my blood. Eventually, I staggered home. It took all my might to get myself to the piano. The room kept spinning. Then I thought of Beethoven composing after he lost his hearing. My situation was nothing compared to that. So I got up, sat at the piano, and, thinking of my sister Baby, started to pray. Remembering my commitment to her, I then dug into it. I used a similar repeating pattern or motif to one in the Bartók piece, perfecting it little by little until it all came together in a sudden flash. It was my first heroic act of rising up to an impossible challenge. I crossed an unknown border of creative strength and reached a new plateau. That alone was the most important victory, though I did tie for first place in the competition. I was now ready to work on a theater piece, but just what kind I didn't yet know.

One day the previous month when I arrived on campus, it was closed and surrounded by police. It was the day of the Kent State massacre, when four protesting students were shot and killed by the Ohio National Guard. There was something dark and ominous in the air. The country was in chaos, and the campus was on edge for action. Later that week I was approached and asked to join MEChA, a new Chicano student activist political organization. I went to a few meetings but was turned off by the militancy of their agenda and approach. I decided I would advance the cause for social justice through my art. I just needed a project.

Around that time, I went to visit a lady friend for the weekend in Healdsburg, some seventy miles north of San Francisco. As we were driving through the Sausalito Tunnel on the way back to the airport my friend's brother pulled out a few sheets of amber acid—Windowpane, pharmaceutical LSD. He worked at a mental facility in San Jose, so the quality was the best. He broke off a square from the perforated sheet and said to just take a corner bite. I tried, but I wound up swallowing the whole thing.

Acid wasn't new to me. I'd first dropped a few years earlier, in '67, with one of the cooks from Chicken Delight. It hit me at Lincoln Park, where I hugged the giant trees for hours. I thought they were the legs of God.

I came on as we were coming out of the tunnel: the view of the Golden Gate Bridge and San Francisco across the Bay was glorious. Everything glowed. I started to rush as we entered the city. We drove through an automated car wash that at first was trippy, but then the giant rolling brushes took on a monstrous face that scared the shit out of me. The effect kept building, until I had to get out of the car. We were stopped at a light. I kissed my girlfriend goodbye, jumped out, and started walking, not knowing or caring where I was going. I just had to move.

I wound up at Washington Square in downtown San Francisco. It was Mother's Day and I watched a pretty young Asian girl slowly walking her very old grandmother along the pathway around the park. I watched them go around and around, transfixed by the idea that every lap around the square was bringing the old woman closer and closer to her death. My heart was pounding and my eyes tearing. I felt like I was a god watching a life expiring before my very eyes. I thought of my sister Baby.

I felt someone put a sheet of paper in my hand. I looked down, my eyes wet with tears, then looked up at the kid who'd handed it to me, who was walking away. He yelled out, "It's a play, man. Come on by. You'll dig it. It starts in thirty minutes." "What? Whe . . . , whe . . . , where is it?" I stammered. He turned around and pointed to the sun. "Straight up to the intersection. It's a theater," he added. Without thinking twice, I got up and blindly started walking toward the sun. It reminded me of the time I'd blindly walked toward the outside shower stall when my face got torched by sulphuric acid. I'd barely made it up the steep street when I saw a poster for the show, *The Civil War,* an experimental theater piece (I didn't catch the playwright's name). The show was sold out, but the kid who gave me the flyer got me in. I sat on the floor and waited for the play to begin and join the psychedelic show that was already blowing in my head.

In walked a chorus of maybe ten actors who stood side by side. The flyer kid was one of them. A small band was in a corner. Footage of African American civil rights marches was projected onto a wall above the chorus. Then footage of drawings of Lincoln being shot appeared, with the chorus singing Southern church hymns. Then footage of JFK getting shot came on the screen while the chorus chanted spirituals; then footage of RFK getting shot, and more singing, and poetry; then Dr. King marching; and finally footage of the Vietnam War and My Lai. I was stunned by the spectacle as the acid hit home. I was still lying on my back, frozen with emotion, tears flowing, looking up at the ceiling, as the audience left, walking right over me. Someone told me to get up to let the people get by, but I couldn't move. The kid finally came and helped me up. He consoled me and thanked me for attending, then invited me to the cast after-party. I accepted.

Poster for my first theatrical work, *Who Are the People?* at the Factory, Hollywood, 1971. Courtesy of the Funkahuatl family archive.

The acid was still on as we walked up and down the steep streets toward the house where the party was being held. My head was blazing, but I managed a conversation with one of the actors about the genesis of the play. I wanted to know how this was done. At the house, we partied as only actors can, wildly dancing, drinking, ego-tripping, and offering up sordid confessions until dawn. I said thanks, goodbye, good luck, and staggered out into the morning fog.

I gave most of my plane money to panhandlers and wound up having to take the Greyhound bus home. The ten-hour ride gave me a chance to come down and think about what had happened the night before. The combination of live music, poetry, chanting, and historical film was a mind-blasting eye opener. I'd finally found my medium: experimental protest theater.

I decided to create an anti–Vietnam War gospel rock cantata and dedicate it to Baby's memory. That was the beginning of *Who Are the People?* I wrote the score for a twelve-member gospel choir, recruited from LACC's New Revelations Gospel Choir; a nine-piece band with drums, bass, guitar, piano, conga, two trumpets, and two tenor saxophones; two modern dancers; three actors; and a troubadour singer/narrator, James Lee Stanley. The showstopper was "A Song for Sister" (written for Baby), sung by gospel diva Betty Perkins. Michael Grey sang lead in the rousing show closer, "The Spirit of Love," which the choir honored me by naming themselves after. The *L.A. Times* called it "a tour de force." I was twenty-eight and on my way, again.

A Song for Sister

Somewhere, a light is shining, somewhere, for you and me
And times when I feel darkness, the shining light of love will shine
    on me.
It fills my heart and soul, it fills the world to know
That fear is for the hopeless / that hate is for the blind
That hope is for the fearless, that love, love, love
Is for the kind people, the good people, the loving people of the
    world.

Miss Santa Barbara and the Summer of 1971

What would my life be without a muse?
A pathetic puddle of rhythm and dues.

MUSES KEPT COMING INTO MY LIFE. What would I be without them?

While feverishly composing *Who Are the People?* I needed to take a few days off to catch my breath and wits. I decided to visit a friend in Santa Barbara for the weekend. I'd brought with me a fresh stash of Colombian Gold, a super-fine strain of marijuana, and mushrooms and was itching for an adventure. I chewed up a couple of shrooms, took a hit of Gold, and blindly headed out for a walk with no destination in mind. I spotted a creek off the road and started to hike into it. The creek was shallow and barely flowing, with heavy vegetation on its banks; birds flew by overhead singing through the air. Suddenly I felt like I was in a tropical jungle. It was a warm clear sunny summer day and I was starting to glow along with it.

Hiking up the creek I looked up and spotted a tower through the trees. It turned out to be the top of the Santa Barbara Mission. As I climbed up the side of the creek, each step felt like I was climbing back into the day when the mission was alive. I finally got up top and saw the expansive mission grounds, its vast open fields and flower gardens below. It looked like a scene out of a western movie in Technicolor. As I emerged, sweating and shirtless with my Afro blowing in the wind, I felt indigenous and free. I *was* indigenous. My dad had recently told me that his mother had indigenous roots. As I proudly strutted across the field all Indio bad, I saw a large sign next to the cathedral that read, "This cathedral was designed and built with Spanish brain and Indian brawn." What the fuck was that about!? Oh yeah, fuckin' colonization.

A group of people stood next to the cathedral beside the racist welcome sign, constructing what looked like a booth under a banner that read, "Welcome to Old Spanish Days." That cracked me up. I felt like I was in some kind of warped racist time trip. As I watched the group work, it became apparent that they were a family, a very blond family: a father, mother, and three teenage daughters. The oldest was wearing a t-shirt, white shorts, and flip-flops. She had a tranquil face, gentle smile, curious eyes, and legs that stretched to L.A. She was an innocent type, and as usual, the dog got restless. I walked straight up to her like a moth to a flame and blurted, "Can I help"? She looked up and smiled. "What are you building?" I struggled to ask. "My family is building this booth for the celebration tomorrow. We'll have woven pieces for sale. We like to crochet." "Oh, that's nice," I said, as a cool breeze sung through my buzzing pores.

I helped with the construction as best I could, given that a psychotropic lust storm was surging through me. I felt like a stoned Brown tornado. Then out of the blue she said, "Wanna play Frisbee? "Frisbee!? Sure! I love Frisbee," and I took off running like an obedient dog, with one eye on the spinning UFO and the other on her beautiful legs. It was fun running like a kid again, like a joyful dog, like a man possessed with life, love, and lust. Panting, I shook everyone's hand as they stared at my Afro and I said, "Nice to meet you, goodbye," like a true *caballero* in the spirit of "Old Spanish Days." Ha! Then the young Nordic goddess said, "Please come by tomorrow and enjoy the day with us. It'll be fun!" Ah man, my heart skipped a couple of beats. "Sorry, I can't. Have to leave for L.A. tonight. But can I call you sometime and ask how it went?" "Yes, of course, please do," and she gave me her number. I firmly shook her hand goodbye, feeling a gentle rush from all parts of my body and the cosmos. I held it for a long time, maybe too long. I didn't want to let go. Something was going on here: her innocence and beauty were a challenge to my integrity—and lust. She just watched me with that slight smile of hers as I let her hand go and trotted off.

I returned to L.A. and jumped into the cantata with a fresh sense of purpose. I felt different, more alive. Oh no! Was it love . . . or just lust again?

I lost no time in calling. "How was the celebration?" I asked. "Oh, it went very well, thanks. It was a good turnout and sales were great. Too bad you couldn't come. We could've thrown the Frisbee around." We agreed to meet at her house the following week; she had a tennis lesson, and I offered to take her and afterward we could hang out. Then I asked, "By the way, how old are you?" "I just turned eighteen. Why do you ask? Does it matter?" "No, I was just wondering." I waited for her to ask me my age, but she didn't. Man, what an innocent soul.

On the drive up, I decided I wanted to experience her in a pure, sober way. So I didn't smoke or ingest anything. As I watched her taking her tennis lesson, I was impressed by her swift, sure movements, like she knew where to hit the ball even before the serve. She was ahead of the game. Was she ahead of me? We came back to her house, then we took a bike ride to Shoreline Park by the beach and ended up at a vacant lot overlooking the ocean. "What an incredible view," she sighed, then continued: "I love the ocean." I replied, "My dream is to build a house here someday and raise a family. I'll be a film composer someday." "I know you will," she said, looking straight into my eyes. "I can feel it."

We rode back to her home and I gave her a light hug goodbye. To my surprise, she gave me a light kiss. Without thinking, I took her in my arms and kissed her long and deep. "Rachuka," she sighed. "What?" "Rachuka! I just made that up. It's what that felt like," she said.

On my next visit, we went to Carpinteria State Beach. She was wearing a bikini that revealed more than I needed to see. We ran along the shore as free as the summer sun, kicking and splashing in the water like two unleashed dogs. We tripped and fell, laughing and rolling over each other into an embrace with the waves washing over us. I kissed her and kissed her as she gasped and gasped, rolling on the shore oblivious to the people around us. It was like the scene in *From Here to Eternity,* with Burt Lancaster and Deborah Kerr. Man, this was it. Yeah, it was lusty and sexy, but man it was beautiful too. But a nagging question persisted: Was I taking advantage of her, of her innocence, just to feed my dog?

An opportunity arose to go to a friend's cabin in Big Sur for a weekend. I told her about it on the way home from the beach and she got excited and said, "Oh! That would be so much fun! I'll—*we'll*—have to ask my parents." "Ask...your...parents?" I wasn't expecting that. "Okay, sure. No problem. I'll come by this afternoon." Well, here was the moment of truth. I decided to take a hit of Gold just to trip on the crazy theater of it all. Of course her parents would say no.

"Daddy, this is Rubén, he helped us build our booth at the mission last month," she calmly said. Her father looked up from reading the paper and checked me out. "Oh yes, hello ... I think I remember you," he said, a bit confused. The mother was sitting crocheting. She looked like Mrs. Olsen, the Swedish neighbor from the Folger's coffee TV commercial. Then Miss Santa Barbara turned to me with a look in her eye as if to say, "Now!" "Sir, 'mam," I said. "Can I have your permission to take your daughter to a friend's parents' cabin in Big Sur this weekend?" I couldn't believe I was asking the question. Here I was, wearing a giant Afro, higher than the sky and barely able to talk, and I'm asking the parents of an eighteen-year-old if she can spend the weekend with me. "We'll be back Sunday night," I persisted. The mom stopped crocheting and the dad stopped reading, and they both looked up in total astonishment. "No, we can't let her do that," he said, while the mom just stared at me, open-mouthed. "But Dad, I'm eighteen now," she protested. "No, I'm sorry. We don't know this young man," her father said firmly. "But, Dad!" "No!" It was like a scene from a movie or a play, but I was in it, for reals. We walked outside. "I can't believe they won't let me go. What do they think would happen? That I'd get eaten by a bear?" We laughed. "Oh well, I'll come by your friend's place tonight and pick you up," she said. "I'll take you to my mountaintop. There's a full moon tonight and the view of the bay will be spectacular. I'll be by at seven."

I was taking a hit as she pulled up promptly at seven in a fire-engine-red Mustang convertible. She was wearing a white mini beach dress that hiked up her thighs as we sped around the sharp mountain curves. My heart raced right along. "I come up here to think and to give thanks to my moon, to honor her," she said. Now I knew I was with a goddess, a pure soul. My lust was merging with a kind of serious innocence, a spiritual love like what I'd once felt for the Southern Belle. We pulled over and parked, got out, and walked out onto a cliff overlooking Santa Barbara below. It *was* spectacular. I took her hand as we walked. She held it tight. I stopped before reaching the cliff, turned my head to her, and softly kissed her on the cheek, then on her mouth. She opened and welcomed my tongue shyly, then eagerly. She got excited, breathing with soft moans. My kisses were focused, deep, and intense. She pulled away, sighing, "Rachuka!"

The moon appeared in all its glory. She smiled and whispered in my ear, "Hello, moon." We kissed, then I let her go and stepped away, not sure whether to proceed or not. She threw me a surprised look, as if to say, "What's wrong?" "This isn't right," I said. "I'm so much older than you." We stood at the cliff, my arm around her shoulder, looking at the harbor lights below, the bright full moon blessing the moment. It was quiet. It was beautiful. She drove me back to my friend's place and I gave her a light goodnight kiss. "Good night, 'Rachuka,'" she whispered. "You are a good man."

I came back to finish the cantata a little older and a little wiser. I invited her to the premiere the following month at the Factory in West Hollywood, a private club that the Rat Pack—Frank Sinatra, Dean Martin, Sammy Davis Jr., Peter Lawford, and Joey Bishop—had opened up. As I was shaking well-wishers' hands after the show I saw her sitting with her two storybook sisters. "Hi, and congratulations," she said. "I loved the musical. The choir was fantastic! What an accomplishment. You must be very proud." "Thank you. I'm so glad you came to the opening. You gave me a lot of steam to finish it." We hugged and exchanged a warm, polite cheek-to-cheek.

A few months passed and I eventually called to say hello and suggest a visit. "That would be great! I'd love to see you again. You can meet my fiancé." I was shocked but went anyway with two friends who drove me there. When we picked them up, she suggested, "How about we go play some tennis?" Somehow I wound up sitting between them in the back seat of my friend's car. It was a long, awkward ride.

He turned out to be an African American fullback on a pro football team. He was a nice guy, actually, gentle even though he was a big burly football player. We headed to the tennis courts, the same courts I'd seen her play on with such fierce confidence the year before. I watched in awe and heartache as they perfectly played tennis together. She was ahead of my game after all. I wished them luck and went on my way.

Frank Zappa and
Ruben And The Jets, 1972–1974

A FEW MONTHS AFTER *Who Are the People?* closed, I ran into keyboardist Bob Harris as I was leaving a phone booth that doubled as my office on Fountain in Silver Lake. I knew him from the days when we hung out with John Beck, lead singer with the Leaves, while he was in a relationship with folk singer/songwriter Judee Sill. We talked about what we were doing and I told him about the musical I'd just staged. He had just returned from touring with Zappa, I think it was the *Billy the Mountain* tour. I told him I'd met Frank a few years earlier, and he suggested we pay him a visit, since Frank and I both seemed to be on a rock theater kick.

As we drove up Laurel Canyon I had flashbacks of working at Chicken Delight back in '66. We passed the notorious Log Cabin where Zappa and his clan once lived along with the GTOs (Girls Together Outrageously, about whom I'll say more later). I don't know how I survived speeding around those curves, stoned and in the rain, delivering boxes of chicken. But hey, it meant at least a couple bucks tip if you got the chicken there hot. So now, just a few years later, I'm on my way to see the wild wizard of rock. Life's a stone trip, all right.

We got to his tree-shrouded home, and surprisingly he answered the door himself. "We met a few years ago at the Shrine for the *Cruising with Ruben & the Jets* album release show," I said. "Yeah, I remember you. You're Rubén." "Right. Sorry I never took you up on your offer to drop off some demos, but I went back to college. I wanna write music for films." He didn't say anything, just "Come on in." We walked into his studio, which burst with guitars and sound equipment. "So, you used to sing a little R & B, huh?" "Yeah in high school in the '50s, then I put together a trio, the Apollo Brothers. We cut a single in '61, sang around town, and did a little TV. We played the Legion once." "The El Monte American Legion Stadium?" "Yeah, with Richard Berry, and the Olympics too." That led to an all-night session of listening to his collection of R & B oldies. Here we were, a couple of grown men tripping on old records like we were teenagers. That was the beginning of our bond: our love of L.A. rhythm and blues.

Then we talked about my discovering modern music composers at LACC, Bartók and Stravinsky in particular. We talked about how they weaved ethnic folk music into new musical and theatrical forms, which was how I interpreted his Ruben & the Jets garage doo-wop band. I saw it as Mexican American rock-theater, though in a very primitive form, which was cool with me. I took a copy of *Billboard* with me that had reviews of *Who Are the People?* and his recent collaboration with the L.A. Philharmonic at UCLA next to it. That got his attention. As the sun was coming up he made a proposal: "How would you like to stage a real Ruben & the Jets? I'll produce the album, and you can tour with the Mothers as an opening band to promote it." I told him, "Thanks, man, that's a damn groovy offer, but I'm not interested in going back to rock 'n' roll. I don't want to move backwards, and besides, too many detours." He stared at me for a few long seconds with those dark eyes, then said, "Take what you know and build your own roads."

I said I'd think about it and get back to him. It sounded cool, but still, the question kept coming up: could I trust rock musicians to pull off this great opportunity? Could I even work with flaky rockers again after working with serious classical cats? Then again, it wasn't like I'd be starting from scratch. There was already an audience for Zappa's Ruben & the Jets. To have an album produced by him and a spot on a tour sounded too good to resist. And I'd be creating a rock-theater piece right in line with my new direction. However, another burning question kept coming up: Was I honoring my sister's memory with this project? Was I keeping my word to create art as a spiritually educating experience? Could I use it as a launching pad that would take me closer to my promises? My conclusion: Fuck, yeah! Give it a try.

I had two tunes that I thought would work: a fast rocker and a doo-wop ballad. A private session was set up at Frank's house.

I called m' man "Flash," who had just returned from Vietnam. "Hey, man, get your boogie-woogie fingers warmed up. We're gonna audition for a once-in-a-lifetime shot!" We went into his bedroom at his parents' home and rehearsed on the old upright piano that we'd used when we started the

Apollo Brothers. His sweet mom, Laura, and his jokester dad, Rudy, were thrilled for him. We worked up "Mah Man Flash," a boogie-rock tune that I'd written for his twenty-fifth birthday, and "Santa Kari," a doo-wop ballad I wrote for the audition. We sounded better than ever.

The session with Frank started out a little bumpy. At one point Flash stopped playing, and Frank said, "Come on, Flash, this ain't Carnegie Hall." "It is for me," he replied, then nodded that he was ready to play again. That time, we got into it and nailed it. Frank smiled, nodding his head up and down. He asked me to put a band together. I said, "I can have a band together in a few weeks."

When we got to the car, I was ecstatic. "Awright, Flash Gordon! You smokedm', man! We're back, Jack!" He didn't say a word. He just drove, staring straight ahead. "What's wrong, man?" I asked. "I can't do it," he said. "What?!" "I can't do it." "What do you mean, you can't do it?!" I didn't know how thoroughly his confidence had been blown away in 'Nam. Unfortunately, the war demons chewed him up pretty bad. He passed away a few years later from too much depression, drugs, and booze. Nobody could play boogie-woogie piano like him. He was the best around. *Rest in peace, my Apollo brother. See you on the rebound.*

I didn't ask Pablo to join the band because he didn't play an instrument. Plus, he had a full-time career gig working as a pressman and he didn't trust the music business after our short-lived career. I could dig it. Instead, he became my number one supporter. He was a true brother. I called Carlos Rodríguez from the band that I put together for *Who Are the People?* to play bass, but he later took a touring gig and passed on the offer. So I called bass player and vocalist Bill Wild of the Du-Vals, who had backed up the Apollo Brothers at Pandora's Box and my *Shindig!* audition. I was reluctant to hire him, what with his history of drugs and booze, but he could play a funky bass and had a soulful voice that I needed for the harmonies. For the sax section I contacted former LACC classmate Clarence Matsui, a Japanese American alto sax cat from Boyle Heights. I also recruited another classmate, tenor sax player Bob "Buffalo" Roberts, and Frank suggested Jim "Motorhead" Sherwood, a former Mother, for the baritone sax parts.

Clarence had been playing with a band from East L.A. that he highly recommended, so I went to hear them play. I was impressed and invited them to come to the audition. They included vocalist and Hammond B-3 player John Martinez, probably the best all-around singer ever to come out of East L.A. Not only could he sing bass and falsetto parts, but he was also a killer lead singer. Then there was vocalist–rhythm guitarist–songwriter Robert "Frog" Camarena and vocalist–lead guitarist–songwriter Tony Duran, formerly of East L.A. '6os greats the Premiers ("Farmer John"). Drummer Bobby Zamora was called in at the last minute. The band sounded great, and Frank dug it.

Zappa was in a wheelchair during this time with a broken leg and other injuries from being pushed off the stage at a concert in London by a jealous fan. This gave him plenty of time to work with the band.

It was my understanding that the members of the band would be signed as "sidemen" and that I would be the leader, sole composer, and lead singer on all material. The band members could be replaced at my discretion. It was also agreed that the project would be a collaboration between Frank and me that would feature original L.A.-style rhythm and blues/doo-wop, jump blues, along with straight-ahead rock 'n' roll and blues—a kind of musical history and repository of Black and Brown L.A. music all wrapped in Mexican American rock-theater. The band didn't get the theater part, though, as I would later discover.

West Coast doo-wop harmony was different in some ways from the East Coast style in that most of L.A.'s singers came out of, or at least were influenced by, the Black gospel church. The harmony blend, which is very natural, smooth, and tight, influenced many East L.A. Mexican American singers, like "Little" Julian Herrera, "Little" Willie G. of Thee Midniters, and "Little" Ray Jimenez, among many others, me included. The East Coast style, personified by non-Black vocal groups like Dion and the Belmonts, Frankie Valli and the Four Seasons, was good, but the vocals and record production had more of a cheery, slick pop sound to it; it wasn't earthy and soulful like ours. Doo-wop harmony comes naturally to Mexican American singers—at least to me—from growing up listening to Mexican *boleros* and singing and harmonizing along with them.

I modeled the Jets' harmonies on those of the Jaguars, a classic L.A. doo-wop group from Fremont High School. The multiracial vocal group of Blacks, an Italian, and a Mexican American epitomized the L.A. doo-wop style for me. Their recording of "Just the Way You Look Tonight" was the template I used to build on.

The Jets were a Japanese American cat, three wild white guys— "Motorhead," "Buffalo" with his ZZ Top hair and beard, and Bill, who could sing some mean blue-eyed soul—and four Mexican Americans. They were quite a crew. My recent composition experience writing gospel parts for *Who*

Are the People? and my early work with the Apollo Brothers gave me the chops to arrange the vocal harmonies for the Jets. Since there were songwriters and great singers in the band, I decided to utilize their talents as much as possible, as both a democratic and a practical musical move. I didn't realize I was also relinquishing my power. Frank wrote two songs for the band, the up-tempo doo-wopper "If I Could Only Be Your Love Again" (with George Duke sitting in on piano for the recording) and a crazy doo-woppish rocker, "The Weenie-Back Wino Walk," which unfortunately didn't make it to vinyl.

Looking back, Frank and I should have told the musicians up front what the project was all about and who I was and my musical history. For all they knew (Bill Wild excluded), I was just another coconut from Hollywood, brown on the outside, white on the inside. I remember one night in Detroit after playing the Masonic Temple, one of the band members called me a "coconut" to my face. It wasn't said with malice, more as a matter of fact. I wasn't offended because I was beyond identifying with one ethnic culture. I'd been living a multicultural existence all my life. I was multicultural before the word was invented, kind of a funky *angelino* rainbow of sorts. So being called a "coconut" was ludicrous. If I'd been raised in East L.A. as a stone Mexican, then moved to Hollywood leaving it all behind, *that* would've made me a coconut. But that wasn't me. So I didn't think I had to tell them anything about my background—musically or culturally. The fact that Frank and I were forming the band together should've been enough cred. But there was always mistrust in the air.

We rehearsed the material for the album for several months, then tested it out playing at Louis Stevenson Junior High in Boyle Heights, Garfield High School in East L.A., and at the Montebello Bowl. My plan was to create a buzz in East L.A. first, then bring the new fans to the Whisky in Hollywood for the debut.

Miss Pamela and the GTOs

ONE NIGHT BUFFALO'S BEAUTIFUL GIRLFRIEND, Miss Sparky, brought singer and sister GTO Miss Pamela to a Jets rehearsal. The GTOs—their name stood for Girls Together Outrageously—were a radical girl group whose album Zappa had produced. Miss Pamela asked if she could sing "Angel Baby" with the band at our upcoming Whisky show. We agreed.

The Whisky was packed. There was a buzz in the air about Zappa's new protégé band. *Were they for real or another Zappa joke?* The pressure was on. Herb Cohen, Zappa's manager and now ours, was at a booth with some celebrities as I walked in wearing a brown leather bomber jacket, tight red corduroy pants, army fatigue shirt with a Chicano Power patch, white boots with hand-painted flames, and a lady on each arm. Hey, it was rock 'n' roll theater, and I was the star and director and itching for some fun. As much as I liked to trip, I never performed stoned, going all the way back to the '50s—maybe a sip or two of brandy before a show to warm my throat, but that was it. There was just too much to handle on stage, keeping the energy high and the harmonies focused, keeping the stampeding herd from going over the cliff. To the band's credit, except for one member no one was a pothead or an alcoholic.

The band blazed on originals "Spider Woman" and "Sparky," an oldies medley, and "Charlena" by the Sevilles. Then Miss Pamela came up, dressed in virginal white with a black push up bra, garter belt, and black-seamed stockings, her long blonde hair nestled on her bare shoulders. She charmed and seduced the crowd with her hot yet sweet looks and nailed "Angel Baby." I was impressed with her performance and the theatricality of it all. For our closer we played the sax-based house burner, Joe Houston's "All Nite Long," with Martinez, Camarena, and me going through some intricate rowdy choreography. We got a great response. After the show, Arthur Lee of Love came up to me and said how much he dug the show, or something to that effect. He was either very stoned or mad, like in crazy, or both. I spotted Miss Pamela and congratulated her on her performance, then asked her out. I had heard about her escapades with various rock gods, but that didn't faze me. I was curious to see just how "outrageous" this GTO could be.

On our date a few nights later, we went first to a fancy piano bar in Beverly Hills for drinks, then to a restaurant at the beach for dinner. It was all very pleasant and polite, not outrageous at all, so I figured it was time to get down. I suggested we drive downtown and find a cheap hotel to spend the night. She was game. We ended up at the Santa Rita Hotel on 11th and Main. It was perfect, straight out of an L.A. noir novel. A fat, cigar-smoking clerk regarded us in bored disbelief. He sat behind a chain link fence next to a cash register that looked like it'd been there since the '40s. The walls were a faded baby blue, with a dim light bulb hanging down from the ceiling on a long cord. "A room for the night," I said. He gave us the key, said, "Fifth floor, bathroom down the hall, elevator to your right. Check out at noon." I pressed the elevator button and pulled the collapsing iron-gate open. The elevator was tiny, barely big enough for four people. "This is fun," I said. "Like out of a Charles Bukowski poem, except this is *our* poem, and *we're* writing it." Her subtle scent and smile made the dog crazy. We kissed hard and pressed our bodies together as the elevator rumbled up.

The room had a single bed, a tiny sink jutting out of the wall, and a small window overlooking Main. "Well, here it is, nothing but the best for a lady . . . and a tramp." We cracked up. We undressed, and for a moment we stared at each other in silence as a blue neon sign flashed on and off, highlighting her snow-white naked body, an immaculate "Angel Baby" goddess. My body was suntanned black and shined sleek as a panther. The contrast was startling. As I reached out for her she put my shadow hand on her porcelain cheek and pulled me toward her. When we lay down, the bedspread slid off revealing a dingy white sheet on top of a thick, yellowed sheet of plastic. Real classy. Then we embraced and ignited as our flames licked the spirit world and kissed the lust. We were more than just two rock 'n' roll souls moaning and howling with the sunrise. We were deities drenched in ecstasy beyond the Santa Rita Hotel, beyond our youth, closer to heaven, closer to God.

We saw each other for a few more weeks. One time she invited me to go see Mikhail Baryshnikov, the Russian ballet god, at the Shrine Auditorium. She was quite a cultured lady, enjoying everything from rock 'n' roll to ballet. Unfortunately, I was too busy with the band to take it further. Who knows what heights we could've hit.

Miss Claremont

THE BAND GOT A GIG in Claremont in early '73 as a warm-up for the upcoming Palladium show where we were opening for Zappa and the Mothers and promoting the new record release. Before we went on, I walked through the audience checking out the crowd, breaking down the white and brown attendance. It was mostly white, and I was curious how they would react to our music, even though it was on Mothers of Invention turf. I noticed the back of a shapely woman in a skintight black pantsuit. I thought I would ask what had brought her to the concert. She turned around as I walked toward her and my jaw dropped. She looked like she'd just stepped off the cover of *Vogue*. She was elegant. She was young. And as usual, the dog was restless.

She was my height, so our eyes met directly. She looked like she could have stepped out of an Ingmar Bergman movie—earthy, with red cheeks and short brown hair. But it was mostly her eyes that stopped me. They were clear and curious. As usual, I was attracted to the paradox of women's purity and sexual confidence.

"So, Miss Claremont, what brings you to this show?" She smiled and said, "Oh, I'm a Zappa fan and I have the *Cruising* album." "I'm surprised you're a Zappa fan, you look so . . . glamorous. You know that the Ruben And The Jets band tonight is not the Mothers of Invention, right?" "Yeah, I know. That's also why I came. I wanted to see this offshoot." "Well nice meeting you. I have to go now; I'm with the band. Can we talk after the show?" "Sure." She smiled as I turned and walked away.

The band played a solid set and we got a very positive reaction from the crowd. I did my best on the oldies medley, directing the crooning to Miss Claremont and turning it up on the sexy "Spider Woman." I felt like we delivered, since we got an encore.

I offered to drive Miss Claremont home, and she accepted. I decided to take a detour into the nearby mountains. "Have you ever been to Mt. Baldy?" I asked. "Yeah, many times," she said. "I love the mountains. They're my second home." I started up the long road, but I really wanted to kiss her, so I pulled over. We found a clearing in the woods. It was pitch black except for the stars and the moon. She leaned against a pine tree and I put my arms around her and pulled her to me. She had full, soft lips and a curious tongue. We were in perfect sync. I wanted to take it higher, but it was getting cold and late.

We agreed to meet at my Echo Park pad before the big Palladium show. I wanted to buy her a fancy dress, so beforehand we went to Aardvark on Sunset in Silver Lake where she picked out a vintage silky-sheer rust-colored outfit. She oozed lust in a demure kind of way as she stood in front of a full-length mirror. I could feel the heat from the mirror as she winked at me. We had dinner, and then I drove to the Palladium.

The show was sold out, with over five thousand screaming Zappa fans. After we were announced there was a loud roar in the hall as we walked onto the stage. I guess we had some fans after all. I was getting a little nervous. Once again, we had to deliver. I spotted Miss Claremont and she waved, a big grin on her face. Man, she looked good in that dress. I turned around, counted off, and jumped into a smoking set of rock 'n' roll fire. I sang my ass off. Harder than at the Legion, *Shindig!,* or the Whisky, and the band blazed right along with me. I saw Frank beaming proudly from the wings as the audience yelled for more. I danced passed him off the stage and he yelled, "Take it!" It was a generous moment. I was surprised that he was so proud. But yeah, of course, the band was his baby, and I was the midwife.

I dated Miss Claremont for a while. Then she got a modeling gig in Italy. The goddesses appeared, then disappeared, momentarily blinding me with lust.

Miss Chino

SOMEHOW WE GOT A GIG at Chino Women's Prison. It was a concert and dance for the inmates. Before we played, I was talking to a bandmate when a very attractive woman approached and asked me to dance to the recorded music coming through the speakers. I asked her if it was all right, and she said yeah. I looked around and saw that the other women inmates were dancing together. It was a bit bizarre. I took her hand and we danced to a slow ballad. She moved like a breeze, fluid and smooth, as she lightly brushed her breasts across my chest. Her warm breath against my face blended with her perfumed hair. It drove the dog nuts. As we floated, not missing a beat, she asked me for my phone number, and like the fun-loving dog I am, I gave it to her.

We talked about her time in prison and what it was like as she held me tighter. She said in a breathy whisper, "It's like your mind is free but your body is in jail. All I do is dream about what I'm going to do with my life." "When do you get out?" "If I behave, I'll be out in a couple months. I want to call you if that's okay." "Hell yeah," I said, not thinking it would ever happen. A woman guard came over and said it was time for the show. The women danced together, swooning during the oldies medley and shaking it to the rockers. It was a horny-dog rock 'n' roll fantasy.

Sure enough, two months later I got a call: "Hey, rock star, I'm downtown at the Greyhound station. Can you pick me up?" I felt a little apprehensive about getting involved with an ex-con, but my crazy sense of adventure led me on. I kept thinking what a great song or poem or movie it might make.

I drove down to 6th and Los Angeles, and there she was standing on the corner, smiling and waving with her suitcase in her other hand. I pulled up and she jumped in. "Hi!" she cried. "Hey, what a trip," I said. "Didn't think you'd call." "Why not?" "Come on, you were in prison." We laughed and she gave me a kiss on the cheek, saying, "Thanks for giving me the right number. I knew I could trust you."

I was living in Echo Park at the time, in an old Victorian with a view of the lake, very bohemian and romantic. We walked in and I poured her a glass of wine, then showed her around. She loved my bathtub. "Can I please take a bath?" "Sure, take your time." I poured her another glass of wine and watched her take off her clothes. Her beautiful body was covered with scars and bruises. I wondered about the life she'd had, what crime she'd committed. I thought, "Man, what am I doing? I can't get into this." But she was soft in a tough kind of way. Plus, she turned the dog on.

I lay down on my bed considering how to proceed. She was singing "Since I Don't Have You" in a soft whisper as I rolled a joint and lit it. I walked into the bathroom and handed it to her. She said, "No thanks, baby. I stopped smoking a long time ago. It makes me do crazy things. And I like you." Man! That tripped me out. What the fuck did that mean?

Watching her dry her ravaged body was beyond any movie I'd ever seen—beyond David Lynch's "Wild at Heart," beyond a Bukowski poem. She saw me staring and said, "It's not as bad as it looks, baby. It's worse inside." I felt myself falling in love with her.

We got on the bed, and as I undressed she started to kiss me on my hands, arms, and chest. We embraced and the jets were lit. The quick intensity surprised me. I'd never known that kind of hungry, unbridled passion. Our breathing became one silent wail as our bodies sang and melted in perfect union, making the gods and goddesses jealous. She started to cry. "What's wrong?" "I can't come," she said, sobbing. "It's been too long. Please come for me. Please come hard for me, baby . . . it's all yours."

When I woke up, she was already dressed and sitting on the bed. "I need to go." I was surprised and disappointed, but I got up and got dressed and we drove off. "Where are we going," I asked. "South Central," she said. "So, what are you going to do?" "I'm going back to work." "Great. What kind of work?" "I'm a cat burglar." "A cat burglar? What's that? You mean you steal cats?" "No," she said, laughing. "I'm a thief. I steal from people while they're sleeping. Gotta be quiet as a cat," she said as she kissed me goodbye. "Hey, cat lady. Call me, okay?" "Bye, baby. Thanks for the ride . . . and the kisses. I love you, rock star." I never saw her again. And yeah . . . she stole my heart.

The Mutiny

BILL WILD'S DRINKING AND DRUG problems got worse, posing a threat to the project, so I fired him. It wasn't easy, since we were longtime close friends. The band got nervous when they saw I had the power to do that. To protect their hides, they called a meeting with Frank and me to reinstate Bill and to remove me from the leadership role. They wanted Tony Duran to be the leader. They fucking "jumped" me out! I thought it was hilarious, even though I was furious. But I bit the bullet and hung in for the sake of the project. I couldn't jump ship midstream. Plus, Ruben And The Jets had a Northwest tour coming up opening for Frank and the Mothers. Tony was a great guitarist, singer, and songwriter, but not a visionary bandleader or a front man. So I had to lead in a subversive way while performing, setting the tone and vibe of the set, a rock conductor of sorts.

My initial distrust was now confirmed. But what really hurt was that Frank took their side. I had a tremendous amount of respect for Frank as a musician and as a man. One big reason I took up the project, aside from our common love for music and theater, was the way he treated his kids, Moon Unit and Dweezil. He was the perfect dad, always ready to compliment them on their drawings or just to talk when they wanted to. He was the role model of a father that I didn't have, nor was, and I trusted him. I could have pushed it and fired the entire band, but I realized he was probably in a production bind, so I let it go and went along for the absurd ride.

Frank was in a hurry to start the album, but Bobby Zamora and Bill Wild weren't quite ready to record all the tunes. So Frank recruited Aynsly Dunbar for the drum tracks on "Mah Man Flash" and "If I Could Only Be Your Love Again"; George Duke played the piano parts. A bass player maybe named Drumbowski performed on those tracks as well. Frank played a blazing solo

Poster for the band's first tour with Frank Zappa and the Mothers of Invention, 1972. Courtesy of Frank Zappa Family Trust.

at the end of "Dedicated to the One I Love," with a great lead vocal by John Martinez. The Latin-tinged groover "Show Me the Way to Your Heart" by Tony was a great surprise. The *ranchera gritos* and alto sax solo on "Flash" were by Clarence Matsui, who later dropped out because we didn't get enough gigs to pay the rent. Motorhead dropped out after the album came out for the same reason. The sessions went well and Frank was easy to work with in spite of his perfectionism, and mine. We were having trouble getting the harmonies tight on a ballad and I kept asking for retakes. In desperation Frank sighed, "Damn, Rubén. Have a little mercy. They're fine." I learned a lot about the recording process—mainly, patience. Recording can be a slow bleed at times, with many painful compromises. Upon completion, Frank asked me what the title should be. *For Real!* was released in mid-'73 on Mercury Records.

The Movie Star and Miss Blue Eyes

I HAD TO MOVE OUT of my Echo Park love lounge because very little money was coming in from the gigs. I'd already spent most of the tiny advance for the record, so I wound up living out of my VW station wagon, parked on the Pacific Coast Highway across from the Malibu Pier. There was a Jack-in-the-Box nearby, which was good for breakfast and a bathroom. When I did have a little extra cash I would hit the bar at Alice's Restaurant on the pier and scope out the lovelies. It was a sweet retreat from the stress and drama of the band, even though I was now homeless.

One day I was sitting at the bar having a glass of wine when a beauty sat down a couple of stools away and spun me around like a spinning top. It was a movie star whose name I won't mention, speaking in French with a lady friend. She was dressed casually, nothing fancy. Her beauty was beyond fashion. I patted down my Afro and thought about my moves as my rock 'n' roll dog yanked his chain.

I slowly drank my wine, setting the vibe to let her get used to me sitting nearby. I raised my glass to take a sip and looked over at her with a friendly smile, momentarily interrupting their conversation. She returned a half smile. "Welcome to Malibu," I said. "Are you from France?" "No, I'm from England but my friend here is from France. I live in Malibu now," she said in a surprisingly warm voice. "Well, like I said, welcome to Malibu. It's temporarily my home too. I'm a musician, a singer in a rock 'n' roll band. I know who you are, and it's a pleasure to meet you. Can I buy you and your friend a glass of wine? The Pouilly-Fuissé is really good here." "Thank you," she replied, "that would be nice." Her friend stepped outside and she went on: "How long have you lived in Malibu?" "Oh, I'm just here for the summer. I'm leaving on a national tour to promote the release of my new album in a couple of weeks, not sure if I'll be coming back." Yeah, it was a little BS about living in Malibu, because I was living in my station wagon outside on the highway. It was half true, though. We chatted a while longer, then, as we finished our wine, she said, "It was nice talking with you. We have to leave now. Thanks for the wine. It *was* good. And good luck on the tour." Her friend returned and they walked out together. "Thanks, I'll be looking for your next movie," I blurted out, trying to be cool as I watched her slip away. I got close, but no cigar. But what could I have offered her in life? Get real, man—nothing but a glass of wine.

Feeling good about holding my own with a movie goddess, I strutted across the street to a liquor store and bought a bottle of wine. I wanted to celebrate my smooth-talkin' groove and see where it could take me next. The dog was restless. I took a couple hits of grass as I crossed the highway, and walked to the beach. It was another perfect day in paradise. The shore was crawling with beautiful hot buttered beach bunny butt. I spotted two in bikinis that looked illegal: there was hardly any bikini *there*. Good gawd a-mighty! I'm not a beach dog, that's not my style. But my ego was flying high, and so was I, and I was sure I could score these two sexy mermaid sirens, at least to share a bottle of wine.

"Hello, what a beautiful day. Couldn't be nicer, huh?" One was rubbing oil on her tanned legs, and she gazed up at me with a faraway look in her eyes but didn't say a word. Then I said, "Hi, my name is Rubén, do you mind if I sit down next to you?" They both stared at me like I was from another planet. One had the most beautiful deep cobalt blue eyes, serene and wise. I was staggered by her beauty as she looked through me with those celestial eyes. I was at a sudden loss for words and felt foolish since they weren't responding to me, only staring. Then Miss Blue Eyes turned to her friend and started flashing her fingers, and her friend did the same. That was it: they were deaf!

They flashed their fingers back and forth while laughing in low, guttural, yet sexy voices. This was going to be the challenge of my life. How the fuck do you seduce a deaf woman? I made a motion like I was writing on a pad. Miss Blue Eyes pulled out a notebook and handed it to me with a pen. I tried to be a *caballero*, a gentleman, in my attempt to seduce her with my naked soul. "Would you like some wine?" I scribbled. "No, thank you, we don't drink," she wrote. I waited a minute, then asked, "What do you do for fun?" "We like to go bowling. We're in a bowling league," she wrote, with the most beautiful penmanship I'd ever seen. I took another hit from the bottle. "Do you ever go out on dates?" I boldly asked. "Yes," she wrote and smiled. "Maybe we can meet sometime and go bowling?" I wrote with sincere confidence. "We're taught not to socialize with the hearing and speaking world." Huh?! "Why's that," I asked. "They cannot be trusted," she wrote in her elegant hand. "When do you go bowling?" I wrote, loading each word with sincerity. "Once a month," she replied. "Would it be okay if I came by?" "Can I trust you?" she asked. I stumbled for a second, not wanting to lie. The look in her eyes spoke truths that I could never know. She was from some other reality, another dimension, too real for me. Maybe she *was* . . . an angel. My heart took a dive into a moment of truth. "Am I real, or am I bullshit?" I asked myself.

"Yes, you can trust me," I wrote. I wanted to know this perfect being.

"Okay, you seem like a good person. I believe you," she scribbled. "We meet on the last Saturday of the month, at the Downey Lanes, at 3 P.M."

For the next few days I struggled, trying to decide whether to go or not. I'm not honest enough. I'm a dog. I'd break her heart. There's no point. But, I thought . . . maybe, I *could* be honest.

When Saturday came, I took a hit, then drove down to Downey Lanes. The place was packed, all the lanes bustling with bowlers doing their thing. There was an eerie but peaceful vibe in the air. There were no voices except for the haunting occasional guttural laughter, lively hands talking and shouting with excitement along with the sound of bowling balls hitting the wooden lanes and the crack of pins getting struck. What a perfect world, I thought, where everybody trusts each other. Maybe this is what heaven is all about. After all, here I was with all these angels.

I searched for Miss Blue Eyes and finally spotted her across the lanes. She looked even more beautiful than at the beach, so poised and confident, so completely in tune, in sync with her unique life force. I realized it was way more than I could ever return. Suddenly I heard someone laugh out loud. It was Miss Blue Eyes, but it wasn't that low gravelly sexy laugh. This time it sounded more like a speaking person's laugh, pure, free, joyful. My heart sank. I watched her for a few more frames, imagined her as my wife, then whispered, "Thank you," and left. I didn't have the heart, the love, or the guts to stay.

Opening for Zappa at San Francisco's Winterland

AFTER WE OPENED FOR ZAPPA and got an encore at the Palladium, by April 1973 we were ready to take on the legendary Winterland in San Francisco. Again, we were the opening band for Zappa, with the British band Foghat second on the bill. It was a full house.

When Bill Graham introduced us, we got a loud welcome. Maybe it was because Buffalo was first to walk out on stage. He had become the most outlandish dresser of the band. He was wearing some crazy zebra-striped pants and a silver glitter shirt with the sleeves cut off and his long ZZ Top/ Jesus hair and beard. Most of the guys wore typical street gear, Levi's and fancy shirts. I had tight yellow bell-bottoms on, a red sleeveless t-shirt with *Rock & Roll* in glitter written on the front, and my trusty white boots with flames. I was ready to work the room.

We started with tunes from the new album, and I was amazed to hear the audience singing along. I looked up then realized there were a lot of Latinos in the house. Then Buffalo's hot, glamorous GTOs girlfriend, Miss Sparky, came out wearing a vintage '20s white sarong over a bold red-and-orange tropical-motif skirt and top, high heels, and a large silk flower in her hair, very Dorothy Lamour. We radiated as we shook it all down to the tune we'd written for her, "Sparky." The doo-wop harmonies sounded fantastic, at times taking my breath away. Buffalo and Tony burned with their solos. Camarena and Johnny sang their asses off, with John's Hammond B-3 screaming through the air. I swear, at moments they sounded like the Young Rascals.

We closed the set as usual with "All Nite Long" and our crazy choreography. The crowd went nuts calling for an encore as we walked off. The shouting continued for several minutes, but there wasn't enough time for an encore. Then to our shock the audience started booing as Foghat hit the stage. Conquering Winterland as an opening band was one of the many highlights of the tour. The band was gaining momentum, confidence, and serious chops.

Con Safos: *The Album*

WE STARTED ON OUR SECOND LP, *Con Safos,* produced by Denny Randell (he'd produced "A Lover's Concerto" by the Toys in 1966), before leaving for the national tour to promote *For Real!*[1] I talked Zappa into creating a set for the cover of the album designed by Cal Schenkel that we could later use as props for our performances. He agreed, and my original idea to create a rock-theater band was finally in the works. The set was a duplication of the corner of Brooklyn and Soto in Boyle Heights, with a lowrider car parked in front of a liquor store. The band was there with Miss Sparky and another girl, lounging and flirting. I stood leaning on a lamppost waving, a big grin on my face. The walls of the store were covered with graffiti that the band and I had scribbled. The "cholo graffiti" used for the album cover's title was created by future Chicano art giant Leo Limón. There was no discussion about the title for the album.

During the Northwest tour the year before, Frank and I had sat together on the bus traveling to Seattle talking about the future. I told him I was writing a musical for the band. "What's it called?" he asked. "I'm calling it *Con Safos,*" and explained that it's a broad Chicano/Mexican American activist street term with various meanings, including a form of self-affirmation, self-determination, exempt from danger, and "fuck you if you don't like it" and so be it. The term is usually written as "c/s" beneath one's name, or tag. He didn't say anything, but later when the album was released, I was surprised

---

1. Upon its digital re-release Bruce Eder of the *Music Guide* praised *For Real!,* as well as the second release, *Con Safos,* stating, "*For Real!* was as much of a masterpiece as *Cruising with Ruben & the Jets* only different—it was less a work of satire than the 1968 album had been, though it still had its moments of great fun amid some genuinely, truly magnificent rock & roll."

Cover for the second Ruben And The Jets album, *Con Safos,* Mercury Records, 1973. Photo courtesy of the Archive of the Idelsohn Society for Musical Preservation.

and happy to see that *Con Safos* was the title. The term and the graffiti were firsts for a major label release. Chicano/Mexican American culture was starting to spread throughout the world.

The Chicano student group MEChA (Movimiento Estudiantil Chicano de Aztlán) at San Diego State University put together a killer lineup for a fundraiser. It was kind of a Chicano/Mexican American Woodstock and I was thrilled to be on the bill. It was the first time I had seen the other bands in person. I was a fan of the production values of Malo ("Suavecito"), Tower of Power ("You're Still a Young Man"), Azteca with Pete Escovedo, and the zany comedy of Cheech and Chong. We held our own, even though I came out and greeted the crowd with "Hello, San Francisco!" That's what the road can do to you.

We later opened for Zappa and the Mothers and the Doobie Brothers at the San Diego Sports Arena. The long tunnel walk from the dressing room to the arena reminded me of the scene in the film *The Brave Bulls* when the *toreros* walked together in a similar dark tunnel to the bull ring, preparing their minds and hearts for the bulls and spectators. The show was similar to that. The band kicked ass that night. We were getting stronger and tighter. There was even a sense of camaraderie in the air. We were ready and excited for the upcoming national tour.

We opened for T-Rex for a couple of dates, for Three Dog Night at the Kansas City Royals Stadium, and for "supergroup" West, Bruce, and Laing with Mitch Ryder in Detroit's Masonic Temple. The Royals Stadium show was our biggest audience ever, with over forty thousand in attendance. It was cool seeing the band name come up on the jumbo screen as we pulled up to the stage in a golf cart. We were not surprised to receive a mild response when we were introduced. After all, we were the opening band and no one had ever heard of us except for die-hard Zappa fans. The band was determined to win them over. We started out with our hotter tunes like "Almost Grown" and "Spider Woman." Miss Sparky came out for her number and was a showstopper as usual, wearing a short white frilly Little Red Riding Hood dress, white socks, and red heels. We left the stage getting decent applause. We felt good about it.

Later that night we partied like a bunch of blood brothers. We went to a bar to eat, and Commander Cody from the Lost Planet Airmen came up to us and said, "You guys look like a band. Who are you?" "We're Ruben And The Jets!" we proudly roared. We got back to the hotel and the clerk said, "There were a bunch of beauties here waiting for you guys, but they gave up and left." We had met them the night before at a restaurant where they were waitresses. I swear they looked like young movie starlets. We invited them to our hotel to meet up after the show. We never thought they'd show up. You never know what starstruck Kansas City women might do to get to Hollywood. Damn! They were fine!

The next stop was New York City. We finally were making the Big Time, although the money still sucked. Walking into Max's Kansas City I noticed an announcement on the entrance wall listing Bob Marley and the Wailers, then us, followed by Bruce Springsteen and the E Street Band. Not too shabby. The Troggs ("Wild Thing") opened for us, and we blew the roof off of the tiny packed room. It was fun hangin' out in the bar at Max's. It was dark, smoky, and loud, with the finest groupies I'd ever seen sprinkled throughout the room. I didn't know where to begin, so I didn't. I drank up my Johnny Walker Black and went to bed early. We were set to open for Deodato in Central Park the next night.

We got to the gig and there was a good-sized audience, around a thousand people. Deodato was a jazz-pop artist who had a disco hit based on the theme from the film *2001: A Space Odyssey*. We were introduced and by the sound of the response there were some Zappa fans out there. We tore into our set with a lot of swagger, winning over the audience. We got an encore. Another triumph. *Variety* gave us a good review. We were on a roll, even though I was singing my guts out with a knife stuck in my back (thanks to the band mutiny).

Meeting Marc Bolan of T-Rex at the Hartford gig was a highlight. He was a real nice guy, down to earth, no attitude. He wore a black cape and cracked a bullwhip during his performance. I dug his flair and style, very theatrical. He said he was aware of our band and that he dug us. That was the best compliment from the tour for me.

The Jets were flying high, and the challenge now was keeping the band from crashing. Even though I wasn't the "leader," I still felt responsible for the project, since I'd started it. There were a lot of hijinks: typical rock-band-on-the-road bullshit of tearing up hotel rooms etc. At one point the band was banned at all Holiday Inns across the country. It was just a matter of time before there would be a meltdown.

And there was. When we returned, management fired half the band, including the guy I had previously tried to fire. Even though there was still some lingering distrust, I agreed to continue and was reinstated as leader, with John Martinez and Camarena remaining. We hired a new rhythm section and played one gig at the Whisky with Sam the Sham and the Pharaohs, and Geronimo Black. Then the three of us did a guest spot with Frank and the Mothers at the Shrine Auditorium, and later we performed for a New Year's Eve show at the Olympic Auditorium with my hero Johnny Otis on piano and his band backing us up.

But I knew I didn't want to continue. I was spinning my wheels. I was burned out.

A while later, I was informed by our manager, Herb Cohen, that Steve Cropper was interested in producing a solo album with me. He was a studio guitarist extraordinaire and songwriter who had worked with Otis Redding, Booker T. and the MGs, Wilson Pickett, and Sam and Dave. He cowrote "In the Midnight Hour," "Sittin' on the Dock of the Bay," and "Knock on

Wood." Yeah, he was a major legend. I still wasn't crazy about continuing in rock, but then I thought, this could be different. I could record with studio musicians and pick my own players for a band to tour with. It would be on more of a professional level all around, and I felt good about that possibility. I could take the theatrical ideas I'd started with Frank to a new level. What David Bowie was doing with Ziggy Stardust encouraged me to continue as a rock theater artist.

It all felt good and I was ready to roll. After two short turbulent years, Ruben And The Jets were over.

Steve and I met, went over possible material, and agreed to do it. Man! I was excited. But then the craziest thing happened: I got wind that he was dating the Southern Belle. I felt a dagger of jealousy go through my heart. A part of me was still in love with her, or maybe it was just that my ego couldn't take it. In any case, I foolishly scrapped the project. I later found out it wasn't true, but by then it was too late. I got burned by my own ego.

Looking back, maybe I inadvertently did have something to do with the breakup of the band. Maybe my self-confidence, coming out of a long history of performing, the classical training at LACC, singing in a gospel choir, and staging a favorably *L.A. Times*–reviewed musical, had given off a hint of arrogance, maybe more than a hint. Maybe that's when the seed of mistrust was planted. Maybe. I continued to be on good terms with Frank, in spite of all the shit that came down. He invited me to record background vocals on *Apostrophe, Live at the Roxy,* and *Zoot Allures* (I sang all the background harmony parts on "Find Her Finer"). Recording with Frank was always taking a leap of faith on his part, since he let me decide how to sing my parts. I always had total freedom. Our musical instincts were always in sync, though, very spontaneous and right on. I finally learned how to record my voice in the studio, thanks to him.

The last time I saw Frank was on a panel discussing rock music in Santa Monica organized by Lee Ballinger, coeditor of *Rock & Roll Confidential.* My talk was on the influence of Afro-Latin music on US pop culture. I think Frank talked about censorship. A few years later I ran into Gail Zappa at the Club Lingerie where their sons Dweezil and Ahmet were debuting with their new band, called Zappa. She told me that Frank was very sick, that I should go visit him. Regrettably, I wasn't able to and he passed away shortly thereafter. I wrote an obit in *Rock & Roll Confidential* praising his courage, genius, sense of humor, and his unswerving love and devotion to his kids. I am grateful for him offering me the opportunity to work with him and for allowing me to experiment with my crazy ideas. I didn't completely succeed at creating the rock-theater idea, but instead the Jets, Frank, and I created two damn good albums. We rocked the fuck out of many shows, getting encores where new opening bands never did. Not bad for a band only two years old. And yeah, gotdammit, it *was* glorious rock 'n' fuckin' roll theater, after all. At least it was in my mind. May you rest in peace Frank, Bill Wild, Clarence Matsui, Jim "Motorhead" Sherwood, and Tony Duran. I'll always love you crazy brothers.

Pilgrimage to Mexico

AFTER THE CHAOTIC NATIONAL TOUR, I was living it up once again in my VW station wagon: tight but cozy. One night while driving along Hollywood Boulevard looking for a cheap place to eat I saw a sign, "We Buy Records," and as Lady Luck would have it, I had a stack of *For Real!* promos with me. As I walked in I saw another sign: "Help Wanted." I sold the records and was told the job was at a wholesale record distributor on Pico by Vermont, right down the street from dear old Berendo. I went there the following day and was hired. Things were looking up.

Shortly thereafter, I moved into the once swanky Langham Apartments in the Wilshire District. The rent was cheap because the formerly ritzy neighborhood (which included the Ambassador Hotel and the Brown Derby) was now in serious decline. But the street still had a very New York look, with 1920s ornate hotels up and down the block. I used to deliver newspapers there on my bicycle at 4:30 in the morning before going to school at Berendo, fantasizing about living there someday. The Langham was the first five-story L.A. hotel to have a pool on the roof. Man, I was in the Big Time!

But the day gig brought me back down to earth real fast. It was hilarious and humbling at the same time, pulling *For Real!* and *Con Safos* off the shelves for the various record store orders. What's that Doug Sahm song title? "You Never Get Too Big And You Sure Don't Get Too Heavy, That You Don't Have To Stop And Pay Some Dues Sometimes."

While working at the distributor and surviving on sweet-and-sour humble-pie tacos, I decided it was time to follow up on another theater piece in the wake of the gospel-inspired *Who Are The People?*, only this time based on the Mexican/Chicano experience. So I enrolled in Chicano Studies at LACC. Fired up by the glorious history of pre-Columbian Mexico, I decided to make a pilgrimage to the land of my ancestors, where the natural and the supernatural worlds are one. Maybe I'd discover a new path into an invisible new world. Maybe I'd discover my true self.

I sold my dear trusty crash pad/station wagon to a Pasadena socialite to pay for the journey south. We'd met a year earlier in San Francisco at a live radio performance of the Jets, hosted by the legendary DJ Tom Donohue. We dated and had a thing for a while. One night I took her for drinks at a fancy bar in Beverly Hills. Heads turned as we walked in. I was probably the first Mexican with a wild Afro to have ever walked in there with an older white uptown lady dressed in all her finery. An older cat with a well-worn ol' show biz attitude was singing old standards at the piano bar. His banter reminded me of Oscar Levant, a '50s composer-pianist with a biting sense of humor. I requested "I'll Be Seeing You" to impress the lady and the piano player. Sure enough, with the cutting wit of Levant he announced it over the microphone: "This goes out to the lady and Mr. Johnny Go Far." It cracked me up too hard to get offended. In fact, I felt a little honored.

"When will I see you again, Mr. Johnny Go Far?" she asked as I kissed her goodnight. "I'm going to Guadalajara soon. Would you like to join me there?" I asked. "Sounds like fun. See you in Guadalajara," she replied.

My man "Flash," Pablo, and I partied all night before I left. Flash made sure he played all of our favorite tunes, just in case I never came back. Damn! Pablo and Flash could dance a pretty mean Pachuko Hop together. They called it the Choke. What a sight! We were having so much fun we barely made it to the Greyhound station in the morning. They said goodbye and wished me the best weed in Mexico. From there I went to Mexicali, then caught a train to Guadalajara. I was on ancestral land once again, and I could feel the gods and goddesses smiling.

The train ride was a long, slow trip into the past, kind of a slippery cinematic time warp. The train was old and rusty and full of peasants and working-class folks. Someone had even brought their goat and chickens on board. The scene reminded me of something out of the film ¡Viva Zapata! The train chugged along, blowing its weary horn as it moved through the various countrysides, some heavy with vegetation, some barren. It was intoxicating.

I finally arrived in Guadalajara, the former home of my father, his brother, and their parents. A deep sense of sadness mixed with a strange sense of pride emerged. I slowly walked through the city conjuring up a history I didn't really know. The air was thick with noise: music, the delicious sizzle of food cooking, shouting, dogs barking, and sirens blaring. My head was spinning trying to stay on.

While waiting at a corner for the light to change I had a brief conversation with a gentleman in a tailored suit. I asked him for directions to the hotel where the Pasadena socialite was waiting for me. He asked me where I was from, probably because of my poor Spanish. "*Soy de Los Ángeles.*" "*Oh, tú eres uno de los pochos de los Estados Unidos.* Oh, you're one of those *pochos* from the United States," using a term for Mexican Americans who drop their Mexican identity and heritage. "*No. Soy Chicano. Nací en Los Ángeles*—I was born in Los Angeles," I proudly proclaimed. "*Peor. Chicanos no tienen cultura. Son cruzados.* Worse. Chicanos don't have culture. They are mongrels," he said, laughing as he crossed the street. I couldn't believe what I'd heard. Too shocked to respond, I drifted into the city in a blurred, pissed-off haze.

This was 1974, and he was in a way right about the culture part: there really wasn't much in the way of Chicano art. You could point to a few novels, including *Chicano* by Richard Vazquez (1971) and *Bless Me, Última* by Rudolfo Anaya (1972), and the required Chicano Studies history book *Occupied America: The Chicano Struggle toward Liberation* by Rodolfo Acuña (1972). There were musicians of the forties like Lalo Guerrero and Don Tosti, and the Eastside Sound from the sixties, but they never made it to mainstream Mexico. Maybe Ritchie Valens did. The great visual artists hadn't emerged on an international level yet. Still, those words cut deep. "Chicanos don't have a culture." What the fuck?!

I felt un-Mexican and ashamed about sleeping with a white American socialite, but I went to the hotel anyway. "Hi, thought you'd never make it," she sighed as she reached out to embrace me. I gave her a little kiss on the cheek and pulled away. "This isn't going to work," I said. "I feel like a cheap gigolo and I ain't digging it." "No, that's not right," she replied. "Don't you know I'm in with love you?" "Sorry, that ain't love. You're confusing lust with love. I gotta go." She freaked out and threatened to jump out of the tenth-floor window, but I calmed her down with a couple shots of tequila. Then, Johnny Go Far kissed her goodbye.

I was awakened the next morning by the sound of loud drums and bugles blaring away. It was the 22nd of November and the streets were filled with marching bands celebrating the anniversary of the Mexican Revolution. Man, those bugles were loud! The brassy sound and thundering drums reminded me of the brass band at the bullfights in Tijuana with my *tata*, so dramatic and thrilling. I checked out of the hotel and went to watch. My spirit was lit. I felt like a Mexican for a minute, and it felt good. ¡*Órale pues México, ahora nos vamos a conocer!* All right, Mexico, now we're gonna get to know each other!

I was set to leave the next day. After walking around in dizzy circles, I finally found the station just as my train to Veracruz was pulling out. "Come on, man, you can make it!" Two hippie cats on the last car had their hands stretched out to me. "Run, man, run! You can make it!" I broke into a sprint and grabbed their hands as the train sped up. They barely pulled me on board. It turned out the guys were drug smugglers on their way to Cozumel for a big purchase. They asked me if I would be their interpreter and offered a lot of money. I said I'd think about it. Man, suddenly the devil was running with me and breathing down my funky neck. This wasn't supposed to happen in *my* movie.

We got to Veracruz and bought some killer weed. It was the strongest I'd ever smoked. We drank beer and smoked in my tiny room while a full-blown hurricane screamed away outside. My head started to leave my body. Then it was blown away into a wild acid-like dream storm. Then, I passed out. I woke up in a deep panic, the wind and rain still blowing fierce and loud. The electricity was out, so I had to crawl on my hands and knees in pitch-black darkness to look for my damn wallet. I couldn't see or feel my hands. The panic was amplified by a pissed-off sense of betrayal. "Of course they're thieves, you fuckin' idiot! They're drug smugglers!"

I managed to crawl outside and to their room through the howling storm. I pounded on the door, yelling, "Awright, motherfuckers, give me my fuckin' wallet!" "What's the matter, man?," I heard through the door. "Give me my fuckin' wallet, gotdammit!" "Hey man, calm down, we don't have your wallet." The door opened, and one of them came out. "Hold on, I'll help you look for it. I have a flashlight." Sure enough, there it was beneath my bed. I let out a shout of relief and joy that could've been heard all the way back in L.A., even though my nerves were shattered. I sure as hell didn't want to end up homeless in Veracruz. I apologized. Then we lit up a joint as the storm subsided. We made plans to meet up in Mérida after I visited Palenque, a sacred city of the Maya. Then we would go to Cozumel for the purchase.

I arrived in Villahermosa, a stop before Palenque, and as I was searching for a hotel I came across a giant stone replica of an ancient Olmec head in a sectioned-off display area. The facial features were very African. It was intriguing. I checked into my hotel, and as I was shaving I heard a rock band playing outside. They sounded pretty good, so I thought I'd check them out.

The music led me to the town plaza. The band looked like teenagers and they were laying down some serious Deep Purple. Then they busted into "La Bamba" and I lit up, hearing "Twist and Shout" by the Isley Brothers in my head. Without thinking twice, I weaved my way through the audience of mostly teenagers and, reaching the stage, walked up to the mic and started singing "Twist and Shout," which basically evolved from "La Bamba"—same bass line and chord pattern. We locked into a surprisingly solid groove, and it cooked. The audience went wild. The crowd was still cheering as I walked off the stage, when a few guys lifted me up on their shoulders and paraded me through the audience like a triumphant matador. What can I say? It was too much, another crazy movie moment.

I wound up sitting with a group of girls, sisters, four of them—all gorgeous—that more or less adopted me after the concert, complimenting me on my impromptu performance. The oldest was Magdalena, the most charming woman I'd ever met up to that time: mature, gracious, and self-confident and genuinely attentive. Is this the way Mexican girls are raised? Well, this one was. I was hooked, but unfortunately I had to leave the next day.

The sisters came to the hotel that night and left a message at the desk to come by their school the next morning to say goodbye. It was a Catholic girls' school. As I walked up to the gate, a group of girls rushed up to me asking for my autograph. Magdalena, together with her sisters, was leading the pack. Didn't she realize I was twice her age? It didn't seem to matter. We exchanged addresses and promised to stay in touch. I never wrote. I didn't want the torture.

I arrived in Palenque the next day and strolled toward the supernatural ancient city. The air smelled sweet and filled me with peace. A long curving path led me through the thick jungle to the main temple, the Temple of the Inscriptions. I recognized it from my Chicano Studies class, but seeing it up close and in person left me awestruck and suspended back in time. Suddenly it was 675 A.D., and men cloaked in jaguar skins were watching me from the bushes and trees as I glided up the path of my destiny. Quetzal birds, revered by the Maya and Aztec/Mexika as messengers of the gods, flew overhead, trumpeting the return of a lost son. Bright rays of the sun cut through the branches igniting the flowers and me, and for a brief moment I felt sacred. I felt a profound, intuitive, instinctual connection to this place, to this history, to my family. I thought of my sister Baby, fell to my knees, and started to pray in my broken way, giving thanks and gratitude. I started to weep.

Slowly I got up and stood in front of the temple, looking up to the top, toward the sun. A soft epiphany hit me upside my head as I started to climb the sacred steps, each step getting me closer to my core, closer to my essential being. With each step I realized I wasn't "American" in the WASP sense, and my only connection to Mexico was ancestrally. *What the fuck am I then?* I sat down and looked out over the ruins and the jungle, watching the quetzal birds flying by. Suddenly I remembered a line from my Chicano Studies class: "*Chicano* is not an ethnic term; it's a political term—a Mexican American activist dedicated to defending the rights of his people." Chicanos are made, not born. It's a choice. So a Chicano *artist* is someone who creates work that celebrates, contributes to, and helps shape the culture. *Hmm, helps shape the culture. Kinda like a sculptor. Yeah, that's it! I'll become a Chicano culture sculptor.*

I reached the top of the temple remembering my commitment to art and to my sister Baby. As I raised my arms to the sun I roared my newfound cultural manifesto across the jungle, tears streaming down my burnt face: "I am Chicano! A radical Chicano culture sculptor! *¡A los que dicen que los chicanos no tienen cultura: Ahora vamos a ver, cabrones!* Now we'll see about Chicanos not having culture, bastards!"

I couldn't sleep that night. Millions of ideas, dreams, songs, and poems swirled through my weary, wasted head. Where would this new commitment take me? What would it make of me? Could I deliver?

I met my hippie friends at the Chichén Itzá Mayan ruins the following day. The landscape surprised me. It wasn't a jungle like at Palenque. In fact, there were hardly any trees at all. It was mostly flat and barren except for some shrubbery. In my Chicano Studies courses I'd learned about the Mayan story. The main pyramid, El Castillo or the Temple of Kukulcán, was a big part of that story, where if you clap your hands at the base of the stairs, you magically hear the call of the quetzal. That effect was designed for sacred ceremonies as a way to communicate with the gods. Another fascinating aspect of the site is the royal ball court, where the losers of a kind of soccer game were sacrificed to the gods. I guess if you lost, you were considered a good sport. That's kinda twisted, but cool.

The Mayans have always believed they were descended from stars and planets and charted the heavens with extreme precision, even building an observatory. My favorite part of the Mayan story is that they mysteriously disappeared. Some say they spent more time looking at the stars than taking care of their crops. The theory suggests that it led to starvation, then civil wars, and sometime around 904 A.D. the mighty Maya faded into the jungle. Even though their magnificent cities were swallowed by the vegetation, their descendants have kept the culture and language alive. It was interesting hearing them speak at the food stands by the highway, their mystical bright voices echoes of a royal past.

That night we decided to take a walk along the highway. We heard there was a hotel down the road and we were ready to party. It was a balmy night. The stars were diamond tripping and the moon was hanging in a lazy tilt when we spotted the Mayaland Hotel. *What the fuck is this? A Mayan Disneyland?!* The hippies cracked up, and we turned around and went back to our campground. It not only embarrassed the fuck out of me, but I felt disgusted that a glorious culture could be so easily trashed and commodified.

The following day we waited for the bus to take us to Cozumel for the big purchase. We were standing in front of the ruins high as the clouds when we saw the bus approach. At the same time, the bus back to Mérida was coming the other way. There I stood, at the crossroads of my destiny. I thought of the blues singer Robert Johnson, who some said sold his soul to the devil. I thought about what I could do with the money as the buses got closer: record a solo album, buy a new car and new clothes, travel the world, and have enough for my old age. It all sounded good, but at the last minute I decided to go home and face my life and my new calling. Fuck the devil!

On the train ride back north I passed a small village and saw a barefoot teenaged girl in a bright red tattered dress watching and waving from the doorway of her makeshift home by the tracks. She had a small smile on her face but a look of desperation in her eyes. Her red dress reminded me of my mother when she took me to my first *Jamaica* in La Veinte when I was four. I thought about the hardship of my mom's parents, *mi nana y mi tata,* coming to L.A. from Mexico with nothing but a commitment to making a new start for the family, to have a better life than was possible in Mexico. I thought of my mom and the hopes and dreams she must have had as a young teenager. The girl waved slowly and sadly. It tore me up, and reaffirmed my decision. Now I too, was coming to the United States with nothing but a commitment and a handful of dreams, like my grandparents and relatives, like all immigrants.

In Guadalajara I transferred to the bus, and at one point we stopped in a little pueblo somewhere by Mazatlán. I spotted a newspaper headline saying

Con Safos (the band). *Left to right:* Sal Rodriguez (drums), Geoff Lee (guitar), RFG (vocals), Tom "Slick" Mancillas (bass). At the Sixth Street Bridge, Boyle Heights, California, 1984. Photo courtesy of Jimmy Velarde.

the rebel Lucio Cabañas had been assassinated by the Mexican army. I didn't know anything about him, but I learned from the article that he was a former schoolteacher fighting the oppressive government for the rights of the poor. I suddenly realized: I wanted to become a revolutionary Chicano artist-teacher. That declaration was the inspiration for my first piece of Chicano sculpture, "C/S," a song poem written for my beloved city of angels and its twisted history with Mexican Americans and Japanese Americans, which I based on Carey McWilliams's book *North from Mexico,* a cherished text from my Chicano Studies class. The title comes from the abbreviation for *Con Safo*s, a recurring theme in my work that has evolved into a symbol of my Chicano commitment, identity, and self-determination.

My new calling and life path were now set. It was as much a spiritual calling as it was political. I was well armed now for the new struggle, with a deeper sense of my ancestral spirit mixed with the need to reveal the untold history of social injustice.

L.A.

Founded in 1781 by Felipe de Neve and settled by Mexicans, Africans, Mulattos, Mestizos, and the original Native American inhabitants the Tongva, later forcibly renamed Gabrielino. The indigenous name of L.A. was Yangna, the Spanish christened it El Pueblo de Nuestra Señora la Reina de Los Ángeles de Porciúncula. L.A.—my city of the angels.

We came to work your fields of plenty. We made you rich. You paid us pennies. We laid your railroad over trails that once were ours. We taught you how to mine your gold, rope your cattle, and irrigate your land. Wait a minute. Your land? *¡Con safos!* What's that strange writing on the walls of L.A.?

March, 1942. It was Taps for the "Japs." You put them all in concentration camps. Who was left to scrape your goat? The Mexicans, why not? We were your favorite joke.

Three thousand years of civilization: Olmec, Toltec, Maya, Aztec. Three thousand years of civilization to wind up in L.A., a people in damnation! *¡Con safos!* What's that strange writing on the walls?

June, 1943, a month of infamy. The almighty Hearst Press discovered a "Menace" to L.A. You'd found your sacrificial "Lamb Special of the Day."

Thirsty for blood and hungry for sales, your headlines screamed: "Mexican Zoot-Suiters Planning to Attack Servicemen. Be Downtown Between Six and Ten."

On the night of June 7th, 1943, your Zoot-Suit Riots began L.A. A mob of sailors, soldiers, and marines marched to the middle of town to hunt those "Dirty Mexican Zoot-Suiters" down. *¡Con safos!*

The LAPD stood by and watched as boys, some only twelve and thirteen, were kicked, beaten, and stripped to "Keep Our City Clean." *¡Con safos!* What's that strange writing on the walls? *¡Con safos!* If you have any balls!

Go 'head "Santo", spray your emblem. Go 'head White Fence, paint your Coat-of-Arms. *¿Vatos locos?* Damn right! *¡Vatos locos!* Die or fight!

Go 'head "Dreamer", spray your epitaph. Go 'head Clover, sign your Treaty of Guadalupe Hidalgo. A treaty that was supposed to guarantee equality.

Go 'head *vatos locos,* children of Aztlán. Spray your metallic blood until all the walls come down!

¡Con safos! Look at me! *¡Con safos!* Know me! I am somebody! I am! *¡Yo soy alguien, cabrones! ¡Con safos!*

Won't you listen to what the walls have to say L.A.? All they're saying is: *¡Que viva Yangna! ¡Que viva Los Ángeles! ¡Que viva mi tierra!* Hey, long live L.A.!

(Loud finger snap, Pachuko style)

La Gypsy

I RETURNED FROM MEXICO with just enough money to pay the rent for my new crash pad at the Langham. Still, I missed my funky old wagon. It kept me humble. Luckily, I got a job right away at another wholesale record distributor on Venice by Vermont, and after another long day of pulling more of my albums I'd go to the Red Onion bar on Wilshire, a few blocks away from my place, to wind down. Of course, I also went there to look at the beautiful waitresses. One night, one came up to me and asked what I'd like to drink. Her low-cut blouse revealed silky olive skin. It called my name. I liked her charm and confidence. I had a hunch she was Mexican: she looked like Magdalena. It turned out she used to be a go-go dancer at Frenchy's in Hayward, a famous nightclub where the Mothers and Tower of Power first got started in the sixties. I dug her hip sense of humor and steady mellow mood. It was just what Dr. Feel Good ordered. We started dating, she moved in, and shortly thereafter we started planning for marriage. Yes, marriage. That's what Mexican women can do to you.

The wholesale distributor owner was a mysterious cat named Rico. He was always dressed in a black leather coat and would walk around the warehouse nervously looking over his shoulder, two bodyguards at his side. He made a killing by buying huge quantities of one of the first big disco hits, "Do It ('Til You're Satisfied)" by the B.T. Express. He was also a good friend with Neil Bogart, who was just starting up Casablanca Records. I was a good worker and we got along. I told him about my musical past and that he stocked my records. That cracked him up.

Other musicians worked there too, so I put together a session to record "C/S" and I played it for him. He dug it and generously set up an appointment for me to play it for Neil, who loved it. He'd just released "Chocolate

City" by Parliament, and liked the spoken-word style. He gave me a contract. I looked for an attorney for weeks to read it over but couldn't find one that I could afford. Neil eventually got pissed off and rescinded the contract for taking too long. It wasn't a very generous contract. But still . . . *I coulda been a contender*—again. Shortly thereafter he released Donna Summer and disco hit the world bigtime . . . and I hit rock bottom again with another bout of deep depression and an anxiety attack that shook me apart. I felt vulnerable, hopeless, and scared. So what do I do when I panic?

I asked "La Gypsy" to marry me—sadly, another desperate, pathetic move.

From "The Star Spangled Banner" to Punk

RICHARD FOOS USED TO BUY his records from me at the wholesaler after he opened his Rhino Records store in Claremont. We became friends through his love of rock 'n' roll and my records with the Jets. One day he offered to finance a doo-wop recording of "The Star Spangled Banner" and "America the Beautiful" as a spoof for the upcoming U.S. Bicentennial. What a great opportunity to mess with American history, to be a radical subversive doo-wop revolutionary. I gladly accepted.

I produced the session (my first as producer) in a South Central garage with Tom Knapp on guitar, Dick Mitchell on tenor sax, David Pinto on piano and arrangements, Hector Gonzalez on bass, Ron Crowe on drums, and John Martinez from the Jets on backup vocals, including bass and falsetto. For the cover I wore a black zoot suit with gold stripes and an Uncle Sam hat, while respectfully holding my shades in one hand. I stood in front of a wall that I'd spray painted *Viva América* on, my right hand over my heart like I was pledging allegiance to it. The cover popped! The wild red-white-and-blue-vinyl single became the second release for the new Rhino Records label, and I held guarded hope that the comedy record would hit. We shot another photo of me in the same zoot suit holding the jacket open with one hand while with the other I pointed to the single tucked inside—like "Hey kids, wanna buy some contraband?"—and mounted those on stands, life size. We put them up at Tower Records on Sunset and other stores around town, marketing it as a solo project. It did make the Melody Maker charts: they called it "A cruddy gem."

I didn't make a dime on that record at the time, but years later I collected royalties when it was re-released in the Rhino Records *Doo-Wop* box set. In

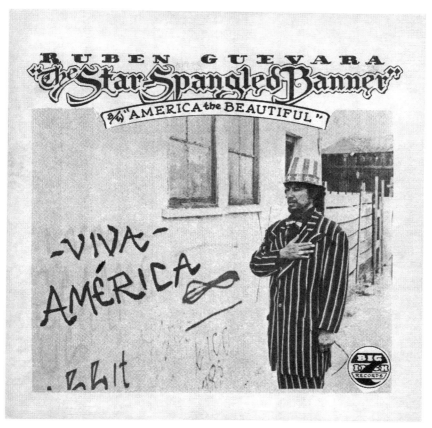

Cover of single vinyl parody of "The Star-Spangled Banner" and "America the Beautiful" for the U.S. Bicentennial 1976. Courtesy of Rhino Records.

the end, I made more from that single than from both Ruben And The Jets albums combined. The real payoff, though, was hearing our "Star Spangled Banner" by accident on Dr. Demento's radio show one Fourth of July while partying with Pablo and "Flash." We danced to it as only rock 'n' roll brothers can.

I took the single to Howard Frank, Lou Adler's assistant at Ode Records at the time. Lou eventually heard it and invited me to a screen test for Cheech and Chong's first film, *Up in Smoke*. I got a gig as a trumpet player in their backup band. The motley mariachi Mexican horn section also included a cook and a busboy from the Rainbow Bar and Grill. That crazy flick led to many later film projects and a long-lasting friendship with Lou and Cheech.

I quit my day gig to work on the film and to promote the single. I felt a new rush of possibility and hope.

My marriage was functioning okay, but something was missing and I couldn't quite put my finger on it. One morning as I was leaving to work on the film I took a long look at "La Gypsy" as she lay sleeping and my jaw dropped. She looked just like my mother! I felt sick with confusion. She woke up just at that moment and asked, "What's the matter, baby? What's wrong? Why do you look so sad?" "Oh, it's nothing," I said. "I didn't get much sleep last night, that's all." "Yeah, I know. I tried to hug you, but you pushed me away." Was it some kind of a weird Oedipus thing? Was I looking for my mother—in Magdalena, in Jackie, La Gypsy? I realized I was and I couldn't take it, so I broke up with her a few years later. That totaled three failed marriages from sheer cowardice. What a wretched dog.

Around this time I met Kim King, the engineer on the recently released *Mink De Ville* album. Willie De Ville was singing doo-wop and R & B and soul like nobody else at the time, and I dug his style and the production by Jack Nitzche. I met Kim through Denny Bruce, an independent record producer and manager of the Fabulous Thunderbirds. Maybe he saw a similarity between me and Willie. He offered to finance some demos, including a new tune of mine, "Homeboy," about the die-hard Chicano-Pachuko experience, and "Back to Babylon" by Moon Mullins, a rocking blues tune about trying to make it in Hollywood. It all made sense. They were great sessions and recordings, but we couldn't place them with a label or distributor.

It was now 1978, and a new scene was starting up in Hollywood called punk. I saw a flyer for a band called the Plugz announcing a gig at Baces Hall on Vermont. I went, but I couldn't get in, so I stood outside and listened. It sounded like distorted metal rock, but I dug the singer, Tito Larriva, who was originally from Ciudad Juárez, Mexico, then El Paso, the birthplace of the *pachuko*. He could actually sing, and he played his guitar pretty damn well. Chalo Quintana kicked it on drums, with Barry McBride holding it all down with his solid bass. Their punk single of the Ritchie Valens classic "La Bamba" turned me around when I first heard it on the jukebox at Al's Bar, a happening downtown dive. "*¡Yo no soy capitalista, soy anarquista!* I'm not a capitalist, I'm an anarchist!" Sounded like revolutionary *pachuko* punk.

I had a chance to move into the basement of a mansion in Laurel Canyon, just down the street from where my face got torched as an infant. The memory kept me on my toes while I headed back into the seductive yet treacherous arms of the Hollywood music scene.

I met Dave and Phil Alvin of the Blasters at the Whisky in 1979, and it turned out they were fans of Ruben And The Jets. A couple of years later they invited my new band, Con Safos, to play at a benefit with them and the Minutemen. The music scene in Hollywood was starting to rise up again after a long dead spell. I dug the fact that punk bands like the Plugz, X, the Germs, and the Alley Cats were playing on bills alongside roots rockers and soulsters like the Blasters, Top Jimmy and the Rhythm Pigs, and Phast Phreddie and Thee Precisions among others. I was still interested in following through with the rock-theater idea but didn't have a clue what it would be. The only rock-theater worth catching was the punk scene, with their loose cannons. I wasn't into the music that much, but I really dug the drama. A punk performance was a life-or-death commitment. Talk about catharsis.

The Whisky and a
New Band: Con Safos

THE CLUES BEGAN TO PERCOLATE when I saw a solo performance by the late Spaulding Gray at the Ford Amphitheatre's little theater in the late '70s. It completely changed my approach to theater and performing. It was just Mr. Gray sitting at a table on an otherwise empty stage. No fancy lights, props, or any type of theatricality whatsoever. The "theater" was in your mind. It was all about the story, just straight-up storytelling, and I was impressed and inspired. It was antitraditional theater and the beginning of what would be called performance art/poetry, then spoken word. I thought, hell, I can do that. I just needed some strong material. I had read about L.A. performance artists like Rachel Rosenthal, Denise Uyehara, Cherie Gaulke, Tim Miller, and Joanna Went in the *L.A. Weekly,* a new rag that covered the arts scene. What they were doing wasn't anything unprecedented: L.A. had a history of performance art that went back to the '60s and Chris Burden, with his notorious exhibitions and live performances that included having a bullet shot into his arm. In the early '70s, there was also a collective of avant-garde Chicanos on the East Side of L.A., Asco, staging their own unique form of guerilla street performance art. I was curious about them and thought about working with them someday.

I was drawn to the form because of the raw, visceral presence that it demanded on the part of the performer. You stood stark naked revealing your soul, spitting out your guts and truth. You didn't need to go through archaic traditional channels to perform. You could just take it to the streets, to warehouses, bars, and art galleries. I liked the freedom of that. You never quite knew what to expect from the work: sometimes it was genius, sometimes a self-indulgent train wreck, with starstruck wannabe actors thinking the performance could be a step into the movies. Consequently there was a lot of *mierda* (bullshit), and the form later lost respect.

I set up a few performances at Beyond Baroque with bassist Hector Gonzalez, at the Improv Comedy Club (stand-up poetry), then later at the Los Angeles Actors' Theatre, and with Los Angeles Contemporary Exhibitions (LACE) at the Victor Building downtown. The performances were primarily collected poems and songs turned into monologues based on my newfound Chicano identity. "C/S" and "Homeboy" were always included. I even started to include shamanic touches that I intuitively connected with, inspired by reading some of Carlos Castañeda's books. But something was missing—some grease, some soul, some funk. So I decided to add a soul band to back it all up.

Independent record producer Harvey Kubernik liked "C/S," the demo I played for Neil Bogart, and put it on his new Freeways Records release, *L.A. Radio.* Later, he invited me to perform at its release concert at the Whisky. I suggested that he include a prominent L.A. poet, whom I'd gotten to know, on the bill. She and I later got involved. It was a stormy relationship, to put it mildly; we couldn't make it work or cooperate in the raising of our daughter, whom I adored. In a 2006 interview she referred to me as "a guy she couldn't pick out of a lineup." I was glad to see she hadn't lost her sense of humor.

As for the concert at the Whisky, Patrick Goldstein, a journalist from the *L.A. Times,* called and asked if there was a rock scene in East L.A. "There is now," I said. Soon after on the front page of the "Calendar" section there was a shot of the East L.A. punks Los Illegals and one of me crouched down wearing a bandanna and shades. He mentioned the concert in the article, and the word was seriously out.

Now I knew what the new rock-theater piece would be: spoken word funk—a few classic East L.A. oldies, a little Gil Scott-Heron–style Chicano poetry, and some James Brown grooves to funkify it all up. This new style of spoken word—reciting poetry with a band—wasn't really new; the Watts Prophets had already been mining that groove in the '60s. But I was going to make it mine. I decided to name the band Con Safos after my song-poem "C/S." The mighty band included Danny Diaz (Village Callers) on guitar, Hector Gonzalez (Eastside Connection) on bass, John de Luna (El Chicano) on drums and background vocals, Jerome Jummonville on tenor sax, and Mel Steinberg (also Eastside Connection) on alto sax.

It felt good coming back to the Whisky with a band that I felt totally comfortable with. Now I could take the failed Chicano rock-theater idea I'd had with the Jets to a new level. Instead of party songs, the songs would be about my new commitment. My second sculptural piece of Chicano culture was about to be shaped and fired.

On the day of the show I had another one of my serial nervous breakdowns. I was broke as usual and needed to buy a large piece of muslin and some spray paint to make a mural backdrop that was to be placed behind the band. At the last minute my dear mother came through with the money, bless her heart. Since I was about to start working on the title song for Cheech and Chong's film *Nice Dreams* (fulfilling my longtime wish to write music for film), Cheech graciously offered to introduce the band. The money for writing the title song, "Nice Dreams," also paid the hospital for the birth of my daughter.

The Whisky was packed. The poet opened with her dark-edged poetry to a warm response. It took guts to walk out on a famous rock 'n' roll stage and read personal poems. Nobody was doing that at the time, except for Patti Smith in New York. Following the poet were the Sheiks of Shake, an underground swamp-blues band that set a funky vibe. The joint was startin' to jump, and so was I.

I took my time getting dressed in my neo-*pachuko* outfit: white zoot pants, pointed shoes, a thin red leather belt, '50s vintage long-sleeved shirt, a wine-burgundy silk bandanna, and shades. I said a little prayer, then I was ready to work another shot in the dark.

Cheech introduced the band, and they tore into Thee Midniters' '60s classic "Whittier Blvd." as I came out dancing my slickest Ruben And The Jets dance moves. In the intense heat of the lights I spray-painted a *pachuko* cross with three rays, and C/S beneath it, on the large piece of muslin I'd hung behind the drums. The red paint against the beige muslin was glorious. It fuckin' popped. The only trouble was, the chemicals from the spray paint got me incredibly high, and after "Whittier Blvd." finished I momentarily blacked out as the lights went down. It reminded me of the sulphuric acid accident I'd had back at the chemical plant. I freaked out and turned to the band in total darkness, my head spinning; realizing I was about to pass out, I started praying with all my might. And then I remembered the shaman Don Juan at the end of *Journey to Ixtlán* instructing Carlos Castañeda to jump off the "cliff" and "fly"—to surrender to what is and let the ego go. The lights came back on and I tore into the set like a released caged jaguar.

After a couple of East L.A.–style oldies, we settled into "C/S." The groove was solid and it kicked my ass just the way I like it—intensely funky. The audience was boppin' their heads and seemed to be digging it. I closed the show with "Homeboy," the capper being the part where the drummer hits a series of rimshots, imitating gunshots, as I struggled to stand while singing the Zappa line " . . . the present-day pachuco refuses to die!" It worked. Cheech came to my dressing room after the show and congratulated me. That was all I needed to boost my sights and spirit to keep me on track. The *L.A. Times* and the *Herald-Examiner* wrote generous praise. I was on my way again.

Miss Aztlán

AFTER THE WHISKY, the band played the local circuit, including Cathay de Grande, the Music Machine, and Madam Wong's in Chinatown. In '82, I moved into former Jets bandmate John Martinez's home in Boyle Heights, right down the street from White Memorial Hospital, where I was born forty years earlier. To celebrate my fortieth birthday I decided to put on a kick-ass party, a rockin' concert-piece of Chicano sculpture.

I met Brendan Mullen, who started the L.A. punk mecca the Masque and was currently booking groups into the Club Lingerie in Hollywood. He agreed to my Eastside Revue idea starring the up-and-coming Los Lobos and the return of '60s legends Cannibal and the Headhunters, a reformed version of Ruben And The Jets, and my new band, Con Safos, backing me and the Jets. The comedian Paul Rodríguez was the MC. That January 23, 1983, there were lines around the block for both of the sold-out shows. Hollywood finally got a heavy dose of Chicano rock 'n' soul thanks to Brendan. May you rest in peace, my good brother!

While I was organizing all that I met Miss Aztlán. My homie, photographer Rudy Rodríguez, had a backstage pass to a *16 de septiembre* concert at Belvedere Park in East L.A. and invited me. When I walked into the hospitality tent and her, my heart jerked and my knees collapsed. She was wearing a traditional white embroidered Mexican blouse with bare shoulders, her long black hair caressing them. I swear she looked like Ava Gardner. Rudy introduced us and she gave me a polite, indifferent smile. Turned out, she was the unofficial beauty queen of East L.A., and rightfully so.

The show was a blast of East L.A. dynamite. Paul Rodríguez was hilarious as the MC; Los Lobos played with total abandon; Cannibal and the Headhunters, with Frankie García (Cannibal) and new members David

Castañeda and Eddie Serrano, thrilled the audience with their perfect harmonies and slick Motown Revue–style choreography. My set cooked with John Martinez and Robert Camarena from the Jets and guest Jerry Tello on backup vocals along with Tom "Slick" Mancillas on bass, Paul Troncoso on guitar, Bobby Espinoza (El Chicano) on piano, Tom Gonzalez on drums, and "Spyder" Middleman on tenor sax.

The door even made some money. I stuck a wad of bills the size of a baseball glove in my pocket. Miss Aztlán was there with a couple of her fine girlfriends and we agreed to meet at the Azteca restaurant on Brooklyn in Boyle Heights for a late-night snack.

I was feeling fat with a fistful of money and was dying to spend it all on Miss Aztlán. Then the mariachis marched in and started to wail. I requested song after song, doing my best to impress the Queen of the Pachuko Hop and her two beauty queen friends. But mariachis don't play for pennies; they play for dollars—many dollars. I barely had enough left over to pay the tip for the feast, but I felt like a millionaire—and like a man. The beauties gave me a ride home, just around the corner, and I made plans to see Miss Aztlán again.

The following week I took Miss Aztlán to a concert at the Roxy that featured Los Lobos and Los Illegals, with Paul Rodríguez as a comic and MC. There seemed to be a copycat gig booker running around. That was cool. It was good that talent from East L.A. was making an impact in Hollywood, with the help of roots bands like the Blasters who were very supportive of Los Lobos and Con Safos. The Blasters even asked us to share the bill with them and the Minutemen at Dancing Waters, as a benefit for the San Pedro Free Clinic.

Unfortunately, I couldn't quite make the connection with Miss Aztlán that I wanted to. There seemed to be a cool distance, and I didn't understand why. It turned out she was looking for a husband who could support her in the style to which she was accustomed. I didn't have the jack. I was barely getting by working as a union extra in film and TV, plus the occasional gig with Con Safos. We gradually parted, and it was extremely tough getting over her—and dealing with my poverty. For the first time I was rejected, and it was about money. My looks and talent were no longer enough.

Gotcha!

I GOT A CALL FROM Central Casting for a film shoot at Olvera Street—doing "background work as an extra."

I'd had to join the Screen Extras Guild when I worked on *Cheech & Chong's Next Movie* as Cheech's stand-in. Basically, the job involved standing or walking through a scene so the cameraman could figure out his moves and the light man could figure out how to light the set. It was interesting to me, seeing how a scene is set up and shot. More interesting than the show biz itself. But joining the extras guild got me in, even if in just a small way.

I was still living in Boyle Heights, so I was close to the Olvera Street location. I got in line at the catering truck for a killer breakfast burrito with ham and sausage, a cup of coffee, and sat down to check out the ladies. As I was taking a big bite, the producer of the last Cheech & Chong movie came by, recognized me, and said hi. "Are you working on this?" he asked. "Yeah. Background," I said. "Great," he said enthusiastically. "Look," he went on, "I have a role for you—with lines. Go to wardrobe and tell them you're the guy for the suit." "Well awright!" I said. "Thanks!"

I headed over to the wardrobe trailer all jacked-up happy. I was going to make some real loot today, maybe enough for the rent and a couple of beers to boot.

"Hi," I said, all bad and proud. "I'm supposed to be fitted for the suit." "Oh, hi," the wardrobe lady replied without looking at me. "Yeah, that rack down there," she said, nodding her head to indicate a cluster of costumes. I walked down the aisle checking out the fancy suits, and yelled back, "Which one is it?" I was eyeballing a shiny black sharkskin suit. "No, not that one," she said. "The chicken suit." "Say what? No, there must be some mistake. The producer told me to pick up my suit. I have lines," I said with pride. I wasn't just another lowly extra. "The suit you're supposed to wear is the chicken suit," she said coldly. I stood there feeling humiliated, but I had to crack up. The situation was just too fuckin' funny. This could only happen to me. *But wait, I have lines!* And there I'd been imagining myself being converted to the Screen Actors Guild rate, which means *mucho* Robert *dinero.* I'd make the rent for *two* months.

I put on the chicken suit laughing my ass off and headed to the set. The assistant director pulled me aside and said, "When the principal walks over to you, he'll hand you a piece of paper and say, 'Give this to Mr. X.' You take it from him and he walks away." "Cool," I said. "What's my line?" "Oh. You're handing out flyers to passing shoppers to come to a fried chicken restaurant. You're calling out in Spanish, *¡Pollo fresco, muy barato! ¡Pollo fresco, muy barato!*" "That's it? Fresh, cheap, chicken? That's *it?*" "That's right. That's it."

The movie was *Gotcha!* I got screen credit: Chicken. Just, Chicken. They didn't even have the decency of calling me Chicken Man. Hollywood, what can I say . . .

Zyanya Records

THERE WAS NOW A BUZZ buzzing around Eastside rockers. So I approached my old friend Richard Foos, who financed "The Star Spangled Banner" and was now president of Rhino Records, to start a subsidiary of Rhino—Zyanya Records ("always" in Nahuatl)— to focus on the history of Chicano rock. I proposed to produce a compilation album on the current East L.A. scene: another sculpture of Chicano culture. He agreed. I suggested that the band that got the best reviews would get to record an album of their own. He agreed to that too. I was able to get masters from the Plugz, the Brat, Mestizo, Felix and the Katz, and Odd Squad. I produced tracks for Thee Royal Gents, Califas, Los Perros del Pueblo, and Con Safos. Well, guess who got the best reviews?

Dave Marsh, rock critic for the *Boston Phoenix* and biographer (Bruce Springsteen, Elvis Presley, and Michael Jackson) wrote: "Con Safos and their track 'C/S' resemble the blustery funk of Fela Kuti & Africa '70." The album, which was called *Los Angelinos: The Eastside Renaissance,* also received rave reviews from Robert Palmer in the *New York Times,* John Morthland in the *Village Voice,* and other critics from around the world. Chicano rock and its history were finally being recognized. We also produced *The History of Latino Rock: 1956–1965,* which included Ritchie Valens, the Romancers, the Premiers, the Salas Brothers, Lil' Ray, the Blendells, Lil' Julian Herrera, Cannibal and the Headhunters, and Thee Midniters. There was a third album as well, with the simultaneous release of *Best of Thee Midniters.*

The three albums showcased the best of East L.A. Chicano rock history and the then-current crop of players. The release party was at the Club Lingerie, with Los Perros del Pueblo putting in a kickass set of Chicano *nueva canción* protest folk, Thee Midniters (without Willie G.) rocking the house, and Con Safos smoking it. I met noted *L.A. Times* journalist Frank del Olmo there that night, who later became that paper's first Latino editor. He had a great time and thanked me for my work. You know, that's what it's finally all about: just shut the fuck up and do good work—echoing Zappa's line, "Shut up and play yer guitar!"

Sometime around 1984, *Los Angelinos* turned up in a Tokyo record store and Shin Miyata (currently head of Barrio Gold Records, a label dedicated to Chicano music) bought it. This was his first encounter with Chicano art and music. The cover had a powerful Siqueiros-like mural by Asco members Gronk and Willie Herrón III, with the band names written below in cholo Graff calligraphy by yours truly. After discovering the album and its culture, Shin moved to Monterey Park and attended East Los Angeles College and took some Chicano Studies classes, as well as studying Spanish. (You never know who's going to listen to your music, so make it good chil'ren. Years later, in the 1990s, a Chicano lowrider and cholo fad hit Tokyo youth with car clubs, and cholo fashion becoming the rage. The trend was started by Shin and others.)

Shortly after the three-album release, I was asked by Dave Marsh to write a chapter on the history of Chicano rock for a book he was editing. "View from The Sixth Street Bridge: A History of Chicano Rock" emerged, with Lee Ballinger assisting with helping me write my first history piece. It was published in 1985 in *The First Rock and Roll Confidential Report: Inside the Real World of Rock & Roll,* edited by Dave Marsh et al. (Pantheon Books). And so began my journalism career, with many articles and liner notes on Chicano music and culture written for the *L.A. Weekly, L.A. Style, L.A. Times,* and a column in *SuperOnda* magazine, among others. At the same time, "The Ballad of East L.A." was published in *The Hip Pocket Guide to Los Angeles* (Harper Colophon, 1985). It was a very busy period, with more cash coming in. My new path and direction were getting more firmly set. The future never looked or felt better.

Cristina, Día de los Muertos, and Chicano Heaven

I FIRST SAW HER at a Jesse Jackson Rainbow Coalition fundraiser at Plaza de la Raza, Lincoln Heights, in the summer of '84. She was an organizer for the coalition, working at the bar. It surprised me that she was serving drinks. She looked like a teenager. I gave her my drink ticket and she handed me my glass of wine with a beautiful smile.

I was in the midst of envisioning a new music-dance-theater piece, *Lil' Ruben G. and Thee Latin Soul Revue,* to be presented at Club Lingerie following the success of the Eastside Revue the year before. That piece had celebrated East L.A. Chicano rock, past and present. It was 1984, and this time I wanted to celebrate Día de los Muertos (Day of the Dead), a custom that goes back to ancient Mexika/Aztec times and one that fascinated me.[1]

---

1. The Aztec ritual was later co-opted and fused with the Spanish Catholic Church's observation of All Saints Day. It's a sacred ritual honoring ancestors, deceased friends and family members, and even pop idols, with *ofrendas,* or offerings, of candles, incense, *pan de muertos* (bread of the dead), *papel picado* (decorative paper banners), and favorite objects of the dead. The altars are adorned with marigold flowers, which symbolize ancestors. The spirits are believed to return on November 1 and 2 to enjoy the gifts. Self Help Graphics & Art, an East L.A. arts center, and San Francisco's Galería de la Raza started the public hybrid Chicanx/Aztec custom in the United States in 1972. On that occasion, the Asco art collective fused avant-garde art with traditional Day of the Dead concepts, and later master *altarista* Dr. Ofelia Esparza led the spiritual altar making, by invitation of Sister Karen Boccalero. The holiday is now celebrated in Mexican American communities all over the country.

Left: Marisela Norte's flyer for *Lil' Ruben G. & Thee Latin Soul Revue* at a Día de los Muertos celebration (1984); courtesy of Marisela Norte.; *right:* the flyer by Rudy Rodriguez for *The Eastside Revue* (1983). Courtesy of the Funkahuatl family archive.

I thought it would be a hip trip to choreograph Mexika/Azteca *danzantes*—a relatively new movement—and hip-hop breakers dancing together for the opening ceremony of the piece. I'd never seen that done before.

I was renting a room in Boyle Heights at the time, and a roommate's boyfriend was a *danzante* in Xipetotec Danza Azteca. I saw them dance and recruited them. Then I met Ultimate Force, a hip-hop break crew at Radiotron, a youth center in the Westlake district and an early incubator of L.A. hip-hop and Graff art founded by Carmelo Alvarez. The youth center evolved out of an earlier hip-hop haven, Radioclub, where I got my first taste of rap with Ice-T laying it down. (I heard echoes of the Watts Prophets.) In short order we started rehearsals at Radiotron.

We got named a Pick of the Week in the *L.A. Weekly,* along with an interview where I was tagged as a "Sub-Culture Sculptor." It was close enough, though I didn't like the "Sub" tag. But in a way it was correct, since Chicanos aren't in the polluted mainstream culture and never will be and that's all right with me. So, I guess I was making progress.

The room was packed and buzzing. Even Prince was in the house. The lights went down as an explosion of indigenous drumming shattered the smoky air. The rowdy nightclub went silent. Sounds of a conch shell trumpeted across the room, calling the Mexika spirit world. A *copalera* carrying a tray of burning *copal* (incense from tree sap) led the entourage of ten *danzantes* dressed in full regalia, tall pheasant feathers swaying above their heads as they slowly marched onto the dark dance floor, their faces painted black and outlined with white skull-like markings. The audience of mostly white Hollywood scenesters watched in awe. The Chicanos in the house smiled with pride.

The sacred ancient fire ceremony honoring Xiuhetecuhtli, the Mexika god of fire, began. Again the *huehuetl* drums roared like battle cannons as the *danzantes* began circling around a small flame lit in the incense burner placed in the center of the dark dance floor. Meanwhile, Ultimate Force slowly entered and joined them, gyrating to the beat of the drums at a respectful distance. The lead *danzante* then reverently approached the flame and placed his bare foot over it. Behind him, with the drums reaching a crescendo, one of the breakers, wearing a football helmet, spun on his head like a spinning top. It was startling. The room gasped. Time stopped. After what seemed like a timeless eternity, the *danzantes* and the breakers slowly exited the dance floor as they and the drumming faded into the darkness.

This was the first time this experimental ceremony was ever witnessed in Babylon. It left a distinct vibe in the air: the suspension of time; sacred ceremonial tradition mixed with a psychedelic, hip-hop, supernatural high. It felt at once sacred and profane, and full of respect. It felt right, since to the Mexika, the natural and the supernatural worlds are one. That's the only reward you get from performance art: you never really know how it's going to fly until you just let it go.

Then Asco hit the stage. Painter and musician (with Los Illegals) Willie Herrón III hung an elaborate mural of his across the stage, while photographer-provocateur Harry Gamboa Jr. projected his noir photos beside it. Then Marisela Norte strolled up to the mic and presented her performance piece *Sleep Walk* to the hushed nightclub crowd. Gronk and guest

Con Safos Band. *Left to right:* "Spyder" (sax); RFG (vocals); Las Angelinas Irma "Cui Cui" Rangel, Suzie Quezada, and Beverly D'Angelo; and at far right (not pictured) Bobby Espinoza (keys), Club Lingerie, Hollywood, 1984. Photo by Gary Leonard.

performer Jim Bucalo then performed Harry Gamboa's enigmatic theater piece *Shadow Play,* accompanied by painter Daniel J. Martinez's hypnotic light design. Babylon got its first dose of Chicano guerilla-theater, East L.A. style.

Next up were the Wild Cards, a neo-*pachuko* band dressed in tailored zoot suits and slicked-back high pompadours who then proceeded to tear the place apart with their smokin' pachuko-boogie-swing jump blues. The joint was now most definitely jumpin', and so was I. Con Safos took the stage with a lethal lineup of players: "Spyder" and Robert Johnson on tenor saxophones, Bobby Espinoza (El Chicano) on keyboards, Paul Troncoso on guitar, Tom "Slick" Mancillas on bass, and Sal Rodríguez (War) on drums. I always wanted some Raelettes of my own, so I put together Las Angelinas, a killer trio of Chicana singers: Suzie Quezada, Irma "Cui Cui" Rangel (Califas), and Beverly D'Angelo. On both sides of the stage were two dancers, Olga Pérez and Bel Hernandez, wearing black leotards, mesh stockings, and stiletto heels, with their faces painted as *calavera* skulls—my twisted funky version of the Phantomettes. The lights went up and the psychedelic ritual of soul continued. The band and I were so fired up that by the time we finished "Land of a Thousand Dances" (the Wilson Pickett version) and got into a killer-tight in-the-pocket groove on "C/S," with Las Angelinas singing like frenzied angels on fire and Olga and Bel shaking their *calavera* tailfeathers, I flew into a new zone: I levitated for the first time. Not too high, about an inch. But it was high enough. The house shook, rocked, and rolled with sacred spirits and pure Chicano soul. I'm sure our ancestors dug it. At least, I hope they did.

I couldn't sleep that night from the adrenalin buzz in my head, so I got up out of bed as the sun came up and took a walk to try and come down. After a tasty breakfast of *huevos rancheros,* I took a walk down Brooklyn and saw a *sastrería,* a tailor shop that specialized in zoot suits. The show had done well at the door, so I decided to have one made. I went in and got fitted for an unbelievable midnight-royal-blue suit and left a $50 deposit. Unfortunately, I never had the rest to pay for it. It would've been my first tailored suit. Was this another metaphor for my life?

As I continued walking down Brooklyn I ran into a friend, Jesús, and he invited me to a party. Hell, yes! I was ready to party! When I walked in I saw the woman from the Jackson fundraiser, recognizing her smile, which lit up the room. Madonna's "Like a Virgin" started to play, and I boldly asked her to dance. She told me she lived with a roommate, someone I knew in fact. Then I asked her who the guy was who was staring at us. "Oh, that's my date," she said. "Oh, cool. My name is Rubén," and she said, "Yeah, Ruben And The Jets." As the song wound down I thanked her for the dance, then took off. I thought that was that.

Later one evening, I stopped by El Café Cultural on First and St. Louis in Boyle Heights, which was run by Mexican socialists Norma and Rodolfo Barragán. I wanted to catch a set by my friends, Chicano *nueva canción* protest group Los Perros del Pueblo, whom I'd produced on the *Los Angelinos* compilation. My *tocayo* and fellow poet Rubén Martínez and I had read there a few weeks before. I dug the vibe of the place. As I walked in, I noticed the beauty from the party, Miss "Like a Virgin," dancing in total abandon to the Chicano movement *corrido* anthem "Mujeres Valientes" (Valiant Women). The song turned out to be about her: a Chicana revolutionary.

I walked over to her after the tune ended. "What a trip to run into you here." "Yeah, I like this place," she said, "with its activists and artists." We danced, drank wine and ate some of Norma's great *chiles rellenos,* and laughed for hours. I was impressed by how relaxed and self-assured she was. Outside as we were leaving, she slid her arms around my waist and hugged me goodnight.

Turned out she was a bilingual elementary school teacher in the Latino Pico Union district downtown, twenty-eight years old. Her name was Cristina. She was born in Mexico City to an indigenous Tarascan mother and an American English teacher with Iroquois ancestry who was also a jazz musician. They'd moved to L.A. when she was ten. She looked Polynesian, Eurasian, Mexican, and Native American, truly a cosmic beauty.

We started dating. Our first formal date was at a New Year's Eve party at the home of Antonio Rodríguez, a prominent Eastside activist and attorney. His mother said we were *"una buena pareja,"* a fine match. That was a good sign—a blessing, in fact—from the revered Rodríguez matriarch. With that, I was formally accepted into the community.

I moved into a single on Boyle, just south of First. We called it "Lovers Island" after a favorite song of ours by the Blue Jays. She introduced me to the Chicano Eastside activist community, starting with volunteering for Antonio Rodríguez in his bid for the 14th Council District and marching in support of the Nicaraguan Sandinistas, the Argentine Mothers of the Disappeared, the United Farm Workers, and immigration reform. It had finally happened: I found my revolutionary soul mate. Plus, she liked to go cruising, listening to oldies on KGFJ. What more could this lucky old dog have asked for?

While working in films when I could as a union extra, I put together another crazy concept concert in the same mold as the Club Lingerie's Día de los Muertos show, but this time emphasizing Chicano art along with the music. *Lil' Ruben G. and Thee Latin Soul Revue, Part II* was created for UCLA's "Mexican Symposium," organized by professor and musician Steve Loza. Xipetotec Danza Azteca and Ultimate Force once again performed their mind-bending magic, and Con Safos performed with Gronk painting on an easel. Las Angelinas sang again too, this time with Geri Gonzalez, who thrilled the packed house with a chilling version of Aretha's "Chain of Fools," and Los Amigos Cósmicos del

Quinto Sol performed their potent mix of political *norteño*-rock. I asked Wayne Alaniz Healy and David Botello, cofounders of the East Los Streetscapers mural collective, to hang their classic mural painting *L.A. Bicentennial Blues* as a bandstand backdrop. Since UCLA provided funding for the event, I was able to commission two monumental murals by Asco members, Willie Herrón III and Gronk, that were hung on either side of the stage, and Barbara Carrasco exhibited her powerful drawings. Marcos Sánchez-Tranquilino followed the opening fire ceremony with a slide show on the history of Chicano art. (This was five years before the landmark 1990 UCLA show *CARA: Chicano Art—Resistance and Affirmation, 1965–1985*, which he cocurated.)

We were cooking and smoking and looking good, and I never felt more secure within myself, my work, and the future. Plus, having Cristina in my life stoked my tired heart with new flames of love, creative fire, and purpose. So a few months after the concert, we decided to live together. We moved into a classic 1920s Spanish-colonial triplex in what was once Brooklyn Heights (now Boyle Heights), a block away from El Tepeyac, a famous Eastside Mexican restaurant. Our new home had polished hardwood floors and arched windows and was by far the most beautiful apartment I'd ever lived in. After a few months of true bliss, feeling grounded with the success of my new life path, I felt confident enough with our relationship that I surrendered my ego and jumped off Castañeda's cliff once again. I asked her to marry me. The dog had found a home.

We planned our wedding to take place in the center of the Sixth Street Bridge, East L.A.'s "bridge of destiny." Talk about a performance piece! I envisioned a large band of mariachis in an arc in front of us facing City Hall, a hundred rows of chairs for family and friends, palm trees in planters, red and white roses along the railing of the bridge, and a line of classic lowriders in all their splendor ready to take the bride and groom to Chicano Heaven. At least, that's what I had in mind. It would've been a trip, but at the last minute we decided to save the money and have a simple private ceremony at the L.A. County Courthouse.

We were both in a daze that morning, not so much because we were getting married but because the night before I'd staged another one of my crazy Día de los Muertos performance pieces at the East Los Streetscapers studio. Cristina had helped me organize the event, another successful Chicano culture sculpture. We celebrated late into the night and barely made it to the courthouse the following morning. Cristina's beautiful, gracious mother,

"Chata," and her husband, Bob "Papa Bert" Manley, attended the ceremony as our witnesses. I made another promise to "love, honor, and obey 'til death do us part." Could I deliver this time? I was confident that I could. This was it. She loved me, in spite of my miserable track record. She was as tough as she was sweet. She was a Chicana.

Born in East L.A.: *The Movie*

WHEN SHE TOLD ME SHE WAS PREGNANT, all I could say was "Thank you to all the gods and goddesses for watching over us and for giving this dog another chance." The news was heavy, but I was ready. After all, it was a miracle.

One day while we were doing our laundry, we heard Cheech Marin's hit single "Born in East L.A." come blasting through the laundromat's speakers. It cracked us up. How inspired, to take Springsteen's "Born in the USA" and flip it into a parody of an illegal Immigration and Naturalization Service deportation. A few weeks later I got a call from him asking me if I wanted to work on his new film *Born in East L.A.* as a culture and music consultant. It came in the nick of time, since extra work was slow. Daniel Stern, an actor in the movie, jokingly dubbed me the East L.A. Cultural Attaché. What a courageous act and how very Chicano of Cheech to keep social issues on the front burner. He could have played it safe and made another stoner buddy movie, but instead he took on the serious topic of immigration but with his zany sense of humor added. I was thrilled and ready to rock.

We were on location in Tijuana for about four weeks. I hadn't been there since the sixties, and before that when I would go to visit my cousins and go to the bullfights with my grandfather. The cast and crew stayed in the Fiesta Americana, a new thirty-story hotel with purified running water. Yes, that's right, purified running water—in all the faucets. I had a giant room with a king-sized bed big enough for a family of ten. It was the fanciest hotel room I'd ever been in. Tijuana sure had changed in the past forty years.

One morning after finishing shooting downtown, I saw the call sheet that read "Location: *La Mesa.*" That reminded me of being a kid and visiting my *tío* Crispín and my cousins, the days when we climbed into truck tires and rolled down the hills at lightning speed, flying through the air like supermen: No fear in my body. No fear of life. No fear of death. Those memories shook me up and made me nervous. Why didn't I feel the same now?

The crew was mostly Mexican, and there was one crewman I'll never forget. His name was Gonzalo. His job was to bring everyone coffee and donuts in the morning and snacks in the afternoon. The catering truck was parked on top of a hill, so he had to walk down the steep trails to the set below. He did that with the tray *balanced on his head!* Every day, three times a day—in the morning, after lunch, and before wrapping—there he would be walking down the trail with his pressed white apron and that tray of coffee, drinks, and snacks perfectly balanced on his head. He looked like an elegant messenger from the gods.

We were in those canyons for several days filming the big exodus scene, where hundreds of immigrants rush the border. What a sweet moment it was watching Cheech direct that scene, an epic Chicano movie moment. I felt proud of him and was proud to be working on the film. It felt important.

When we finished in Tijuana, we moved location back to Los Angeles—to Chicago Street off First, just a few blocks from my apartment in Boyle Heights. On one of the lunch breaks Cheech invited me to join him in a sweat at the corner Russian bathhouse. It was the oldest bathhouse in the city at the time, having opened at the turn of the century. We talked about the movie and how it was going. He said he was happy with it. I said he was making history. He laughed and said he was just making a movie. I said, "Man, it's more than just another movie. It's a powerful statement on immigration. You've put a human face on it. That's pretty damn important." He said, "Thanks. We'll see." Later we went back to Tijuana to wrap the movie. Then I came home to await the birth of my son.

On June 11, 1987, Cristina glowed when she told me it was time to go to the hospital. Her joy radiated all through me and lit me up like a Christmas tree. She was calm and still smiling as I held her hand, waiting for the next contraction to hit. An hour after we arrived at the hospital, it was time, and she was wheeled into the delivery room. All seemed to be going well until I noticed the doctor anxiously call for another nurse. There was a problem with the delivery. I looked at Cristina and she had turned a ghostly yellow-green. I felt so panicked I couldn't even pray. Where was my childhood bravery, my lack of fear, flying through the air? Where was Superman?

Miraculously, Cristina's heartbeat slowly improved as our son entered the world bellowing his arrival. She managed a faint smile and asked to hold him. The doctor cut the umbilical lifeline and handed her the tiny baby. She held him close and kissed him. A nurse then handed him to me to give him a bath, to wash off the sacred blood. Our son, Rubén Gabriel Guevara III, would now join his brother Ben and his sister in changing the world.

THE PROMO TOUR

When the long black limo pulled up to our apartment building, all the neighbors came out to see what was happening. Cheech had asked me to join him on a promotional tour for *Born in East L.A.* in Mexico, and the limo came to pick me up. I felt like a movie star for a minute. Cristina walked me to the car with Rubencito in her arms and we kissed goodbye. My head was spinning with good and bad memories as the limo drove through my neighborhood on the way to the airport. I especially remembered the humiliation in Guadalajara. How would a movie made by a *pocho* fly in Mexico?

The first screening and press conference were in a fancy hotel in Mexico City. We were greeted cordially, but I was still nervous as the movie began. Thankfully, the comedy scenes lifted my spirits. There were actually laughs in the house. But when the great exodus of migrants streaming across the border came on screen, I experienced an emotional meltdown, remembering my trip to Mexico, my mothers' parents migrating to L.A. to make a new life, remembering that girl in the red dress waving at my train, waving at her hopes and dreams. It all hit me hard, real hard, and by the time the movie ended I was in tears, shaking in another puddle of rhythm and dues. After a few minutes, the publicist, Maricela Palafox, gently tapped me on the shoulder and said I needed to go to the table in front for the press conference. Her voice sounded like she was a thousand miles away. I walked to the table in automatic–pilot zombie mode. My mind was shattered, blank. I was too spun out to panic.

I gradually came to as the reporters asked Cheech about his motivation for making the film. He said the US sends billions of dollars in aid to help support economies in other countries they call "favored nations." Why, he asked, couldn't the US government treat Mexico as a "favored nation" and help it grow economically so there wouldn't be so much immigration? Awright, Cheech! That woke me up. I wanted to say something about the disrespect we've felt from Mexicanos. I was desperately trying to think of what to say, but nothing came out. Not until we hit Monterrey.

I'd stayed up most of the night writing a speech and was in another zombie daze when I arrived for the screening and press conference. As Cheech

Cheech and me at the screening and press conference for *Born in East L.A.,* Mexico City, 1988. Courtesy of the Funkahuatl family archive.

and I were entering the theater I asked him if I could make a statement during the Q & A. "Go for it," he said. The movie rolled, there were some laughs, and when it ended there was modest applause. At the press conference, after a few general questions, Cheech introduced me. I took a deep breath, jumped in, and started the speech in perfect *pocho* Spanish:

> "*Mexicanos queridos,* I want to talk about the renaissance of Chicano culture—not Hispanic, not Latino, not Mexican American, nor *pocho* as we are known by some of you. As you know, the word *Chicano* was originally a pejorative term used by the Mexican upper classes to describe *los de abajo*—those of the lower classes. During the civil rights movements of the sixties, Mexican American students decided to take that derogatory term and turn it into one of respect and commitment. They called themselves Chicano, and that fueled the emerging Chicano civil rights movement. The term *Chicano* is not an ethnic term; it is a political term. Chicanos are Mexican Americans who commit to enrich their culture and community through politics, education, science, and the arts. Chicanos are made, not born. It's a choice.
>
> "*Mi gente:* like many of you, we are mestizos, a powerful mix of Spanish, Arab, African, and Sephardic blood mixed with Asian and the blood of the indigenous peoples of the Americas. As you know, the Mexican philosopher José Vasconcellos described us as *la raza cósmica,* the cosmic people.[1]

1. José Vasconcelos, "La Raza Cósmica" (1925), in *Aztlan: An Anthology of Mexican American Literature,* edited by Luis Valdez and Stan Steiner (New York: Vintage Books, 1972).

"Now, with all due respect, there has been a long, unfortunate misunderstanding and lack of respect for Chicanos and Mexican Americans, your children to the north. We've been called *pochos* without a culture, and *cruzado* mongrels, as I was once told in Guadalajara on a pilgrimage and homage to my ancestral roots.

"We were not traitors because we left Mexico. It was the Revolution that forced my grandparents to the United States. And, we have never lost or cut our roots with you. And as for not having a culture, well, I have news for you: we've been busy. We now have internationally recognized artists, including painters Carlos Almaraz, Gilbert "Magu" Luján, John Valadez, Chaz Bojórquez, Wayne Alaniz Healy, David Botello, Barbara Carrasco, Margaret García, and Judithe Hernández, to mention only a few. Also writers and poets: Oscar "Zeta" Acosta, Rodolfo Anaya, José Montoya, Rodolfo "Corky" Gonzalez, Richard Vázquez, Rodolfo Acuña, Gloria Anzaldúa, and Cherie Moraga, among many others. And musicians, among them Lalo Guerrero, Don Tosti, Ritchie Valens, Carlos Santana, and Los Lobos. Theater and film artists: Anthony Quinn, Ricardo Montalbán, Luis Valdez and El Teatro Campesino, Edward James Olmos, Pepe Serna, Kiki Castillo, Evelina Fernández, and now, Cheech Marin with his new movie *Born in East L.A.*[2] It has taken a while, but now it can be said without a doubt that Chicanos have created and continue to create a magnificent and vital culture, *¡una cultura chingona! ¡Y—que cabrones! Gracias. ¡Con safos!*"

Surprisingly, I received a rousing ovation. Some even stood. A movie theater chain magnate came up to me and gave me a vigorous Chicano soul-brother handshake. Then he offered to fly Cheech and me to Guadalajara for the next screening—in his private plane.

The publicist, the magnate, Cheech, and I boarded the plane and took off. We celebrated by drinking the best tequila and smoking the best weed and cigars—two Chicanos and two Mexicans flying through our ancestors' sky as high as the clouds, etched by our shared scarred history. My work was done. Mission accomplished.

We landed in Guadalajara and Cheech and I thanked our host for his generous offer of flying us there. I then turned to Cheech and said, "Man! That was a stone trip. Probably wasn't that big of a deal for you. You probably

2. Had I been more awake when I wrote this speech, I would have included more Chicana artists, writers, and musicians in the lists. Beginning with painters Josefina Quezada, Yreina Cervantes, Santa Barraza, Carmen Lomas Garza, Patssi Valdez, and Judith Baca; writers and poets Ana Castillo, Norma Cantú, and Lorna Dee Cervantes; musicians Lydia Mendoza, Linda Ronstadt, Rosie Mendez Hamlin, and Vikki Carr; and in theater and film, Lupe Ontiveros, Alma Martinez, Rose Portillo, and Dyana Orteli.

fly around in private planes all the time. But, damn! Chances are it'll never happen to me again, not in this lifetime anyway. Thank you, man. Thank you for asking me to come along and for letting me add my two cents' worth back there in Monterrey. I appreciate it more than you know." "You are very welcome my brother," he said, and then, mysteriously, he told me to meet him in front of the hotel in about two hours. "Groovy," I said, wondering what was up. "See you then."

A couple of hours later we jumped into a cab. "Where are we going?" "We're going to a *sastrería*. They specialize in mariachi suits. It's the best tailor shop in town." We pulled up and walked in. I'd never seen so many fine mariachi suits in my life. But it made sense, since Guadalajara is where mariachi was born. "What kind are you going to get," I asked. "I don't know yet. Go ahead—pick one out for yourself," he said. "Say what!? Are you serious!?" "As serious as a heart attack," he said with a big Cheech grin on his face. I found a handsome charcoal-black suit with small silver buckles to clasp the jacket and a row of them along the side seam of the pants. I'm sure my father would have chosen the same. The tailor took some measurements and went into a back room, then came back a while later with the altered garment. I finally got my first tailored suit! Cheech was fitted too, and soon we were both fit to start a trio: *Trio Los Mas Locos—The Loose Cannon Trio*. All we needed was Tommy Chong.

I got to the hotel and checked a map of the city and its neighborhoods, and lo and behold, there was the Colonia Ladrón de Guevara, the rich neighborhood my father ran away from as a kid. The map showed that there was even a hacienda there. How crazy was that? I thought of wearing my new mariachi suit and walking up to the front door and announcing the return of a lost Ladrón, *¡y que!* But unfortunately I didn't have the time to visit. I did, however, go to the cathedral designed by my ancestor on my mother's side, the architect don Martín "El Alarife" de Casillas. The white marble inside the church gave it an unearthly celestial vibe, like being in the clouds. He is interred there, and I tried to conjure up his spirit as I strolled through the iconic seventeenth-century structure.

The screening went very well, with a full house of press, and the response was enthusiastic. Everyone was excited by the positive response and the reviews. To celebrate, Cheech invited his attorney, the late Peter López and his beautiful wife, actress Catherine Bach, for a dinner in one of the finest restaurants in town. We partied, feasted, and proudly celebrated a new chapter in Chicano cultural history. We had left our mark, and it was deep. And, I was one proud and grateful Brown dog.

With Cristina and our infant son, Rubén Gabriel Guevara III, Boyle Heights, California, 1987. Photo taken by Adriana Rivera, courtesy of the Funkahuatl family archive.

I took a plane to Mexico City to spend a few days with Cristina and our new son at her *abuelita*'s modest apartment complex in Colonia Obrera. As the cab pulled up, I saw her waiting for me outside. Man, she looked so beautiful, smiling that killer smile. What can I say? It made my heart jump and shout. How much better could a dog's life get?

The following day we visited the famous floating gardens of Xochimilco and took a leisurely boat ride through the canals. Boats filled with musicians floated by, serenading us with classic Mexican folk songs. Cristina knew most of them and sang along. It was one of the most heart-wrenchingly beautiful days of my life, watching Cristina cradling our infant miracle son in her arms and looking so happy. But sadly, our Chicano Heaven was about to become as fragile as the flowers growing on the banks and as muddy as the canals.

When we returned to Boyle Heights, I began experiencing bouts of depression, feeling isolated because of all the attention my son was getting. I was no longer the adored one, and it was tough to accept. But of course, our son had to come first. So our time and attention went exclusively to him. We became full-time parents and foolishly left the marriage behind.

A few months later, on October 1, 1987, the Whittier Narrows earthquake hit and mercilessly shook our beautiful apartment up and down like a toy paper house. I was sleeping on the couch when it hit and went into a serious panic. I crawled on my hands and knees down the hallway, struggled to climb onto the bed, and rolled on top of Cristina and Rubencito while the house violently shook. I thought it was the Big One, that we were history. Rubencito was barely four months old. With my arms tightly wrapped around Cristina and the baby, I managed to pray for us to be spared, and waited for the building to collapse. The building shook up and down, up and down, like a berserk jackhammer. Then, it stopped. Stunned, I couldn't let go of them and hugged them even tighter, waiting for the aftershocks to hit. They weren't as bad. Then, there was just silence. The silence after a hard earthquake is like hearing for the first time. The air is still in shock, almost dead. We immediately packed the car and split for Santa Barbara for a couple of days. Our apartment was spared, but the foundation of our psychic world, our love and marriage, were seriously damaged.

A few months after the nerve-shattering earthquake, Cheech scored a sweet deal for a variety show at NBC. Sweeter still, he asked me to come on board as a music consultant. I had produced three tunes, two *banda* and one mariachi, for the *Born in East L.A.* soundtrack and was eager to do more. This was a major break for me, and I was finally able to breathe a little easier. But then, a few months into production, bam! An invisible demon aftershock hit: the Writers Guild went on strike, closing down all TV and film production. Hollywood came to a standstill, and inflicted on my marriage a blow that seriously undermined our emotional and financial stability. Seeds of resentment, mistrust, and insecurity were firmly planted. Yeah, there was definitely trouble in paradise.

After a few weeks of panic-filled job hunting, I finally got hired as a security guard. My car died a few days after I started, so I had to take two buses from Boyle Heights to Hollywood at five in the morning to get to work by seven A.M. The ride gave me plenty of time to plan my next move—and plenty of time to worry. One early morning as the bus stood idling at a red light at Brooklyn and Soto, I noticed the mural *El Corrido de Boyle Heights* by my homies the East Los Streetscapers. The mural lit me up for a minute, and I wrote the following poem.

Brooklyn and Soto

5am on a bus to work
car was dead
birthday morning
life flashes by
waiting for the light to change
sitting
numb
drifting
fading
remembering
empty
hopeful
ephemeral fame
when out of my funk
I hear a woman singing
across the street
in a mural
"el corrido de boyle heights"
singing
a ranchera as if her life depended on it
singing from brooklyn & soto to the moon and back
singing through centuries of Mexican joy and sorrow
singing through my finite skin
feeling it dance in the atoms of my dying bones
tasting it in the memory of my scarred soul
she is singing to me
"You are a Singer
Sing your Life
Live the Song
Be the Music"

The light turned green, and I got back on track.

Caliente y Picante

THE STRIKE FINALLY CAME TO A MERCIFUL END. Cheech's show started up, the dark clouds parted, and the Hollywood gods smiled on us for a change. Man, Cristina and I were so happy. But the smiles didn't last long. After taping a couple of shows, the program was canceled, and we were hit with another heartbreaking emotional aftershock. It forced Cristina to go back to work as a teacher again, and that didn't fly well with her. I had promised her that she would not have to work for the first few years after our son was born so she could give him all of her attention. Thankfully, Cristina's *tía* Hortencia helped with babysitting while she worked and while I nailed an occasional extra gig. It started to get tense at home, real tense, and I went into a deep dark funk.

We decided to move into an apartment in Cristina's parents' triplex in Mid-City, to save money in order to buy a house. We sadly packed and left our cherished Boyle Heights apartment, with so many beautiful memories, along with occasional rocky ones, indelibly tattooed on its innocent walls. I often drive by there, and the building always brings tears to my eyes. One lasting haunting memory stands out. After the freaking earthquake, one of the neighbors' geese was so frightened it ran away, leaving its mate behind. Every early morning thereafter around 3 A.M., loud sorrowful honking cries rang out as the goose walked down the middle of the street looking for its mate. It was chillingly eerie and sad. "Cristina, do you hear that?" "Yeah. It's hard to lose your mate. Even geese know that," she sighed.

We moved and tried our best to make the marriage work. Then out of the blue I got a call from a Mexican American film producer who offered me a gig as musical director for an HBO/Cinemax special titled *Caliente y Picante,* a first on Latin music. It was truly a gift from Chicano Heaven. It saved not only my sanity but also my shaky marriage. The lineup was a who's who of the field at the time: Celia Cruz, Tito Puente, Rubén Blades, Carlos Santana, Jerry Garcia, Linda Ronstadt, along with Daniel Valdez and the group Mariachi Los Camperos de Nati Cano. Jerry Garcia wasn't exactly "Latin music," but I guess the producers thought since he had a Spanish surname it would work to have him on the show. One day before rehearsals, I had to meet with him to go over his set. Man, he was one cool cat. As laid back as you could ever get. Not in a stoned-out way, just simply at peace with the world, with a very calm and calming spirit. He was a delight to work with, very accommodating, with no rock star ego bullshit. He was a true star, a real sweetheart of a man.

The lineup was missing one important component of "Latin" music—Tex-Mex—so I brought in the "Jimi Hendrix of the accordion," Esteban "Steve" Jordan, a.k.a. "El Parche." We had become good friends while filming his performance cameos in *Born in East L.A.* He was very excited about doing the gig. Everyone was. I felt good about adding his music to the mix.

The producers were having trouble confirming Carlos Santana for the show and asked me to call him. I did, and luckily he knew of my compilations on Rhino Records and was also impressed with their recent John Coltrane release. After a long meandering conversation he finally agreed to do the special, then asked if his father could have a guest spot with Mariachi Los Camperos de Nati Cano. Since his father was a former violinist with a mariachi group in Mexico, I thought that would be great. So it was set that his father would be included in the show. The producers agreed and flew them both down with lodging at the Biltmore. It all looked fantastic, and I was a hero—for a minute.

The special was taped over the course of two sold-out shows, which also served as a fundraiser for the Educational Issues Coordinating Committee, a Chicano youth advocacy group launched to support the 1968 East Los Angeles school walkouts, or "blowouts" as they were also called. The producers generously set me up with a room at the Biltmore too, and Cristina and

Rubencito came along to spend the night. I felt like a man who was finally in charge of his life.

The first show went very well. But during intermission for the second show, Steve Jordan lost it and got recklessly loaded. When it was time for his spot, he staggered on stage, barely able to walk, never mind play or sing. I couldn't fuckin' believe it. Then the director told me to go out and get him off the stage. How the fuck was I supposed to do that?! I was furious as hell but still managed to walk out with a forced smile while dancing to the music. I locked my arm under his and started jamming, singing along like I was a surprise guest. I slowly turned him around to the beat and started walk-dancing him off the stage as the band kept playing. It worked. I had to make it work. It was one of my toughest moments ever on a stage. But hey, that's rock 'n' roll.

I had suggested to the producers during rehearsals that a salsa version of "America the Beautiful" would be cool for the finale, a groovy way to send a message that América was not just the United States, but North, Central, and South as well. Luckily, they agreed. But I had to get the performers to agree. My idea was that Celia and Rubén would each riff back and forth on what made América a beautiful place. Celia agreed, bless her heart, but Mr. Blades declined because he didn't want to "offend" anyone. Before we were ready to film the finale, the director at the last minute decided that each artist would introduce the next artist as they came on stage. When I asked Carlos to do that, he said, "I'm a musician, not an MC." I reminded him that the request came from the director, not from me, but he still declined. Once again, Celia was the only one who agreed. She welcomed Tito onto the stage and they rocked the house, with Celia improvising away on what América meant to her in her own inimitable, charming way. She was a consummate professional. By all accounts the show was a success, with standing ovations for both. After we'd wrapped, everybody was ready to party. I celebrated like a king with my dear family that glorious night. The next morning Steve came up to me in the lobby and apologized for his stunt. I told him thanks and wished him a safe trip back home to Corpus Christi.

When it came time to mix the sound for the show the producers offered to fly me, Cristina, and our son to New York. We were thrilled. Here was a fantastic opportunity to heal our faltering marriage and boost my burned-out self-esteem. Richard Carey, one of the show's producers, picked us up at Kennedy airport. As we drove through Manhattan, rocking memories came flooding back of Central Park and Max's Kansas City with the Jets. Now, sixteen years later, my skills had brought me back to supervise the mixing of a TV special. I was making progress, and it was about time.

We drove north out of the chaotic city and through thick forests on our way to Bearsville, just west of Woodstock, where we stayed the night at Richard's beautiful farmhouse. Echoes of the 1969 Woodstock music festival, *the* twentieth-century rock event, rang in my ears, a reminder of the transformative impact that rock could have on the world. Here I was in the middle of all that history, trying to do the same thing for Latino music.

The following day Richard drove us to the legendary Bearsville Studios, founded by the renowned Albert Grossman, manager of Bob Dylan, Janis Joplin, and the Band. The studio had a long history of recording future major artists. The Band was one of the few non–R & B bands of the sixties that made a strong impression on me. Their American roots mix of country, folk, rock, R & B, and soul was a unique sound that no one had ever captured before. I particularly liked "Tears of Rage," "The Weight," and "I Shall Be Released," which sounded like stone gospel to me. I felt the presence of their genius in the studio, and it humbled and inspired me.

The mixing sessions went very well during the day. At night I would return to our idyllic bungalow in the woods, where Cristina and Rubencito would greet me with much-needed love. This was the way my life was meant to be: making music and making love. This was the life I felt we deserved. It was a healing time for us and for the marriage, the most beautiful time we ever had together as a married couple and as parents. I had never been so happy before in my life, or since. But another aftershock was about to hit.

When the producer first hired me, I agreed to defer my fee until the show was released on video. After months and months of waiting and making phone calls that never got answered, the show was finally released on Rhino Records. Great! Surely I would get paid now, since I had worked with that label before and had a close relationship with them. But it turned out that the deal was made as a direct buyout for the show. One of the producers—not the one who hired me or Richard

Carey—had taken the money and split. I never saw a dime. Although the visit to Bearsville and the few fleeting moments of Chicano Heaven with Cristina and Rubencito were well worth it, not getting paid as musical director and sound mixer wound up striking another blow to the marriage.

Performance Art

IN ORDER TO KEEP MY HEAD ABOVE WATER, I had to find creative ways to maintain my sanity, to not drown in a dark funk. Performance art had always seemed to me an exciting option. I felt the message of Chicano affirmation was important and needed to be heard, even if it didn't pay the rent. A series of performances kept me alive during this period. In 1989, I joined pioneer performance artist Tim Miller and *el mero mero performero* Guillermo Gómez-Peña, along with Emily Hicks, Elia Arce, and my *tocayo,* poet Rubén Martínez, for a performance event at the short-lived but significant Latino cultural space Macondo Espacio Cultural in the Westlake District. Our piece, *Arte Fronterizo Conceptual,* spoke of the absurd state of political affairs in Mexico and the United States. Then Gómez-Peña invited me to perform at Tijuana's hip artist colony El Nopal Centenario, along with Rubén Martínez and radical Tijuana performance artist Hugo Sánchez. The performance consisted of the four of us sitting in a semicircle, taking turns reading random sentences from our writings. We read round and round, faster and faster, reaching a screeching crescendo until we imploded. It was a trip: pure, visceral spontaneous combustion. The same year, Gómez-Peña and the Border Arts Workshop invited me to perform with them for the inauguration of Highways Performance Space in Santa Monica. I led a large group of performers down the middle of Olympic Boulevard through my old La Veinte barrio, reclaiming the land of the Tongva and the Casillas and Gutiérrez clans. We walked into restaurants and bars with me chanting the words *con safos* to the four directions while waving *copal* smoke in a sweet moment of reclamation. The Casillas market was still there. One of the restaurants was next to the alley where I had walked with my mother, holding her hand, on our way to my first *Jamaica,* her long black hair flowing, her red dress aflame.

Performance art had a redeeming way of mixing spiritual ceremony with personal and cultural history, allowing me to relive it and momentarily be back in it—precisely in the moment. It became my spiritual practice and medicine. There were moments when I felt my ancestors singing in my DNA, whispering through eternity and making me feel at peace, at one with everything. This is what some people call a liminal space, the space between the natural and the supernatural world. Which is groovy, but it was too bad it couldn't support my family. Still, I pursued it against all odds. ¡*Con safos, cabrones!*

To France with Aztlán, Babylon, Rhythm & Blues

I WAS ANTICIPATING THE UPCOMING Quincentennial 500-year celebration in '92 of Cristóbal Colón "discovering" the so-called "New" World. I
thought it was time to create another experimental theater piece to challenge
this claim. I'd never followed through with restaging a theatrical production
of *Who Are The People?* and that remained a thorn in my side, though I had
tried to a degree with Ruben And The Jets. This would be the follow-up. I had
read about the burning of the Aztec and Mayan libraries and other atrocities
during the invasion of Mexico back in my Chicano Studies days. That violent
history inspired the title and subject of the new piece, *La Quemada:* The
Burning—an unconscious metaphor for my life. To my surprise, I later found
out that I have Tecuexe[1] ancestral roots in the small community of La
Quemada, Jalisco, through my maternal grandmother's Casillas lineage. The
original settlement burned down, and was subsequently named La Ciudad
Quemada (The Burnt City). It has been associated with Chicomoztoc, the
Chichimeca mythical place called "The Seven Caves" where the Aztek/
Mexika remained for nine years during their migration to Anáhuac.

I formed the performance art group Modern Mesoamerican Ensemble
and recruited Luis Pérez Ixonestli, a pre-Columbian wind and percussion
virtuoso; poet Alma Cervantez; and two Mexika/Azteca dancers, Lazaro
Arvizu and Olga Pérez. I also commissioned a set design by Chicano artist

---

1. The Tecuexe tribe belong to the Chichimeca people, who were known to be expert
artisans, carpenters, and musicians. They participated in the Mixtón Rebellion of 1540–42
against the Spanish invaders.

Clavo, by John Valadez. Program for traveling Chicano art show *Le Démon des Anges*, Espace d'Art Contemporain, Lyon, France, 1990. Courtesy of the Funkahuatl family archive.

Arturo Urista (cousin of the poet Alurista). The piece debuted at the Southern California Library for Social Studies in '88. We restaged it in '89 at Highways, with a set by Magu and Arturo and two aerosol spray paintings by Leo Limón, and again in '90 at UCLA's Schoenberg Auditorium as part of the landmark Chicano art show *CARA: Chicano Art—Resistance & Affirmation, 1965–1985*. For the UCLA performance, I invited poets Max Benevídez and Salomé Esparza, procured the talents of Magu and Arturo once again for the psychedelic set, and featured Luis Pérez and his brother Javier Arellano, who mixed ancient Mexika dance ritual with modern movement. Patssi Valdez was in charge of makeup and costumes, and the awesome lighting was by José López. It was a killer show. Everything worked—the text, the message, the music, the choreography, the costumes and makeup, and the lighting. It was a triumphant *rasquache* piece of work.

The ball kept rolling in the winter of 1990 when Leo Limón, bless his heart, later suggested to French curator Pascal Letellier that I be included in the closing of the landmark Chicano art show touring Europe, *Le Démon des Anges* (The Demon of the Angels). The show included many of the main Chicano painters of the day, who previously had little or no European recognition. This was the first tour of Chicano art ever to reach Europe, and man,

I was so proud to be a part of it and of its evolving worldwide fame. *Órale,* Chicano art power! Check me out! I was on my way to Europe with my wife and son, with all expenses paid! Performance art was taking on a more serious tone, and it was finally getting some respect from Cristina.

After a sleepless all-night flight, we arrived seriously jet-lagged but in good spirits. Here we were in Paris, the city of love and lights! I hoped the visit would fire up our marriage. Our hotel was in the Latin Quarter and looked like something out of *Les Misérables,* with its eighteenth-century architecture and antique furniture. It was like a movie set, with us as the stars: a Chicano family living a fantastical dream come true. We were up all night taking turns reading to Rubencito, whose sleep schedule had been turned upside down. He especially loved the alphabet books, pointing to the letters and pronouncing them after us. We loved it too.

On our first full day, we went to Meudon to visit the studio of Rodin, the French father of modern sculpture. His studio was nothing fancy, but you could feel his immense talent by looking at his drawings. There was a sketchbook with his famous *Thinker,* and a *Voltaire* encased in glass, which fascinated Rubencito. (We'd encouraged his interest in art and books from the start: they were his favorite toys.) The mockup of Rodin's famous piece *Gates of Hell* in the courtyard was mind bending. The figures seemed to move. Although strictly speaking they were still, his genius pushed them onto a different, animated plane. Again, Rubencito was mesmerized.

The following day I went for a walk through the fabled Latin Quarter looking for coffee while Cristina and Rubencito took a nap. I was curious why they called it "Latin." It turns out it got its name from the Latin language, which was once commonly spoken in the area, going back to the Middle Ages. It was now called the Algerian Quarter, after the many immigrants who had settled there after Algeria won its independence from France in 1962. It hit me that their struggle to make it in France echoed that of Mexicans coming to the United States after the Mexican Revolution. In a way, they are France's Mexican Americans.

As I walked along the River Seine wondering how many lovers had strolled along the same path, I came upon the cathedral of cathedrals, Notre-Dame. Its towering immensity stopped me in my tracks. The only other cathedral I had seen that came close to its majesty was the one in the Zócalo in Mexico City, Catedral Metropolitana de la Asunción de María. As I drew near, I remembered the film *The Hunchback of Notre Dame.* I looked up at the massive doors and beyond, at the precisely carved stone ornamentation, then up toward the top of the cathedral, where I saw small statues of people that looked like they were in motion, like in Rodin's *Gates of Hell,* like in a flip-book. Then I saw the steeple where Quasimodo brought the beautiful Esmeralda and rang those giant church bells as if imitating his beating heart in her honor. Thinking of the story made me wonder what kind of a life I would have had if my face hadn't recovered from the sulphuric acid burn back in '64. I guess that's why the movie moved me so much, along with the sheer genius of Charles Laughton's acting. He portrayed the hideous Quasimodo with a heart and rendered him human and vulnerable. What a lesson.

Remembering Quasimodo ringing the bells reminded me of a story my dad once told me. When he was a kid in Compostela, Mexico, he used to sneak up to the church tower and ring the bells at odd hours so no one would know exactly what time it was. He was severely punished by the priests, but he did it repeatedly and was never caught. That pretty much sums up my dad: always getting away with being mischievous.

Walking back to my hotel, I passed by the bookstore Shakespeare and Company. A poster was taped to the front door announcing a reading by East L.A. homeboy Luis Rodríguez, and it was going on right then. What a crazy surprise! I went inside and heard him read. He was great. It was inspiring to hear poems about East Los Angeles so far away from home. It occurred to me that we were on a similar mission of spreading the word on *chicanismo.*

I first met Luis through the great Chicano poet Manazar Gamboa. Gamboa was the director of Beyond Baroque, a literary space in Venice and an early incubator of L.A. poets. He'd also formed the Latino Writers Workshop with Luis. When Luis, Manazar, and I met in 1980, they were in the middle of planning a fundraiser for the workshop, and they asked me if Con Safos could play. I gladly agreed. The event took place at Self Help Graphics & Art in East L.A., my first introduction to the important art center. But damn, what a far-fetched far-out run-in this was! Two Chicano artists from East L.A. in Paris doing their thing! What were the odds of that happening?

I invited Luis and his wife, Trini, to a reception later that night at the home of Pascal Letellier, curator of *Le Démon des Anges.* We, together with Cristina and Rubencito and painters Magu, Eloy Torrez, Margaret Guzmán, and Yolanda Gonzalez, partied all night long—East Los style.

With the release of his award-winning memoir *Always Running* a couple of years later, Luis went on to become an internationally recognized poet and writer. I've never met a more committed Chicano. In my view, he and his generous, giving, and committed wife, Trini, embody the full manifestation of *chicanismo*.

My traveling Chicano *familia* were having a ball, and so was I. Paris was all it was made out to be, a romantic city living and breathing its art and culture (in spite of its abuse of the Algerians). The following day we were off to Lyon for the opening there of *Le Démon des Anges*, the last stop on its European tour. We were excited, and I was ready to rock.

I'd created a solo piece, *Aztlán, Babylon, Rhythm & Blues*, for the performance, an edited solo version of *La Quemada*. The plan was to make a statement about the invasion of Mexico by Spain and its repercussions as succinctly as possible—to create a mysterious trancelike environment, to mesmerize with ceremonial ritual, to communicate with the bare minimum of text. My homeboy Magu was part of the *Démon* exhibition and was in Lyon for the opening, so I asked him to join me in the performance. We met in the lobby of our hotel, an ancient refurbished convent with stone walls several feet thick. Voices and laughter made a strange cool echo in the halls, and I wondered what it must have sounded like when the nuns sang Gregorian chants. We carefully went over the piece, making sure he knew his cues, and after a couple of trial runs I felt we were ready to kick some serious butt.

I was dressed as one of the immigrant orange vendors seen on many L.A. freeway ramps in the '80s, wearing exaggerated tattered work clothes, my face painted with indigenous streaks of color, carrying a bag of oranges, and with a travel bag slung over my shoulder. I entered from the back of the room shouting, "*¡Naranjas, naranjas fresquecitas!* Oranges, oranges very fresh!" and made my way past the audience to the front of the room. I stayed focused. I had to deliver, not only for my *raza* but for my marriage.

I launched into "El Indocumentado," a poem about the ironies of Columbus's arrival and its consequences. First, Columbus mistakenly thought he was near India, consequently naming the indigenous people Indians. Then came the arrival of conquistador Hernán Cortés and his customary greeting by the Aztec emperor, Moctezuma, who some say believed the invader was the returning Toltec God-King Quetzalcoatl, as had been prophesied. Then, the forceful subjugation by the "holy men," the Catholic priests, or, in the present day along the U.S. border, the Immigration and Naturalization Service. I lit my *copal tlapopochhuiloni* (incense burner), blessed the room and the four directions, and began building an altar with objects I pulled out of my bag: the Chicano rock compilation album *Los*

Angelinos; a flyer for a Carlos Almaraz art exhibition; a handful of Día de los Muertos sugar skulls; several oranges; and some candles that I lit later.

Then I went and stood in front of a seven-by-seven-foot piece of butcher paper that would be turned into a mural by Magu while I recited my poem "Beasts of Burden." He began by putting a red FSLN (Frente Sandinista de Liberación Nacional) bandana over my face. Then, with my legs spread and my arms outstretched against the paper, he spray-painted an outline of my body to symbolize an executed Sandinista. He pulled the paper from the wall and rolled me up in it, and ceremoniously carried the "dead body" into the dark room, where he laid me down in the middle of the aisle. Lighting some sage, he performed a stylized Native American burial ceremony—Chicano-style— offering the smoking sage to the four cardinal points over my cocoon tomb. He then spray-painted indigenous symbols and C/S on the rolled mural.

Unfortunately, the chemicals in the spray paint got me loaded just like back in '80 at the Whisky—something I didn't foresee happening. There was no way I could tell him to stop, and I freaked out for a minute thinking, *What if I faint?* I just held my breath and waited. Soon, Chicana artists Margaret Guzmán and Yolanda Gonzalez assisted as midwives as I slithered out of my cocoon tomb, high as a kite, as Funkahuatl, the Aztec God of Funk. In funky ritualistic movement, I relit the *copal,* then faced the audience in silence for a few minutes. I needed a little time to regain my consciousness. The silence was staggering. I slowly rose and led the audience into the exhibition gallery, waving my lit *copal* burner while reciting sections of "C/S." It was a glorious entrance. I felt like an angel on a mission from Chicano Heaven.

First I stopped in front of the East Los Streetscapers' monumental (15' × 16') mural *L.A. Bicentennial Blues,* the same one we hung as a backdrop for *Lil' Ruben G. & Thee Latin Soul Revue II* back in '85 at UCLA. It depicted an exhausted East L.A. boxer sitting on his stool waiting to answer the bell for round/year 200, still fighting to get a piece of the American Dream, with the crowd screaming for blood in the background. That struggle continues. I waved my burning *copal* with tears flowing and shouted, *"Con safos,"* instructing the audience to repeat it after me. My voice cracked with emotion.

The East Los Streetscapers was a pioneer East L.A. mural collective, and its founders, the painters Wayne Alaniz Healy and David Botello, had become two of my closest friends. To offer this blessing in their—and Chicano art's—honor in a land so far from home, on a continent whose people had invaded our ancestors' home, was a powerful *reconquista* payback moment. Too bad the performance wasn't in Spain.

An important aspect of my work is collaborating. *Top:* Here I am in collaboration with Gilbert "Magu" Luján, *Aztlán, Babylon, Rhythm & Blues,* for the closing of the traveling Chicano art show *Le Démon des Anges,* Espace d'Art Contemporaine, Lyon, France, 1990. *Bottom:* Later on that tour we undertook a group collaboration for *Rencontre de l'art Chicano et de l'art Zydeco*/Encounter between Chicano and Zydeco Art, in conjunction with *Transmusicales Festival,* FNAC, Rennes, France. *Left to right:* Yolanda Gonzalez, RFG, Eloy Torrez, Margaret Guzman, Patssi Valdez, and Francis X. Pavy. Both photos by Cristina Shallcross; courtesy of the Funkahuatl family archive.

From there I led the audience through the gallery, stopping in front of each painting or sculpture and repeating the ritual of waving the smoking *copal* and chanting "*Con safos*" together. At the end of the performance/tour, I placed the smoking ceramic burner on the floor, knelt, and thanked the audience for their respectful attention. I blessed them with a final wave of *copal* and closed by declaring "*¡Que viva Aztlán!,*" with the audience repeating after me, and added one last "*Con safos*" to seal the sweet moment. I knew I'd go to Chicano Heaven now. But more important, I hoped Cristina was moved.

The reception was held at Le Petit Bistro, one of Lyon's finest *bouchons* (a traditional Lyonnais restaurant specializing in meats). The French are known for making food into an art form. Man, lemme tell ya, they don't mess around. Cristina, Rubencito, and I joined some of the exhibiting artists, curator Pascal Letellier, the gallery staff, and a TV crew. Before the culinary parade and the ritual of eating art began, Magu and I slipped outside to fire up our taste buds with a little marijuana. The ancient cobbled street was narrow, lined with buildings that were hundreds of years old, featuring wrought-iron balconies and tall carved wood and iron doors. Again, the movie camera in my head was rolling. "Hey Magu, can you believe it? Two Chicanos about to be seriously wined and dined in France, and all because of our art." Magu smiled, took a long hit, passed me the joint, and said, "Yeah, bro', how sweet it is. We're being treated with respect, Chicano royalty. Too bad it's not like this in the U.S." As I handed him the joint I replied, "Yeah, but we're getting it started, holmes."

First they served wine, grapes, and trays of every kind of cheese possible. This part lasted around two hours. The idea is to have a conversation—an engaged, relaxed conversation—while eating. The food merely serves to enhance the dialogue. The bottles of wine kept coming, and we kept drinking, talking, and laughing. Then the appetizers appeared: *escargots* looking like they were meant for a king; duck *paté;* sausages; tripe soup (it didn't taste like *menudo!*); chicken liver salads; stingray fish; vegetables in a bone marrow sauce—and all this before the main course! Eventually the succulent pot roast arrived along with casseroles of offal (animal organs), and finally dessert: lemon meringue pie and caramelized apples. Everything was presented exquisitely, intricately molded, carved, and curled like nothing I'd ever seen before. It was sculpture; it felt like a shame to eat it. Another hour or so passed, with more drinking, talking, laughing, and eating. Funny, you'd think that after drinking so much wine you'd get drunk as a skunk and pass out. But it didn't happen. Instead, you eat slow, savoring the food like when you're making good love. Gotta give it up to the French, they know how to get down and turn a meal into an orgiastic feast for the eyes, tongue, and soul. But man, I sure could've used some good ol' homemade Mexican salsa.

As we were leaving the restaurant I was introduced to one of the dinner guests, a professor from the Sorbonne who taught a class on Chicano murals. That totally floored me. She congratulated me on the performance, then she blew my mind even more by inviting me to the Centre Aztlán in Paris, which she'd founded. Unfortunately, I never made it. But dang! Can you believe it? *Chicanismo* was sure getting around.

To my surprise, I got a call from a local TV station in Lyon to take part in an interview with an underground Algerian youth Graff crew. There had been several clashes between them and the police over tagging in the previous weeks. It reminded me of similar struggles with East L.A. youth at home. The station sent an attractive woman reporter (I love how the French kiss you on both cheeks when they greet you) and a cameraman to film the interview. We arrived at a burned-out building covered with very interesting, original Graff and were met by members of the crew. They led us to their encampment in the basement. I was struck by how much they looked like Mexican American kids. They could've gone unnoticed in any East L.A. neighborhood. But then I remembered: many Mexicans have Arab blood—*la raza cósmica.*

They graciously received me as a brother. We discussed their struggle, then I asked for a can of paint and sprayed a *pachuko* cross—a Christian cross with three rays shooting out from the center—on the wall behind me. I explained that hard-core Mexican American *pachukos* of the '30s, and later the *cholos* or gangsters of the '50s, wore the cross as a mark of distinction and honor, in the form of a tattoo on the left hand, in the webbing between the thumb and index finger. I also explained the *pachuko* credo to them as I'd learned it from Chicano poet Alurista: "The *pachuka* and *pachuko* don't care to make something beautiful in their lives, but rather to make *of* their lives a work of art." I sprayed *C/S* beneath the cross, giving its meaning: "If anybody writes anything against my *placa*/tag, it goes back on them tenfold. This protects the writer like a talisman while saying, 'Fuck you if you don't like it.'" It was, I said, a symbol of self-affirmation and determination. When I finished, there was silence. Then one of the boys walked up to the wall and sprayed the Muslim crescent moon next to the *pachuko* cross. Everyone cheered. Finally, I showed them how to give the Chicano hand shake and said goodbye. They were beautiful kids and it was a beautiful moment.

My dear friend Gilbert "Magu Courtesy of Guevara Family Archive." Luján and me at my sixty-sixth birthday concert, Eastside Luv, Boyle Heights, California, 2008. Photo by, and courtesy of, George Rodriguez.

On the way back to the car, the reporter complimented me on how well I'd communicated with the Graff crew. They had been trying to set up a meeting for weeks, she said, but without success. It took the *Démon des Anges* show to get their permission, since they were fans of Chicanos and *cholo* graffiti. One never knows where or when you will be appreciated.

After Lyon, we decided to go to Arles to pay homage to Vincent Van Gogh at his museum there, with Magu joining us. Again, more narrow cobbled streets and beautiful old buildings. There was a very peaceful vibe as Magu and I strolled through town sharing a joint the first night. No wonder Vincent dug it there. You could hear and feel inspiration in the air, a kind of soft whispering from the muses. I was seized with a strong, inspiring recommitment to my work. Recalling Vincent's suffering, I realized that mine was pale in comparison. "Hey Magu, do you think you have to be a little crazy to be an artist?" I asked. "I don't know, man. But trying to make a living by making art can sure *drive* you crazy." We both laughed. But still, the question haunted me.

Later that night when I returned to our hotel, the roof caved in. I discovered to my horror that we were almost out of money, and Cristina totally lost it. I'd never seen her that furious before. It shocked me. She screamed at me for being a fuckup and putting her and our son in jeopardy, with no money for food or a place to stay. Looking back, I can't blame her. That night I started coming down with the flu, probably from all the money stress. Plus, I was supposed to perform a couple of days later, in Rennes. It was a living nightmare, mind-bending awful, and I fell into a deep, painful panic. The following day, I had to get away from it all, so I met up with Magu again and we walked down to the Roman ruins to smoke a joint. "Hey Magu, do you think the Romans threw Christians to the lions down there?" "Aww man, don't talk that kinda shit! Let's talk about Van Gogh," he said as he passed me the joint. "Okay," I said; "I wonder if he sat and smoked weed on these ruins and painted those fields across the way, all blazing in the sunlight like wildflowers on fire." "Hell yeah, weed and wine, the perfect combo," he said. "Hey man, do you think he really cut off his ear over some chick?" I asked. "I don't know. But if he did," he replied, "I sure hope he was high when he did it. You know, to kill the pain with some laughter. Hey man, don't bogart that joint, awright?" It was fun hangin' with crazy Magu. He could be hard-headed, but if you got him high enough he loosened up. And he sure could philosophize your head off. I loved that crazy *vato*. May he rest in Chicano Heaven as high as a satellite.

Some Haiku for Magu

Hey Magu what's new?
Are you dancing with angels?
Real tight and real slow?

Playing some James Brown?
Please, Please, Please, In a Cold Sweat?
Try Me, Out of Sight?

We met at LACMA
Los 4 in Seventy Four
Chevy hood looked good

Perritos and cars
Cruising became an art form
Aztlán your palette

Your humor was art
Glowing, radiating love
Whimsy, light, passion

The spirit of art
A mystical mystery
Penetrating hearts

Magulandia
A place of visions and dreams
Cosmic *locura*

An artist shaman
Conjuring liminal grace
Magu *por vida*

"Le Démon des Anges"
Chicano art hits Europe
We partied till dawn

Dinner in Lyon
We smoked and drank to the gods
Ate like emperors

Collaboration
You wrapped me in a mural
I rolled out a god

Funkahuatl sang
Leading the crowd to Aztlán
Dancing with tears, joy

So, what's new Magu?
Getting ready to join you
Just a few more years

Gotta live real, real
Live life as a work of art
Breathe the art of life

Your art is spirit
Chicano Buddhist brother
Thank you for painting

Thank you for living
Thank you for being Magu
Now, get to work Holmes

c/s

We left Arles early in the morning and arrived in Paris early that after-noon, tired and silent. I was still fighting the flu and in a daze over my mar-riage falling apart as we continued together on the trip. It was tough carrying Chicano and Mexican history and culture on my back while trying to save my family. My plate was full, and it was heavy. Magu had continued on to Barcelona from Arles, so there was no more laughter, no more trippin', no more fun. Rubencito became my only source of joy.

We didn't linger in Paris, but soon left for Rennes on a bus loaded with performers for the upcoming international Trans Musicales music festival. I was booked to perform the following day at FNAC, a book-and-record store, in conjunction with the festival and another art exhibition Pascal had curated, *Rencontre de l'Art Chicano et de l'Art Zydeco* (Encounter of Chicano Art and Zydeco Art). That show featured Patssi Valdez and Eloy Torrez (*Le Démon des Anges*), as well as Francis X. Pavy from New Orleans. Pascal had a keen eye for finding great unrecognized art, and this show was no exception.

The festival producers had asked me to help them book Esteban Jordan. They had a Latino component to the show that included pioneer Chicano hip-hop artist Kid Frost and the Mexican American Elvis (El Vez), and they wanted Steve to round out the bill. I reluctantly called him and asked if he was inter-ested—and if he was, I told him he had to promise to stay sober. He agreed.

I thought I'd extend an olive branch to Cristina, who had cooled down on the long bus ride, and asked if she wanted to go to the concert that evening. Her sister Blanca was with us and could take care of Rubencito. She agreed. Man, it was a blast of fresh air, hanging out with her after the bitter argument in Arles. It definitely stoked the love flames. We danced like kids to Mr. Jordan—who thoroughly redeemed himself—and to the music of the Wild Tchoupitoulas and the Preservation Hall Brass Band. It felt like the night back at the Café Cultural in Boyle Heights, the night we fell in love. We were look-ing good too, like rock stars, in our black leather jackets and scarves. We laughed, danced, flirted, and fell in love again. Life couldn't have been better.

The next day it was time once again for *Aztlán, Babylon, Rhythm & Blues*. My spirits were up, and I was ready to roll. Since Magu wasn't around, I asked Patssi and Eloy, who were there for the Chicano/Zydeco show, to collaborate on the adapted piece with me. The space was packed, and I was nervous; it wasn't an art audience like at the gallery in Lyon.

I began the piece the same way, entering from the back carrying my bag of oranges and shouting "Fresh oranges for sale" in Spanish. When I reached the stage, I lit my *copal* burner, pulled the sacred objects out of my travel bag to build the altar, and blessed the room and the four directions. I slowly removed my shirt standing in front of a large piece of muslin, with Patssi joining and painting abstract imagery on my chest while I recited excerpts from "El Indocumentado." Eloy and Francis then started painting a mural next to us, with Margaret Guzmán and Yolanda Gonzalez assisting. Another short poem, "Beasts of Burden," followed, and I closed again by reciting the poem "C/S" while relighting the *copal* and blessing the room, repeating "*Con safos*" to the four cardinal points. After a long silence with me simply staring at the audience, I stepped away. The room exploded in applause. The performance felt fluid, magical, and powerfully beautiful.

Later, at a small reception in my dressing room, I noticed a strange-looking man with round wire-rimmed glasses. He reminded me of a German SS officer. He was talking with Pascal very intently while staring at me. It felt weird. Was I about to get arrested? Then they both came over and Pascal introduced him: it turned out he was the director of the Centre Pompidou in Paris. He said he was impressed with the piece, shook my hand, and clinked my glass of wine with his. Oddly, he never smiled, just stared.

Meanwhile, back on the home front, our financial status was becoming an issue again. So I frantically asked the promoters of the festival to lend me enough money to cover the costs of the hotel and some food. They responded very generously. Regrettably, I wasn't able to pay them back in full—yet another strike against my integrity.

Cristina, Rubencito, and I took the train to Paris, had one last silent modest dinner, sadly said goodbye to the city of love, and flew home. It was a very long flight. We returned home with our marriage smoldering, barely alive. It was right before Christmas and I didn't have a dime. I hit a low that was lower than I had ever hit before, a deeper, dark funk. What a contrast between being considered a cultural hero in France, while at home I was nothing but a failed husband and father and not worth a shit. So it was back to solitary confinement while I looked for a job.

The following year, 1991, Marietta Bernstorff from SPARC (Social and Public Art Resource Center) in Venice, California, invited me to perform the original full version of *Aztlán, Babylon, Rhythm & Blues* for SPARC's anti-Quincentennial show *Encuentro: Invasion of the Americas and the Making of the Mestizo*. The performance received a favorable review in the L.A. Spanish-language newspaper *La Opinión*. But it wasn't enough. I had to come up with a new plan if I was going to save my marriage, and I had to do it fast. What I came up with was to go back to L.A. City College, earn enough credits to

Funkahuatl in solo work, *Aztlán, Babylon, Rhythm & Blues*
for *Encuentro: Invasion of the Americas and the Making of the
Mestizo,* regalia designed and created by Patssi Valdez, Social
and Public Art Resource Center (SPARC), Venice, California,
1991. Photo by, and courtesy of, Aurelio José Barrera.

transfer to UCLA, get a bachelor's degree, then take CBEST (the California
Basic Educational Skills Test) and become a K–12 substitute teacher.

I continued with my solo work to considerable acclaim, as well as hosting
a radio show on KPFK called *Artes en Los Ángeles* that focused on the
Chicano art scene in L.A., but it still didn't pay the rent. Even so, I couldn't
understand why Cristina didn't see the value in what I was doing—spreading
Chicano history and culture, enriching it. After all, she was a hard-core
Chicana activist; her university mentor and Rubencito's *padrino* (godfather)

was "father" of Chicano Studies and *Occupied America* author Rodolfo Acuña. I thought she would appreciate and value my work. But what I couldn't see was that she was reacting as any mother would: she was looking out for our son, and I wasn't doing my part. The painful struggle and our constant quarreling finally took its toll, and we decided to separate.

I left with great sadness in my heart just two weeks before the 1992 L.A. riots. I rented a room at the East Los Streetscapers' downtown studio. My intention was for us to part for a while, cool down, and take a hard look at our marriage. After several attempts to patch things up, to no avail, I felt that it was hopeless. Chicano Heaven was closing its gates, and the angels were crying and singing the blues.

Validation Crisis

I WAS INVITED TO A PARTY at film producer Nancy de Los Santos's home in Echo Park that summer of '92. In the kitchen, I noticed a woman who looked like a rock 'n' roll rebel. She came over and clicked her can of beer to my glass of wine. "I like your work," she said. "I saw a video of your *Aztlán, Babylon, Rhythm & Blues* at UCLA." We chatted for a moment—she said she was an artist—then she wandered off. Yes, she looked very young, but she liked my work, and I needed to hear that.

There was a hip place in Little Tokyo, the Troy Café, a hub for the downtown and East L.A. art and music community. It was run by sometime Asco collaborator Sean Carrillo and his wife, Bibi, daughter of Fluxus pioneer Al Hansen. Their son, Beck, worked there occasionally, helping set up bands and working their sound system, before becoming a rock star. I walked in one night and there she was, sitting at a table with some friends. They invited me to join them. We talked about Chicano art and history and the progress we were making. She struck me as a committed avant-garde artist-activist, and I wanted to help. She invited me to the opening of her upcoming exhibit at the Social and Public Art Resource Center (SPARC).

SPARC occupied the space that once was the Venice jail, and the installation used a jail cell as its canvas, with volatile writings against the US government pasted on the walls. It was a strong political statement. I was impressed.

Yeah, you could say there was also some midlife-crisis bullshit going on. But here was a new generation being influenced by my work, and, weak fool that I was, I found that moving. The fact that young Chicana artists were still mining *chicanismo* was inspiring. Isn't that what it should be about—to pass the *pinche* torch?

Eventually Cristina got wind of the fact that I was seeing the artist and blew her top. It was volcanic and ugly. Hell knows no wrath like an angry betrayed Chicana. The fact that we both had hot tempers didn't help. There was no communication. No negotiation. The fighting escalated, causing excruciating pain and suffering for everyone involved, an ongoing monstrous living nightmare. Although it had been clear to me that it was over, I couldn't see that it wasn't over for her.

Looking back, I realize that I wanted validation as an artist and as a man. But real men and artists don't need validation. What a pathetic, twisted, weak, egocentric fool I was. For that, the dog was severely punished.

That Christmas Eve, I went to Suehiro's, a Japanese restaurant in Little Tokyo that Cristina, Rubencito, and I used to frequent. The two sisters who owned the place, Junko and Yuriko, would buy Rubencito art supplies for Christmas every year, so we felt a friendly family bond. His drawings on napkins were taped to the walls and had started a trend, with customers doing the same until all the walls were covered with napkin drawings. On this night, I sat at the counter and ordered a bowl of rice and miso soup. That's all I could afford. Then Junko handed me a bulky napkin with my name written on it. "For you," she said. "You forgot last time." I opened the napkin, and there was change that I'd neglected to take when the three of us had eaten there last, before the separation. I ordered a full dinner . . . and broke down. It was our first Christmas apart from each other. It was a very sad, long night, the longest of my life.

During the separation, Cristina continued to realize her dream of becoming a singer. She became known as Machaka Khan, in Alice Bag's quirky performance art group Cholita, which included cross-dressing lead singer Vaginal Cream Davis. I was very happy for Cristina and hoped that performing would help her get through the breakup. I caught them at Club Lingerie one night, and she was great.

It reminded me of when we were still together and I wanted to support her ambition of becoming a singer by inviting her to perform with me on a few occasions. Back in the summer of 1990, she sang with me and Irma Rangel at the last concert of Con Safos at the California Plaza's small amphitheater, with a set designed by Magu. In late 1993, she danced during a spoken word performance of mine to a track by Fela Kuti at the Women's Building in an event curated by Coco Fusco. Apparently, it was a thorn in her side that I didn't validate her enough as an artist. That hurt both her and the marriage.

I wrote this piece searching for solace, reflecting on the legacy of my neighborhood—the love that comforted and nourished me, and the undying inspiration that motivated me to focus on my promise that I made in Palenque.

From the Heart of América: The Corner of Brooklyn & Soto

Heading east on Sixth Street, from downtown L.A. you eventually come to the Sixth Street Bridge, a bridge of destiny.

Crossing the bridge—where east meets west—I look down and see the L.A. River smiling up at me, yet with a tear in her eye . . . reflecting the joy and sadness of a long and sometimes painful history of our beloved, unpredictable city of multihued angels. Alongside the river I notice the tracks of the Southern Pacific railroad, tracks that were laid over trails that once belonged to the indigenous Tongva/Gabrielino, then Mexico, tracks that brought our *familias* here. Tracks of the American Dream laid on the backs of ethnic American history.

The Sixth Street Bridge of Destiny leads you out onto the legendary Whittier Boulevard. At Whittier & Soto, if you make a left and go north about a mile, you'll arrive at the heart of the universe, the *corazón* of Boyle Heights: the intersection of Soto & Brooklyn.

Brooklyn Avenue, now Avenida César Chávez, is the grand promenade of Boyle Heights. Where you stroll your *ruca* (lady) or your *abuelita* (grandmother) or cruise your *ranfla* (chariot), to impress and express your love, pride, and joy.

The soul of Boyle Heights is reflected in its music, in the murals, in the food, in the faces of the children and los *viejitos,* the elders—and in its history.

Welcome to Boyle Heights: Los Angeles's original polycultural community. Imagine eating a giant kosher teriyaki burrito filled with guacamole, lox and sour cream, rice and beans, from Manuel's El Tepeyac, Canter's deli, and Otomisan Japanese restaurant on First, while dancing to a Jewish klezmer–*corrido*–boogie-woogie–doo-wop–hip-hop–shuffle with taiko drums keeping the beat. Can you hear it? Can you taste it? Can you dig it? Can you take it? Good. Welcome to Boyle Heights.

Welcome to the mural capital of the world, Soto & Brooklyn/César Chávez, where three murals heroically stand as sentinels of Chicano art and identity: *El Corrido de Boyle Heights,* a wild and passionate rendering of a wedding and reception by mural pioneers and masters East Los Streetscapers; Paul Botello's passionate homage to Picasso across the street; and across the street from that, *Boycott Grapes,* Willie Herrón III's defiant tribute to the United Farm Workers and their ongoing struggle.

If you look and listen closely, you can hear a certain unique kind of music sweetly oozing and singing from the walls through the murals. A certain kind of eternal *angelino* music, harmonizing with life and death, joy and sorrow, gently floating down through the streets, through the cafes, bars, restaurants, and department stores. From barrio blasters and car radios, a uniquely American cultural phenomenon is being tattooed onto the thick, exotic air.

The rich and glorious history of Boyle Heights is a metaphor and a microcosm of the elusive American dream for an autonomous and harmonious multicultural society. Russian, Jewish, Italian, African, Japanese, Chinese, and Mexican American cultures organically took root and meshed in this fertile, multiethnic community, creating a rich human and cultural legacy that continues to flourish and inspire.

While Boyle Heights is held in place by very real physical, economic, and social borders, there are no human borders. In one form or another, the soul of Boyle Heights will find you, lift you, and take you away. Away from a broken heart, a broken home, a broken dream. The music of the legacy hears you. It touches. It heals.

I continued doing my thing, collaborating with homeboys John Valadez and Harry Gamboa Jr. In some twisted way, performance art had a redeeming value: it temporarily made me feel like a god, even though I was a dog.

Jammin' with John Valadez

BACK IN '83 WHEN I was getting ready to release *Los Angelinos: The Eastside Renaissance,* I went searching for an artist to design the cover. The *L.A. Times* had just run the Pulitzer Prize–winning series "Emerging Chicano Artists," and one installment featured a photo of John Valadez on a fire escape at the Victor Building downtown. I decided to see if he might be interested. The first time I saw his work was when he was sharing a studio with Carlos Almaraz on Spring Street, downtown, a few years earlier. John was not there when I arrived, but a large 6′ × 4′ graphite-on-paper drawing roared across the studio like an epic Chicano movie that transformed an ordinary-looking barrio kid into a bigger-than-life cultural hero. The life-size portrait was infused with a kind of hyper-real humanity; it was a loving testament to *chicanismo,* enriching and ennobling Mexican American culture with every perfect stroke. I saw an immense talent at work—a genius.

When I tracked him down about the album cover, we discussed some possibilities but couldn't decide on an image. I eventually wound up using a photo of a Los Tres Grandes–inspired[1] mural at City Terrace Park by Gronk and Willie Herrón III.

John and I stayed friends over the years, and in '94 I rented office space while running Arts 4 City Youth, a free arts program that I founded the year before, out of his studio at the Victor Building. While there, I witnessed the painting

---

1. Los Tres Grandes refers to the three major figures of the Mexican muralist movement, Diego Rivera (1886–1957), David Alfaro Siqueiros (1896–1974), and José Clemente Orozco (1883–1949).

of his monumental—pushing contemporary art's envelope to the max—masterpiece, *Pocho Crudo,* a chilling portrait of the charred face of an infant wearing a Native Mexican headdress on its head. This searing commentary on genocide struck a deep chord in me, evoking the memory of my own face burning as an infant. This cat could blow as good as any painter I knew, as fierce and fearless as James Brown could sing. He became a hero of mine.

In 1992, we got a chance to jam together—Chicano rock meets Chicano art—in a fashion art show curated by Gloria Westcott at the Park Plaza Hotel, a reemerging classic 1920s Art Deco building in the Westlake District. John cut up various *piñatas,* stitched them back together, and turned them into an explosive psychedelic mix of bulls, celestial beings, and various comic book characters that morphed into a dreamy freaky Frankenstein *piñata* suit. But it was more than that. The suit symbolized (as I saw it) a fractured culture trying to piece a new one together: a Chicano-Angelino culture. The dressing room was in the basement of the hotel and was buzzing in a flurry of flesh and fashion. My head spun in disbelief as I watched some of the men turn into beautiful women. A few were even flat-out fine, drop-dead gorgeous. As they slithered into their tight, glamorous high-fashion gowns embellished with outrageous designs, I felt disoriented. What the fuck was I doing here?! It looked more like a drag queen event. As I was getting into my suit, one of the beauties next to me said, "Oh, I get it, you're *La Reina de la Piñata,* the Piñata Queen. That is so fabulous!" "Thanks, very kind of you." What else could I say? I painted my face, hands, arms, and feet in indigenous streaks, tightened up my suit, and now Funkahuatl, the Unknown Aztec God of Funk, was back ready to rock and shock.

I walked out into the packed house shaking my maracas and chanting *"Yaaang-na!... Yaaang-na!"* which flowed into *"Naaa, na na na naaa, na na na, na na na, na na naaa,"* the opening chant from "Land of a 1000 Dances" by Cannibal and the Headhunters. That segued into a poem about the potential of L.A. becoming a feast of transcultural Angelino love. From the loud response I got, those in the house probably thought I was preaching trans-*sexual* love. I guess in a way I was.

I closed by dancing a ritualized two-step to the funky tribal Vodou groove at the end of Al Green's "Love and Happiness" as it soulfully oozed out of the huge house speakers. Stepping it up as a bolt of Reverend Green's electric soul shot through my body, I started boogalooing down the dragstrip-runway tossing handfuls of cellophane-wrapped candy into the loud crowd. This wasn't exactly a typical runway fashion art show moment, but it didn't seem to matter. The ultimate mind blower was when I looked up and saw the flying candy shooting sparks as pieces flew out in a huge arc over the audience and caught the shine of the spotlight drenching them in light. I went into a liminal-like space-soul-funk trance, watching myself as if suspended in space and time flying through a supernova meteor shower on acid while grooving to the Righteous Reverend Al Green swooning away. What can I say? Those are the moments one lives for: a brief instant of ecstasy in transcultural-sexual soul funk church. Can I get a witness?! Can I get an Angelino Amen?!

Yangna (From the Yangna Hotel)

Yaaaaaaaaaang-na! (shake maracas)
Yaaaaaaaaaaang-na! (shake maracas)
Yang Naaaa na na na naaa na na na naaa na na naaa na na naaa na
    na na naaaaaaaaa!
I am born of
Crushed bone, blood, mud, *mierda,* marijuana, Malinche,[2]
    machismo, a White and Brown Madonna,
Manifest Destiny, domestic violence, gangs, drug abuse, Chicana/
    Chicano and American Indian Studies,
media, madness, mushroooms, and muuuusic (shake maracas)
My name is Funkahuatl, the Unknown Aztec God of Funk.
I've come to re-funkify you, L.A., with some love, happiness,
    rhythm & blues
I've come to eat from your polyethnic banquet, my Queen of the
    Angels, *mi reina de los pinche ángeles*
Feed me your Thai-Mex chicharrones and your sweet potato pie *con
    un liquado de mango*
Stir-fry my heart, my brain, my soul, with your feast of infinite
    possibility

2. La Malinche (c. 1496/1501–c. 1529), also known as Malinalli, Malintzin, or Doña Marina, was a Nahua woman who acted as an interpreter and advisor for the Spanish conquistador, Hernán Cortés. She was one of twenty women given to the Spanish as slaves in 1519. She later became a mistress of Cortés and gave birth to his first son, Martín, who is considered one of the first Mestizos. Her reputation has changed and evolved over the years; she is seen alternatively as a traitor, as the quintessential victim, or as the symbolic mother of the Mexican people. The term *malinchista* sometimes refers to a disloyal compatriot.

Touch, taste, drink, eat, and saaaaavor your pregnant promise of
  transcultural love and happiness
Now, get down!
Let's get funky!
Let's eat, L.A.!

The Yangna Hotel, another modified anti-Quincentennial jam, followed at the Jansen-Pérez Gallery in the Wilshire District, my fiftieth birthday gift to myself. This time John created a makeshift cardboard box house like the homeless build on Skid Row sidewalks. Mexican tabloid magazines were scattered around it. Next to it, he placed a ceramic sculpture of a stereotypical sleeping Mexican under a sombrero commonly sold on the U.S./Mexico border. It was about a foot and a half tall. He created another psychedelic piñata full of candy, only this time I wore it on my head as a giant headdress over a football helmet, the intention being to break it open at the end and once again throw candy out into the audience.

I opened with the usual four-directions *copal* and *con safos* blessing. After I finished reciting "Yangna," with the Isley Brothers' "Fight the Power" blasting out of my boombox, I pulled out a small bat and started hitting myself over the head along with the beat, trying to bust the piñata open. In between hits, I took a moment to relight the *copal*—and wooosh! The headdress went up in flames! Once again, my desire to start a fire threatened to burn me up. With the headdress piñata blazing away and me dancing to the groove, I continued hitting it with the bat, trying to put out the flames and bust the candy loose at the same time. The candy finally started flying out of the piñata with every hit and landing on the floor, where the mostly white audience scrambled for it on their hands and knees like hungry children. Then, every time "fight it" was sung, I took a swing at the sleeping Mexican sculpture: "fight it"...*Bam!*..."fight it"... *Bam!* When it was finally smashed to bits, a bouquet of plastic roses popped up out of his sombrero, as if they were an incubating, unbreakable dream. The audience ate their candy, cheering the new accidental Fire God of Funk as I closed out with another four-directions blessing, firmly sealing the moment. Again, sometimes you just never know what will happen in a performance. That's the beauty of it. That's the only payback. It's always enough. It has to be.

Fast forward to 2009: I was visiting John at his Boyle Heights studio while he was working on *Muertadores IV* (Dance of the Dead), a surreal *Pietà*-style pastel painting of a dead matador on a cloud surrounded by a bevy of beautiful

Muertadores IV, pastel by John Valadez. I wrote a poem inspired by this painting as a collaboration for the art show *Intensidad,* Avenue 50 Studio/Gallery, Los Angeles, 2009. Courtesy of the artist.

women, above a cemetery in which three matadors stand in stylized poses.[3] He was going to show it at an upcoming group show, *Intensidad* (Intensity), at Kathy Gallego's Avenue 50 Gallery in Highland Park. The show featured three other painters, Barbara Carrasco, J. Michael Walker, and Elizabeth Pérez, and I had been invited along with three other poets, Gloria Enedina Álvarez, Peter

3. Pietà is a Renaissance style of art that depicts the dead body of Jesus cradled on the lap of his mother after the Crucifixion.

J. Harris, and Abel Salas, to write a piece based on a chosen artwork in the show. Of course I chose John's. I imagined that the women on the cloud were murdered women from Ciudad Juárez. They were consoling the dead matador while the other three *matadores* on the ground, gesturing as if making cape passes at an imaginary bull, ushered the dead souls of the buried murdered women onto the heavenly cloud above. The resulting haiku poem was written to honor the hundreds of slain women of the ongoing and deliberately unsolved femicide in that godforsaken town. *Que descansen en paz,* may they rest in peace.

Traje de Luces / Suit of Lights

The warm night calls you
"Tonight, a Dance for Lovers!"
Corrida de luz

Strokes of life and death
Dance in the darkness of light
Dance with destiny

Aztec virgins scream
Hearts explode into fire storms
Souls cut, scarred, bleeding

¡Matador! Say it!
"¡Las mujeres de Juárez!"
"¡Descansen en paz!"

Fury transcended
Ignites the light in terror
Dries God's bleeding tears

Life, love, ecstasy
A dance for lovers only
Xikan@ Heaven

John finally had his own retrospective solo show, *Santa Ana Condition: 1976–2011,* at the Museum of Contemporary Art, San Diego (La Jolla) in 2012, thanks in part to Cheech Marin's generous support. It included the inspiring graphite pencil drawing I first saw back in 1980. Tough *Los Angeles Times* art critic Christopher Knight named *Santa Ana Condition* one of the ten top art museum exhibitions in L.A./Southern California for 2012. My homie had arrived big-time. Chicano art was now out of the barrio . . . but the soul of the barrio was not out of the art.

Arts 4 City Youth and Trying Again

IN THE SUMMER OF 1993, during the dreadful separation from Cristina, I was contacted by Juan Carrillo, a former member of the Rebel Chicano Art Front (who played on their initials to also call themselves the Royal Chicano Air Force), an art collective then working with the California Arts Council. He said that there was state money available for a free arts program for youth in East L.A. This was ironically a result of the L.A. uprising. I thought of the rebel Lucio Cabañas and my Chicano commitment back in Mexico to use art as a revolutionary tool for changing and enriching community. I told Juan I would do it if it could take place in the housing projects. He said that would be fine. All I had to do was write up a proposal with an itemized budget. My proposal and budget were approved, and Arts 4 City Youth (originally called the Summer Arts Recovery Program) was launched. Our mission statement announced our aim: To develop a new generation and community of culturally sensitive artist-leader visionaries who would lead Los Angeles into the twenty-first century creating inter-barrio and cross-cultural dialogue, respect, and unity through the arts.

My vision was to let the kids write, paint, film, dance, and photograph their own life stories, using their own words and images. It was a healing process for me and I think for the kids as well. Running the program and deepening my involvement with young people took me out of myself, and I needed that. Nearly two decades later, over nine thousand youths have participated in the program in schools, housing developments, and parks in Pico-Union, Downtown, Boyle Heights, and East Los Angeles. Concerts cosponsored by UCLA's World Arts and Cultures program were presented at many elementary schools, including Magnolia Elementary Avenue School in Pico-Union. Many of my artist friends have served as mentor-instructors, which has provided them with much-needed cash. An arts revolution was in progress, and I heard echoes of approval from Mr. Cabañas.

Working with the kids and watching their joyful development, however, was a painful reminder of how I wasn't around to nurture my own son's talent. So for the sake of my son—and my own self-respect—I asked Cristina to take me back. She accepted.

That fall, I transferred to UCLA where I enrolled in the World Arts and Cultures program. It felt odd being a student with kids half my age. I was old enough to be their father. I had turned fifty the year before.

While I was at UCLA, Rubencito displayed his genius on his first day of first grade. The three of us were standing in the back of the classroom, which was filled with students and parents. When the teacher finished her orientation remarks on how she approached teaching, she asked if there were any questions. Rubencito shot his arm up, and the teacher said, "Yes, the boy in the back." Everyone in the room turned and looked. With complete self-confidence and a clear voice he asked, "I want to know what happened to the dinosaurs and when did man begin?" The teacher was momentarily speechless, then said, "Uhhh, we will try to get to that." Man, I felt so proud I got tears in my eyes.

When Rubencito was in the second grade, I saw him up late one night working on a project. I thought it was a homework assignment, but it turned out to be one of a series of seven comic books that he created—both drawings and text—based on the R. L. Stine *Goosebumps* series, only this was a parody. He called it *Skin Crawlers* and centered it on his schoolmates and teacher. His teacher and the school librarian were so impressed with the books that they exhibited them in the library. He was only seven years old. That's when I knew he was an artist. I *had* to stay and make the marriage work.

UCLA

I FIRST SAW SANKAI JUKO, the Japanese butoh dance company, in the fall of '93 while attending UCLA in the process of trying to salvage my marriage. The performance obliterated everything I thought I knew about theater. It was beyond Western theater, beyond most of the absurdists, experimentalists, and surrealists. I thought my work was crossing new boundaries, but it paled in comparison to Sankai Juko. According to the program notes, "Butoh is theater of the sub-conscious, inspired by the criminality of the French novelist Jean Genet, the French surrealist movement as well as the anti-censorship of the Marquis de Sade." It was also inspired by the U.S. atomic bomb attacks at Hiroshima and Nagasaki that ended World War II. I was transported into an uncharted space watching the performance—no, not a performance in the traditional sense, more like an apparition in which the subconscious was revealed in a new aesthetic dimension, taking me into an inner world of pain and an outer world of transcendence at once. A majestic pre-recorded soundtrack of Ligeti-inspired space music accompanied the carrying and lifting of seminude shaved-head bodies wrapped in white robes and covered in white ash in honor of the victims of the atomic bombings. They moved as in a slow-motion dreamtime, their tortured, gaping mouths, faces, eyes, arms, and hands reaching for and touching an invisible deity. They seemed like shamans "dancing" in liminal space. No words were spoken. None were needed.

I was struck numb. Written text and dance theater had suddenly become useless, obsolete. It took me weeks to come down from the buzz. I grew new skin. My speech pattern changed. I looked at people in new ways, sometimes through them. I floated when I walked. I had to learn how to be normal again, how to be human.

LAX/94: Fire Ants for Nothing, a collaborative video performance. Video and photograph by Harry Gamboa Jr., Los Angeles, 1993. Courtesy of Harry Gamboa Jr.

I learned that as he was dying, one of the pioneers of butoh, Tatsumi Hijikata, had climbed onto his deathbed and danced his final dance before close friends and family. I reimagined that moment in a collaborative performance with Harry Gamboa Jr., *Fire Ants for Nothing,* in which I portrayed a homeless man dancing on my sidewalk deathbed. Working with Harry was always an exercise in freefall improvisation and fearless leaps of creative faith. The direction was to react to the word *futility,* as in the Sisyphus myth. I imagined the futility of trying to make a living as an artist, always haunted by the shadow of winding up broke and homeless. I pulled out a new large plastic mattress bag and wrapped it around me, covering my entire body, poured water over my head, then started crawling on my hands and knees on the sidewalk, going deeper and deeper into a trance. There is a scene where I looked into the camera appearing absolutely crazed, hopeless, and scared— which was exactly how I felt my life had been up to that moment and how it might continue to be. As I crawled along, tears burning my eyes, I came across an ant crawling next to me and I repeated, "I am *not* an animal! I am *not* an animal!" I held my hand over the ant, following it, when Harry gave the direction to crush it. I did, reluctantly—then I collapsed. I felt I had also crushed myself, my spirit, my soul.

Butoh-inspired performance art provided a creative channel for me to experience life, death, and rebirth: moments of leaving my pain, moments of leaving the planet, moments of being a god.

UCLA's World Arts and Cultures program enabled me to hone my performance chops and experiment with various cultural performance styles. This also kept me from jumping into my dark funk tank and drowning in it with my demons, which were always right below the surface staring at me with menacing grins. All this while I tried like hell to keep the dog in check. Gotdamn! Those UCLA women were fine! But hey, I was old enough to be their father. So a new mind and lust set emerged: platonic friendship. It humbled the restless dog.

While fighting with my demons, trying to keep my marriage intact, I had to make some sense out of my life. What was it for? What was I living for? What was I dying for? What was my mission? What happened to my revolution? I had to make something out of my lust, anger, and despair or else blow up and drown. The following was an attempt to do that. It was performed as a butoh spoken-word experiment in a choreography class.

I began on my hands and knees, dragging and pulling my travel bag across the studio dance floor in a glacially slow slide. The idea was to make the bag look heavy and full of trauma, the slow movement agonizing. Then I stopped and slowly started pulling out my trauma, the items I'd used in my performances in France. I built an altar, my grave, and finally, my tomb. After it was built, I did a Hijikata-inspired death dance around my grave-bed, then slowly lay down to expire. After a long, slow death in stylized movement, I lay still for a few more minutes, then, slow as a sunrise, I rose from my tomb and began speaking the poem "My Name Is Fuck You If You Don't Like It" (updated here to the present) in a remote spirit voice, without anger.

I closed as usual with lighting and burning sage, then stared straight ahead toward the class. I whispered *"Con safos"* to the left, center, and right while waving the smoking sage for a few seconds. The room was silent. No one moved. They just stared back at me. Confused? Awestruck? I don't know. After a few more minutes of dead silence, the class was dismissed.

My Name Is Fuck You If You Don't Like It
Dedicated to oppression[1]

My name is "Fuck You If You Don't Like It."
I breathe through fire and stone
I breathe through ashes of flesh, blood, and steel.
I breathe through centuries of invasions, genocide, colonization,
    slavery, Manifest Destiny,
incarceration, and perpetual occupation

My name is "Fuck You If You Don't Like It"
I breathe through tears of terror and pain.
Tenochtitlan: the burning of Mexico City in 1521
Texcoco in 1535
The holocaust of the Caribbean: over 30 million indigenous souls
    took flight between 1500 and 1530
Maní, Yucatan: the burning of the Mayan libraries and where
    Spanish soldiers were ordered to hang village women because
    their beauty distracted them
Little Big Horn
Wounded Knee
The Trail of Tears
In 1942, during World War II, over 120,000 innocent Japanese
    Americans were put in US concentration camps
The 1943 L.A. Zoot Suit Riots by US servicemen
The U.S. atomic bombings at Hiróshima and Nagasaki
The Bloody Sunday March in Selma
The 1965 Watts Rebellion
Vietnam My Lai village massacre by US troops
The 1968 massacre of protesting students in Tlatelolco, Mexico City
The 1970 Chicano Moratorium riot started by L.A. sheriffs at
    Laguna Park, East L.A.
Nicaragua
Guatemala
The invasion of Panamá
The invasion of the Persian Gulf
The invasion of Grenada

1. Carey McWilliams identified C/S as a sign of defiance of oppressive conditions among
Mexican Americans. In *North from Mexico: The Spanish-Speaking People of the United States*
(1948).

The invasion of Iraq
The invasion of Afghanistan
The 1992 L.A. rebellion that led to Ferguson and Baltimore

My name is "Fuck You If You Don't Like It"
And I will not be con-formed, re-formed, de-formed.
I will not be re-moved, re-built, or re-birthed by force, guilt, shame,
     or despair

My name is "Fuck You If You Don't Like It" and I am not a
     multicultural performance artist
I am Black, Brown, Yellow, and Red brothers and sisters
I am a witness
I am a testament
I am memory
I am a sacred vow
I am a weapon
your conscience
And fuck you if you don't like it.

During this hectic time I reactivated Zyanya Records, featuring Chicano and
Latin rock from the United States, Latin America, and Europe. The follow-
ing compilations were released that addressed sociopolitical issues.
¡Reconquista! The Latin Rock Invasion (in collaboration with Emilio Morales
and Maria Madrigal of La Banda Elastica, 1997) featured twelve 1990s con-
temporary world rock bands: Maldita Vecindad y los Hijos del Quinto Patio,
Santa Sabina, Cuca, La Castañeda, Fobia, Caifanes, and ¡Tijuana No! from
Mexico; Divididos and Los Fabulosos Cadillacs from Argentina; Seguridad
Social from Spain; Mano Negra from Spain and France; and Negu Gorriak
from País Vasco. In 1998 ¡Ay Califas! Raza Rock: The '70s & '80s was released.
It featured eighteen classic California bands: Santana, Los Lobos, Cheech &
Chong, Tower of Power, Malo, Tierra, Azteca, Cold Blood, El Chicano, The
Plugz, Ruben And The Jets, War, Con Safos, Los Illegals, Sapo, Yaqui,
Cruzados, and Daniel Valdez. My commitment to cross-cultural activism
through the arts pulled me up and kept me from sinking deeper into the dark
pit of despair.

Journey to New Aztlán

HANAY GEIOGAMAH (KIOWA), founder and director of the American Indian Dance Theater, was my professor in playwriting and Native American Studies at UCLA. He and avant-garde opera-theater director Peter Sellars, who taught performance classes, were my senior thesis advisors. I had met Peter and become friends with him during the time I curated a Mexican *banda* performance at Olvera Street for the 1989 Los Angeles Festival, which he directed and co-curated with UCLA professor and World Arts and Cultures department chair Judy Mitoma.

My 1996 senior thesis, "Journey to New Aztlán," argued that an ethnic artist could stay true to his or her political and cultural truths while experimenting with performance traditions outside the artist's own cultural background. *Funkahuatl Speaks,* the performance piece that emerged from the thesis, fused elements of Japanese butoh dance, Native American ritual/neo-shamanism, East L.A. rhythm and blues, and the history of Los Angeles. I used the same large plastic mattress bag that I'd used in *Fire Ants for Nothing.* I started the performance by lying still in the bag upstage, then I poured water from a water bottle over my head. I slowly slid toward the front of the stage. The idea was to look like an amoeba moving at the speed of a snail, leaving a trail of life-memory ooze behind. When I reached the front I slowly pushed my outstretched fingers through the plastic, then pushed my wet face through, as if in childbirth. With my head slowly emerging, I breathed loudly and stared at the audience, a startled look on my face. I slowly slid out through the torn plastic, struggled to stand, produced my travel bag, and pulled out my *copal* and lit it, then in a tired whisper called "To all the directions, around, above, below, and within; and to all the gods and goddesses who got kicked out of the cosmos for not answering prayers because they were too busy having fun: God bless them all." There was one line I dug in the intro: "Gods and goddesses wouldn't exist without our pain. We created *them*."

I then recited the song poem "C/S," with East L.A. classic doo-wop ballads "The Town I Live In" and "Together" playing low on my boombox as if in a distant dream, and ended as I did at the fashion art show, with Al Green's "Love and Happiness," throwing candy from around the world to the audience while Rubencito handed out fruit from various L.A. cultures. To my surprise, everyone got up and started to dance and sing along with the Reverend Green's primal screams. It was a beautiful sight, a beautiful night indeed.

Unfortunately, the high from the performance didn't last. My past affair haunted the marriage, undermining my ability to focus in school—though somehow I kept that together. The arguments and shouting increased, which our son had to listen to and endure. With so much emotional turmoil always in the air, several months later I decided to spare my son further anguish— and I left for the last time. It was another heart-shredding decision: the most wrenching experience since the death of my sister. But it felt necessary, for everyone's sanity.

I might have failed as a father with Ben and my daughter, but I was determined to keep a strong relationship going with Rubencito. I made it a point to let him know that I was still his father, that I loved him, that he wasn't the reason for me leaving. We would just have a different kind of family. And we did. I provided regular child support; I took him to museums, concerts, art galleries, and, our favorite thing, the movies, as well as taking him to and from school until he graduated and went off to college. Even with my limited resources, I contributed to his college expenses. He attended UCLA on a partial scholarship from Warner Brothers film studio, then transferred and graduated from NYU's film school with honors in 2009. The relationship with my son during this depressing time was my only heart oasis. Rubencito was a gentle, good-hearted kid with a great sense of humor, always making me laugh—the only real laughter I knew. The only love I had. Still, he has not forgiven me for leaving the marriage.

I "walked" my graduation ceremony in June 1996, though I didn't technically graduate until the following fall quarter. The event was in the main quad in front of the campus centerpiece, Royce Hall. While sitting looking up at the magnificent building waiting for my name to be called, I remembered the first time I saw the campus on a YMCA field trip in '54. I didn't know what a university was. I was told it was a school, but that was hard to believe. It looked more like a movie set, a magic realm of kings and queens from medieval times. I never thought I would someday be sitting there waiting to "graduate" from that marvelous kingdom. My mother, sons Ben and Rubencito, sisters Linda and Loretta, brother-in-law Paul, nephews Billy, Chris, and Andrew, and niece Sara were there. My dad didn't make it. Cristina did.

When my name was called, I marched to the stage feeling like a redeemed, if somewhat ravaged, warrior-artist. I managed to graduate with honors, making *cum laude* after dropping from *magna cum laude* because of my personal chaos. The following week I participated in the Raza graduation ceremony organized by students of Chicana/Chicano Studies. It was a moving reminder of what the Chicano civil rights movement had accomplished. It felt good being among my fellow Chican@ children. We'd come a long way since my Mexican pilgrimage and commitment to my art in 1974.

To graduate formally, I needed to create a final solo choreographed performance piece the following December. The class was taught by David Rousseve, dancer and artistic director of the acclaimed modern dance group REALITY. I had left my marriage a couple of months before and was living in my car close to campus. I was homeless, but I was so wrapped up in preparing the piece in my car that it didn't register as a big deal. I was preparing for something more important: my death.

I performed the *butoh*-inspired piece called *Mi Familia Cósmica/My Cosmic Family: A Dance of Life and Death* in December of 1996. I again wrapped myself completely in the now-tattered plastic bag, my face painted with jagged indigenous streaks, wearing the clothes of a homeless man, in bare feet. The performance, in front of the dance building, was in very slow, focused motion. It began at the bottom steps with my birth from the plastic womb-bag, followed by a stylized enactment of the burning of my face as an infant. I turned to my right, attempting to walk a child's first wobbly steps, proceeding in a semicircle halfway up to the top of the steps, my toes turned inward as I walked on the sides of my feet, legs slightly bent. At the top I stood almost upright, creating the idea of midlife, and recited the poem "Mi Familia Cósmica." I then descended, still to my right, in a continued semicircle, my legs becoming weak with old age, my body now bent, legs wobbly, as I headed to my birthplace/grave at the bottom of the steps. There I reached up to the sky in gratitude, whispering *"Con safos"* while imagining dancing on my deathbed like Hijikata, then looked up and stared at the audience. I murmured, "Now live ... and dance ... to your ... *Music*," and slowly crumpled and dissolved back into the plastic bag. There's nothing like living out your own death, facing it straight in the eye. Performance art gave me a brief, illusionary sense of immortality and a brief handle on my life. Without it, I'd probably be dead for reals.

After finally graduating, I found a small room in the Little Tokyo Hotel. It felt good to move out of my car and not have to look for places to shower and shit every morning. I liked my room, even though I had to share a bathroom down the hall and a community kitchen. It felt like I was on a vacation in Japan—a cheap vacation, but as close as I'd probably ever get to Tokyo. Still, in reality it was nothing more than a clean flop house.

A couple of days after moving in, right before Christmas, I was parking my car at Yaohan Plaza shopping center in Little Tokyo, when out of nowhere a bolt of panic and depression hit my gut like a spiked cannonball on fire. I went down in flames. It was deadly awful. I felt my life had come to an end. Barely finishing school and leaving my wife and son after three long, exhausting years of trying to keep it all together had finally taken its toll and left me emotionally and spiritually dead. I was fifty-four and broke, with thousands owed in student loans; I saw myself heading straight to poverty and Skid Row, as I had prophesied. I sat in my car immobilized, staring out, my eyes burning, my mind numb, my heart bleeding, my gut twisted in knots. I knew if I didn't get out of the car I would collapse in that dreadful terror and die. I reached for the door handle with everything I had, turned it, and dragged myself out. I had to force myself to move, walk, and breathe. This was no performance art piece that I could control, and Superman was nowhere around.

Shaking and taking deep breaths, I managed to get to the second floor, where I used to take Rubencito to buy him Godzilla toys. There was a play area with kids running and jumping around. Rather than going into a deeper funk, I miraculously managed a smile, remembering the times he'd played there; I could almost hear his laughter as I spun him, clutching his precious Godzilla, on the minicarousel. It brought tears of laughter, love, and strength.

I survived the next few weeks on automatic pilot by mostly staying in my room, coming out only to eat and teach a poetry class once a week. There was no life to live for, no future. I managed to get through that grim, bleak Christmas mainly thanks to a warm visit with Rubencito and Ben. That was a lifesaving turning point. They became my reason to live so I could at least die with some honor.

For My Son Ben on His 40th Birthday

Pacing
Waiting
A tight knot of nervous expectation

Time
Frozen in a sweat
Me and your heartbeat
Dancing with
Doubts
Wonder and
Dreams

Will I make it
Can I be a father
Can I go the long haul
Will I pass the torch of
Integrity
Compassion
Wisdom
Forgiveness
Love
Manhood

March 26, 1962
I'm nineteen and
In love
Music singing in my heart
That life is beautiful
Young love knows no fear
A holy gift

Mr. Guevara
You have a son
Congratulations

I run to your mother's side
She's pale
Drained yet
Smiling

Little
Tiny

Sparkling
Angels
Flew 'round and 'round my room she said
Singing
Love is the sacred language of the
Heart
Love is the
Music of the
Soul

Standing with your
Grandmother
In front of
A glass wall
Witnesses to
A room full of new
Life
Voices
Roaring their
Arrival

We stand in silence

Then . . .
I see you

Singing your
Perfection

I tremble in
Awe
Watching you sing your
Song
Watching you sing your
Prayer
Watching you sing your
Heart out
Proclaiming your
Birthrights

Will you be there
Will you always be near
Will you read me stories

Will you take me with you
Will you really be my Dad

I shake as I
Breathe deeply and smile

Haiku for My Daughter

Memories rush in
Love wrapped in tears and laughter
Some things never change

Pushing your stroller
You looked around in wonder
Where am I going?

The swings in the park
Your curls flying through the air
Eyes wide dancing joy

You looked at flowers
Petals sang with your fingers
Magical music

The park, you and me
Memories etched in my heart
A long time ago

Now you're two years old
Hawaii was your new home
I went to visit

A park was near by
The swings again called your name
Same glee and laughter

The visit ended
We lost contact for a while
Always in my heart

Holidays flew by
Your birthday top of my list
Wished you love and light

Thirty-six years now
A strong woman of the world
You have made your mark

Father and daughter
An indelible blood bond
Irrefutable

For My Son Rubencito on His 18th Birthday

You emerged into the world
Proclaiming your presence
While your mother fought to stay alive

Both of your cries
Were an affirmation
A confirmation of life, love, and destiny

The nurse wrapped you in a bright white towel
Blessed, tattooed with a mother's greatest gift
Her sacred blood

With the holy crimson water still clinging, singing
Onto your immaculate skin
I plunged you into a bowl of water
A baptism of love

You grew to love music
To sing
To draw
Skills that created confidence

Eighteen years have passed
You're a tall, talented, strong soul
With a smile and heart that lights the universe

Graduation ceremony
Visuals, dance, music, and theater
A grand opera of artistry, sweat, tears, and dreams

The future is not tomorrow
The future is not over the horizon
The future began when you arrived on the planet
When you were received with unconditional love

Remember, parents and kids are not perfect
Their love is

So, create with soul
Be kind
Be and live the future
As a warrior of wisdom and truth

The Enchantress

AFTER A SAD AND SOMBER New Year's Eve, and my meltdown, in January of 1997 I received a phone call out of the blue from the California Arts Council with an invitation to attend a three-day retreat on building stronger nonprofits. At first I didn't want to accept: I couldn't handle being around people. But the more I thought about it, the more I thought, why not. Maybe I'd pull out of my funk and get back on track. So I went.

The retreat was on a beach near Santa Cruz. It was paradise. I reconnected with Juan Carrillo, who'd originally contacted me to start Arts 4 City Youth, and his coworker Lucero Arellano. By day there were workshops; by night there were social gatherings with other nonprofit directors and artists. All this activity was a good distraction. I slowly came back to my old self. I got a new sense of hope.

On the last day of the retreat, Gustavo Vazquez, a photographer, invited me to go to San Francisco with him for a book-signing reception for our mutual friend Guillermo Gómez-Peña. It sounded good. I hadn't seen Guillermo since we collaborated at Highways' inauguration back in '89, and San Francisco sounded like fun. The dog was slowly waking up.

At the bookstore, my eyes shot to a tall, elegant raven-haired beauty across the room wearing a black velvet dress. Our eyes met and kissed for a second. It was electric. I turned and saw Guillermo and we greeted each other with warm *abrazos*. I congratulated him on becoming a MacArthur Fellow back in 1990 and for the release of his new book, *Friendly Cannibals,* a collaboration with Chicano visual artist Enrique Chagoya. He then invited me to join him for a group dinner at an Italian restaurant after the reception. It was held in a dark medieval-looking room, where a long table was decorated with lit candles giving off a gothic glow. We sat down, and lo and behold, taking the chair directly across from me was the beauty. She was even more beautiful up close in the candlelight, positively enchanting. My heart stuttered. Guillermo introduced us, and she extended her hand; as I held it I recognized love's sweet soul music singing through my body. It felt good to hear. I didn't want to let go. As we talked about the life of an artist, she listened to what I had to say. She really listened, and I really needed that. I loved the way she would tilt her head as she pondered an idea, smile, then graciously offer her point of view. The dog was definitely charmed.

After a delicious dinner and our long conversation, I said that it had been a pleasure to meet her, and she smiled as if she had known me for a long time. We exchanged numbers and promised to stay in touch. Stay in touch? Hell, I wanted her forever. We corresponded over the next few months and planned to meet the following June. It was a very long wait.

We planned to meet for coffee in Chinatown. Man, I felt like a nervous young cat on a first date. While I was rehearsing different hip greetings, she suddenly appeared out of the blue brisk *San Pancho* air, her long black mane blowing across her beautiful face. She was wearing a simple sleeveless blouse, blue jeans, sandals, and no makeup. Her flawless beauty had a certain vibe, more spiritual than flesh or flash. I momentarily lost my mind and voice, and all I could say was hi as she greeted me with a smile and a polite cheek to cheek. We ordered coffee, then walked over to a sidewalk table. As I nervously put my cup down, the table collapsed, spilling our coffee all over us. But I managed to pull off a Superman lick by grabbing the table just before it completely collapsed on the sidewalk. She just smiled a killer Mona Lisa half smile, like it was no big deal. I got us two more cups like nothing had happened. We savored our coffee, our conversation, and each other. Man, it was easy to talk with her. No ego, no attitude, just a loving, lovely human being. Her voice tasted like wet mint, her words and manner spun a web of music from another world, not from the outside or inside, but from some uncharted space beyond my knowing. I flat out fell in love with her.

Just as the sun pierced through a cloud, I looked down and saw her toenails, painted a bright candy-apple red suddenly ignite and shoot white sparks of love through me, like when Frankenstein got those electrical shocks bringing him to life. Stunned, I wasn't sure how to deal with it. But like Frankenstein, I had to figure it out. We continued to talk and laugh and I continued to wonder: How do you love an enchantress?

It was getting late and I had to catch a plane back to L.A, though I didn't want to leave. I finally managed to say goodbye and after another sweet, polite cheek-to-cheek we again promised to stay in touch. I glided down the steep Chinatown streets one inch off the ground, dancing like Frankenstein might have danced with love for the first time. I was resurrected. I was a new man. It was a miracle. But, after all . . . love *is* a miracle.

We did stay in touch, writing letters to each other. Then she sent a book of love sonnets by Pablo Neruda that permanently cemented my love of poetry, and of her. They became the medicine that fed the wild, enchanted dog. I never declared my true feelings for her, though, because my heart was burnt to a crisp. Ultimately, distance and our busy lives kept us apart, except for a brief dinner seven years later. Although what we shared was short lived, what we had will last until the last love poem is written. Sometimes love can exist—and last—only in the heart of a poem.

Candy Apple Red Toenails

The radiance of your
beauty
magic
humility
Struck and lit me
Gentle eyes that could see and heal through pain
Danced in perfect grace
While the skin of my weary scarred soul
Flinched and pulled
Then whispered,
"Surrender . . . it's only love"

Querida

Te mando la luz de mi sendero / I send you the light of my path
Te mando la luz de mis sueños / I send you the light of my dreams
Te mando la luz de mi corazón / I send you the light of my heart

A Mission District Haiku

Waiting for the night
As the full moon sought the sun
I felt my heart sweat

Seven years had passed
Eighty-four moons reflected
Since our smiles first met

We ate in dark noise
Dancing and reaching for light
We sensed a kind trust

I offered my hand
You carefully offered yours
A link without rust

Walking to your car
My bones shivered and rattled
Then glowed from your smile

Friendship a rare gift
Manifestation of love
Sacred without guile

Writing these poems salvaged my heart and resuscitated my life. Now I was ready to continue as a culture sculptor.

América Tropical

IN 1997, SHORTLY AFTER I returned from San Francisco the first time I met the Enchantress, playwright Oliver Mayer cast me in a production of his new play *The Road to Los Angeles: A Populist Posada* at the Social and Public Art Resource Center in Venice. This was an opportunity to try out my performance chops in a theatrical setting for a change. The play, based on Mexican master muralist Davíd Alfaro Siqueiros's 1932 mural *América Tropical,* commemorated the artist's hundredth birthday. I had the massive task of portraying his spirit. This was the challenge I needed: butoh meets Funkahuatl!

The cast went to visit the mural at Olvera Street, to get a sense of what we were trying to evoke in the play. The mural was then at the end of the first phase of conservation. Because of its political subversiveness, it had been censored by the L.A. City Council and consequently whitewashed.

We walked into the small shed that was protecting it. A black velvet stage curtain covered the 18' × 80' masterpiece. Assistants standing at each end of the mural, with me in the center, reached for the ropes that were hanging from the top and slowly pulled. The curtain rolled up as if a play was about to begin. I wasn't ready for the impact the silence and the imagery would have. A drama as vivid and visceral as an acid flashback hit me as the curtain went up, like the hurricane back in Veracruz. The mural still had immense power.

In the 1960s the whitewash paint had started to peel, revealing the mural underneath. Now with the conservation in progress, most of the original mural could be seen. It reminded me of photos I'd seen of the ancient faded Mayan murals at Bonampak, which could still enthrall the dead.

A sonic field of energy was made visible. Violent histories between Mexico and the United States were juxtaposed onto each other, creating an aural and visual cacophony: an indigenous Mexican strapped to a double cross, with an American eagle hovering overhead as if circling prey before the kill; two Mexican revolutionary soldiers on either side, aiming their rifles at the eagle. The drama of the painting was overwhelming, and I felt dizzy with electric currents of anger and awe.

Siqueiros was inspired to paint the indigenous figure at the last minute because of the deportations, or "repatriations," that were occurring in Los Angeles at the time. They infuriated him. After it was unveiled, the mural was censored and whitewashed. According to art historian Irene Herner-Reiss, Siqueiros then offered to replicate just the central image of the indigenous Mexican on the cross and send it to La Plaza de la Raza as a gift to the Los Angeles Mexican American community in an act of solidarity, but he died before he could do so. The mural subsequently became an inspiration and cornerstone for the emerging Chicano mural art movement of the early '70s.

In the play, the moment of truth came when I walked, in butoh posture and pace, into a bright ray of light that shot up from the floor and across the room. I slowly made my way, bent over, my face contorted, and reached out to grab the light, finally pulling myself into it as if I was returning to the source of our beginning. Going into a Don Juan zone, for a few minutes I *was* the ray of light. I lingered longer than I should have. I didn't want to come back.

After the performance, a woman came up to me and introduced herself as my cousin, Donna Guevara-Hill. I was floored: she was my *tío* Xavier's daughter. We'd never met before. She had become a theater director and headed a youth program, the Migrant Youth Theater Project. I told her about my theater background, and she graciously hired me to direct six plays, one every summer for the next six years, with kids from migrant families throughout L.A. County at different universities and theaters. Three of the plays were folk tale adaptations, Chinese, Arabic, and Inuit, and three were originals based on their parents' true stories of coming to the States and raising a family in a hostile land. We had eight weeks to write it, block it, and perform it with a full tech crew of lighting and sound. The kids always came through. I loved those students and their work. The art revolution kept rocking along, and the beat was deep.

About a year later, I got word that my father was in town from Panama to treat his recurring asthma. I hadn't seen him in over ten years and was looking forward to seeing him again. When I arrived in South Central, though, I couldn't believe I was at the right address. I thought the person answering the door was a homeless dude, unshaven, wearing a black wool gangster beanie. He greeted me warmly, but I still didn't recognize him, or didn't want to. "¿M'hijo, cómo estás? Son, how are you?" I was shocked. He looked as if he had aged thirty years since the last time I saw him. He looked . . . old . . . very old. We talked about his medical condition and he explained that he was in town with his wife, Nelly, to deal with it. I told him I would help him by taking him to his doctor visits.

I drove home feeling deeply unsettled, sensing another meltdown like the one after graduation. I started breathing deeply. I started praying. When I returned to my Little Tokyo hotel room, I collapsed in a tearful torrent of sadness and fear. The horror of seeing death up close in my father's withered face reflected my own mortality. I fell to the floor sobbing with a frightening fierce intensity. As with the last meltdown, I knew if I didn't move, I would die. This was not a performance I could simply pull out of. I truly felt my life was over as I lay there, immobilized, drenched in tears and terror. But with the grace of God and all that is merciful, I put my hands on the floor and with the feeble strength of a dead man fighting for his life slowly pulled myself up, rising from my deathbed, a sobbing resurrected Superman. It was now time to live again, so I could properly die.

What triggered those attacks? Maybe being wrapped in sheets screaming for weeks, so I couldn't scratch my burnt face as an infant? Watching the car tire skid to a halt against my head on the pavement as a child? Being thrown off the Santa Monica pier so I could learn how to swim? I remembered the terror of abandonment I felt one day in the second grade when my mother didn't come to pick me up from school as she had promised. It was a long, tearful walk home. Maybe the trigger was the violent, tragic death of my beloved sister. Or my face getting burned again by sulphuric acid. Could it be the destructive fights with women? My failure as a providing father and husband? Maybe all of it.

So why didn't I just pull the trigger and end it? Because I get a kick out of my whacked-out sense of humor, my wild sexual encounters running the dog, and my love of a good story and needing to know how it might play out. Also, like I said before, because of my sons. There are still times when my life gets too dark and heavy to rise up from, and those times still haunt me like a shadow on fire. But then, there's always another story lurking around the next corner, the next smile, that eases the obsession, if only temporarily. The dog serves that purpose with its lusty madness. It's all about how you deal with the lust and the madness. As a dirty dog? Or an impeccable dog? Your choice. Your karma.

Miss Mongolia

AFTER A FEW MONTHS AT the Little Tokyo hotel I moved into a more spacious room. One hot day as I was climbing the stairs after walking my existential dog, I noticed the door of my old room was open, and sitting on the bed watching TV was a dark-haired beauty. The blue light beaming from the screen washed over her outstretched legs, which were barely covered by a short white nightgown. I stopped at the open door and said, "Hi. I used to live here." She just covered her legs but didn't say a word. The TV continued flashing its bluish glow, creating a sexy strobe-light effect on her knockout face and body. I got tongue-tied and managed, "Sssee you around." She just nodded her head, staring at the TV in a distant daze. The dog barked goodbye.

The following day the door was open again. I knocked. She was dressed in a white terrycloth bathrobe, with her hair pulled up and wrapped in a white towel like a turban. My knees flinched and the dog stirred. "Hi again. Are you a student?" I asked, since most of the tenants were. This time she answered. "Yes, I'm studying English," she said in an indifferent tone. "Oh, that's great! Where are you from? Japan?" "No, I'm Mongolian." That caught my attention. "I've never met a M-M-Mongolian before," I stammered. "I only know Mongolian barbecue." She laughed. I was making progress. "What's it like there?" I continued. She didn't answer that, but instead said, "My grandfather is a Buddhist priest and I took care of him. Now my younger sister does." "Oh, really? Wow, a Buddhist priest. I've studied a little about Buddhism. I think it's a very useful philosophy, very practical. In fact, I taught a *haiku* poetry workshop last month to a group of Buddhist priests here in Little Tokyo," I said, trying my best to impress. "Oh, are you Asian?" she asked, checking me out. "No, I'm Chicano," I said proudly." "I don't know what that is, but yes, Buddhism is very useful." "Why did you leave your country?" "I wanted to come to America to become a model. But first, I need a portfolio." "I have a friend that's a really good photographer," I blurted. "Would you like to shoot some photos with him?" "Oh, thank you. That's very nice of you," she said, her face finally coming alive. "But I have no money." "That's okay, I'll take care of it," I said, feeling like a big shot. After all, she was a granddaughter of a Buddhist priest. And once again, I was old enough to be her father.

I called my homie Francesco Siqueiros and told him about the Mongolian model. "And no, *ese,*" I said. "It's not a dog shoot. No dog-monkey business. She's serious. And besides, her grandfather is a Buddhist priest. So, sorry, *ese,* you can't seduce her." He agreed, and we set up a time the next weekend.

When I stopped by to pick her up, she answered the door looking like she'd just finished shooting the cover of a Japanese high fashion magazine. I was a little puzzled that she could afford such an outfit when she said she didn't have any money, but she explained that the dress was a gift. "Is it okay?" "Perfect," I said.

As we drove to Francesco's studio I tried not to stare at her but rather keep my eyes on the road while the dog chomped away at his chain. It was a painfully long ride. We finally arrived, and Francesco's eyes popped out. "Hey, *ese,* be cool. Go get your *babas* bag (drool catcher) and your muzzle." We laughed. She demurely smiled.

He shot a few rolls of her sitting on his couch, then he suggested we go to the roof, via a ladder from his bedroom. She climbed up first. I was behind her and couldn't help looking up her dress as she made her way. She looked down and caught me staring but didn't say anything. I thought it was some kind of cool Buddhist acceptance thing, but I turned away anyway. Homie maintained as a *caballero perro,* a gentleman dog, and finished the shoot without scaring the lady away. On the drive back to our hotel I invited her to get something to eat but she said she couldn't. She had an appointment. I walked her to her room and said "See you in a week or so with the proof sheets. And . . . sorry I looked up your dress." She just smiled and shook her head.

A week later I had the proofs. When she came to the door, she was wearing that terrycloth bathrobe again. I asked if she'd like to come to my room to look at them. "Yes, but first I take a shower. I will come over right after." When, a little while later, she knocked, she was wearing the same bathrobe, with her wet hair rolled up in a towel. Strange, I'd've thought she'd change into some regular clothes before coming over.

Her scent was pristine, pure, and untouchable as she walked past me. The dog moaned, and I pulled him back on his chain. She walked over to my bed and sat down. I pulled out the proof sheets and we looked them over. She picked several shots, then abruptly fell back on my bed, sighing about how tired she was. Her robe opened slightly, revealing her divine legs. I tried with all my might not to look, or to think that she might be seducing me. "No, no, no. She's the granddaughter of a Buddhist priest, for chrissake!" She laid there for a few seconds. Was she waiting for my move? Or was she just really tired and stretching her back? The dog started to bark. I was torn in two. What if I made a move and she wasn't trying to seduce me? How fucked up would that be? After a few more seconds of dead silence, she got up and sighed. "I have to go now." We set up another meeting when I would give her the finished prints. I watched her stroll down the hall to her room, barefoot, naked under her robe. All the while the dog was chewing on his chain.

Francesco got busy with other projects and couldn't develop the prints right away. I stopped by to tell her but there was no answer. Another week passed and I still didn't see her, so I went to the manager and asked him if he knew anything. He said, "Oh, you mean the hooker? She move out. She go to Monterey Park."

Sometimes you just gotta get the dog out by any means possible. That whacked-out episode inspired this poem later that night. It helped to keep the dog karma down.

Sacred Hearts

Had to turn the car around and look again. Seventh and Kohlor,
  Skid Row, downtown, in front of the Olympia Hotel. Spider
  Woman incarnate, back-combed raven hair in flight, eyes as
  dark as a nun's secret, standing tall in a tight black see-through
  miniskirt, spike heels, black mesh stockings, and a baaad
  attitude. She was the shadow side of beauty. Feline. Primal.
I pulled over and asked her to get in. "Hey, Night Train, wanna take
  a ride?"
She turned away, then reached for the door handle and got in. I
  couldn't take my eyes off her nipples, fresh as ripe sweet peas
  pressing hard against her black silk top. But it was her dark green
  eyes that pulled me closer. Green as Mayan cenotes, sacred,
  sacrificial death pools. I stepped on the gas and drove off.
I noticed her body. It was trim, tattooed, and finely toned. Her satin
  brown legs were long and lean. No cuts, scars, or bruises.

I headed east on Brooklyn, past Self Help Graphics & Art, then
turned left on Hazard past the Anthony Quinn Library and up
the hill to City Terrace Park. Drove to the east side of the park
and found a secluded spot with a dazzling view below. "Heaven
Must Be Missing an Angel" by Tavares was playing on the radio.
I looked over, and she threw another one of those seductive *bruja*
looks, so dangerous it could shatter stone.

As I moved my mouth toward her, she slowly opened hers and
received me. Her lips were full, soft, determined. Our wild
tongues danced and met and melted in sweet surrender. She
caught and started to suck my tongue, firmly holding on as I
moved my hand further up her dress. Her body subtly jerked. It
turned me on.

She sat on my lap facing forward as I rubbed her in a light circular
motion while I slowly entered her. Her moans came from a deep,
dark place as she hit her first orgasm, then another, and another,
as I held mine back, waiting for the perfect moment.

As I continued to gently stroke her she hit another one, then
another. I stopped to let her catch her breath, but her body
continued to jerk sporadically, raising our white-flame heat
higher. We locked in sync as her moans went from an intense
purr to a primal growl, momentarily startling me as we finally
exploded and evaporated in a hurricane of fire.

We started to scream together as an owl flew by and covered the
moon, our bodies numb in divine delirium collapsing into each
other.

I was awakened by her sobbing, first softly, then louder, calling out
some dude's name, "Antonio, Antonio," as she held me tight,
her arms trembling, as tears, saliva, lipstick, dead memories, and
running mascara mixed into a bittersweet nectar of lust dancing
with love in the immaculate virgin moonlight.

I looked into her shattered, soulful eyes, gave them a soft kiss, and
said, "Hey, Night Train, *¿que tal mi chula?* I like you . . . a lot" as
Aretha Franklin's "Ain't No Way" came on the radio, caressing
and penetrating through our sweaty, sinful pores and straight
through our sacred hearts.

Teaching Poetry

WHILE I WAS ATTENDING UCLA I began teaching poetry at Metropolitan State Hospital in Norwalk, a facility for the mentally and emotionally challenged. I needed the money. When you arrived at the main gate, an old wooden sign with the name of the hospital carved in old English letters greeted you. It looked like something out of the TV show *The Addams Family,* spooky and absurdly humorous at the same time.

I didn't think I would be there for more than the eight-week contract, but I ended up teaching there for sixteen years. The "clients," as they were called, were actually not that nuts—not any more than me and many of my friends. So it was easy to work with them, once I got over their disabilities and quirky ways. Their illnesses for the most part were due to chemical imbalances, as well as from emotional and drug abuse. They all had the potential to express themselves, unless they were overly medicated, which unfortunately was the norm. The hospital came under federal investigation in the early 2000s because of several suicides and family complaints about overmedication being used to control the clients. One of my students, a young teenage girl, hanged herself. She was a great poet.

Over the years, I became friends with many of them. One young man had been an engineering student at UCLA, but he flipped out over the stress of school and the pressure to succeed. He was eventually released after our workshops ended. In 1999, I was invited to teach full time, working with kids who were moved to Metro from Camarillo State Hospital after it closed. I accepted. How tough could it be teaching six boys, ages eight to ten? After all, I had a boy of ten at the time, Rubencito. I thought this would also be a great opportunity to practice a more Buddhist attitude.

On the first day of school, right before lunch, a fight broke out between two boys in my classroom. As that pair punched away, the others turned over my desk and their desks and threw their books and papers all over the room. My assistant, a "psych tech," pulled the alarm, and other staff arrived and pulled the boys apart. As they were taken back to their unit, one of the boys yelled out at me, "I know my rights! You're a fake teacher! You're not accredited!" He was then strapped onto a gurney and wheeled into a small room that looked like a jail cell. My heart broke as I looked through the small window in the door watching him squirm and cry. Was that what I went through when I was wrapped in sheets so I wouldn't scratch myself when I was burned as a baby?

I sat literally trembling during the lunch break. What the fuck was I doing there? I didn't sign up for this. I wanted to split, but was torn; shouldn't I stay and try to work with these boys? I couldn't bail on them like everyone else had in their lives, even if it cost me my sanity.

Each morning, the boys would line up at the classroom door and I would greet them and ask if they were ready for the day. This greeting also served as a way to see where their heads were at and if they were overmedicated. One day there was a new kid who was last in line, and when I said, "Good morning, welcome to class," he replied, "Fuck you, white bitch!" I just stood there speechless, holding my breath, and remembered that that kind of "bad behavior" was an example of SED—severe emotional disorder—and his attack was based on defense and survival mechanisms. So I used the moment to practice Buddhist teachings, like putting the ego aside and not taking insults personally. It was the toughest thing I've ever done, but I kept at it.

I lay awake nights trying to figure out how to get through to the boys. I had meetings with the principal, but got no real ideas except for the formulaic approach: "if they act out, send them to their unit." How was I going to get them interested in learning English, science, history, and math while keeping order in the classroom? I finally resorted to the approach I always use in teaching poetry—I ask the students what they are interested in, what matters to them. It turned out the boy who yelled at me was interested in poetry and math. I brought him my poetry books and we read them together. Two others were interested in sports, so I brought them *Sports Illustrated* magazines to read and had them create collages of their favorite athletes. Soon I was making progress and breathing easier.

After a training session on State Standards, I realized that I could combine art with the basic threads of math, English, history, and science. A light lit up. Why not have the boys design and paint a mural? I spread out a long piece of butcher paper, enough to cover the four walls of the room. It served as a daily reminder that we'd have something fun to do later. First we did the basic stuff, like science in the morning; in the afternoon we painted—for example, different vegetables that were indigenous to the Americas: squash, tomatoes, chiles, corn, and beans. That satisfied the science component. They painted the vegetables flying around Aztec and Mayan temples that were adorned with the number systems of those cultures. That satisfied the history and math components. The poet wrote a poem about ancient América, and other students wrote powerful adjectives on the mural. That satisfied the English component. We eventually presented the mural and poem at a Multicultural Day celebration. The principal was blown away; she'd never seen anything like it.

I finally had the students' trust and respect. A few months later, the poet earned enough positive behavior and school work points to become Student of the Month, twice. Another tough kid—he'd cut up a girl's face with a broken bottle—also earned the award. The new student changed his attitude when he saw his peers doing well and becoming students of the month, and he improved too. I lasted the full school year, though there were still many times I felt like quitting. The poet and the tough kid were released early because of their behavioral improvement and put in foster homes. The rude boy, I heard several years later, was killed in a drive-by shooting.

I wasn't rehired because I never turned in lesson plans. I thought they were useless, and in that setting, they were. But I later learned that without them, the principal's job was on the line. She had no choice. The school was eventually closed because of the irresponsible medical care the kids were getting.

Later in 2000, I came back at the invitation of the arts facilitator, Yvonne Cherbak, to teach poetry to the adults in the prison section and in the Spanish-speaking Latino unit separate from the prison. Walking into the wards (later called "units") was always an adventure, not to mention a demanding exercise in empathy. Some of the Latino students would be lying in the hall having conversations with themselves or yelling at the walls. After a while you get used to it and it all becomes normal—because it is to them.

A beautiful blind Latina therapist was assigned to help me facilitate the poetry class in the Latino unit. Watching her walk down the halls with her white poodle seeing-eye dog, a bright smile on her face, was like something out of a Fellini movie. She moved and looked like a saint, and so I called her "La Santa." As the class continued to grow in popularity, a nurse was added to help out as well. She was a big, tall woman, a Latina with blazing red hair. The left side of her face was tragically disfigured from a fire when she was young. (Fire follows me like a shadow.) Still, she had a beautifully radiant smile.

I had recently received the anthology of Pablo Neruda's love poems from the Enchantress and I decided to bring it to class. I asked the red-haired nurse to read, since my Spanish wasn't that great. She stood beneath a lone light bulb in the dreary room of pale, lime-green walls. She wore a green dress and looked beautiful in all her tragic splendor. I had chosen "I Don't Love You As If You Were a Rose" for her to read. The class of seven was silent. She read as if she was on a grand stage at the Metropolitan Opera, eloquent, poised, in love with each word. Again, I thought of Fellini. I watched La Santa listen intently, wondering what was going through her mind: Memories of a former lover? Of a broken heart? A longing for love? I had never seen a blind person cry before.

The flame-haired nurse finished, her eyes wet. The class remained silent. I softly said, "Gracias." Then I went around the table and asked each student what they liked about the poem. Many had never heard a poem in Spanish before. Some seemed in a daze. Some just smiled.

I got to a young man who I knew couldn't speak very well and rarely tried. I had known him for several years and was impressed with the images he would draw during class. I hadn't intended to ask for his response, but something inside said to ask anyway. He put his pencil down and slowly said in Spanish, "Love is bittersweet. Love heals and scars. Love is life." The nurses were astounded. He had never spoken that coherently before. That was one of the greatest poems I'd ever heard.

While I was still working at Metropolitan I was also teaching at other schools, including Crenshaw Community Day School in South Central. One of my poetry students had been killed in a drive-by shooting and the class was in a state of shock. Earnest was not a gang banger; he was just at the wrong place at the wrong time. I had to pull them out of their depression, so I wrote this poem. I read it to them the day before the funeral.

Dedicated to Earnest (1985–2002), and for my poetry students in Mr. Carter's class at Crenshaw.

A Poet's Job

The young man said to me,
"It doesn't seem real, Mr. G. He was just here. Now he's gone. Just
like that."

"Death makes you ask tough questions," I said. "Like, what is
real? What lasts? Look at me. What do you see? A man. Alive.
Breathing life. Will I last? No. Will you last? No. Does anything
last?" I asked the young man.
"Yes, Mr. G.," he said. "Our spirit."
"Yes, exactly. And the poet's job is to keep that spirit alive, through
poetry. That is job one.
Poetry that sings painful songs of joy.
Of reaching into our hearts and tearing out pieces that will light the
world.
Poetry that reminds us of Earnest's spirit, his dreams, hopes, fears,
tears, and laughter.
Poetry that reminds us of our stupidity, our brutality, our inhumanity.
And poetry that reminds us of our beauty, of our Light, of our Soul.

"And you, young man, you have it in you to write about it. Because,
you . . . are a poet."
"Naw, Mr. G. Not me. I'm no poet."
"Yes you are, young man. Because your heart is connected to the
spirit of life. To the spirit of poetry. And even though we poets
are mortal, remember that poetry . . . is immortal.
It can never die because our spirit needs it.

"Now, go write a poem for Earnest.
He needs to hear from you.
His spirit is probably in a dazed frame of mind.
Trying to figure out what happened.
Trying to figure out how to get back to school.
How to get back home.
How to deal with not being able to return.
"Be brave and write that poem, young man.
Poets are warriors of the heart.
Ease Earnest into a peaceful frame of mind.
Let him know that he is missed, that he is loved.
Let the world know that his spirit is still alive."

Inner City Lessons

ONE OF THE MOST GRATIFYING moments while teaching poetry occurred at Trinity Elementary in South Central. I was assigned to a fifth-grade class, a younger group of students than at Metropolitan. One of my approaches was to give the students an assignment, have them write for half an hour, then everyone would read their work, which I saw as a way to build character, self-confidence, and of course reading skills. This was also part of the state teaching standards for literature. And at the end of the eight-week program, there would be an assembly with parents invited to hear them read. This created tension and anxiety. One girl started to cry when her turn came to read. I told her that it was okay, and she sat down. Afterward I told her that she didn't have to read in class if she was too nervous but to at least read the poem at home, privately. She was a very sweet girl and I was taken by her sincerity and shyness. She actually wrote a very good first poem.

The classes didn't go well. One student complained to his parents that the assignments were too difficult, that I didn't explain the assignments well, and that he was forced to read. The students were English learners, and I kept that in mind by speaking Spanish when necessary. This student just didn't want to do the work.

One assignment, designed to teach similes and metaphors, involved using the senses in a poem. I asked the students to choose a favorite powerful word such as *love, hate, war,* etc. Then I asked, What does it taste like, smell like, sound like, feel like, and look like? What would it say to you if it could speak? What kind of funeral would you have for it if it died? How could it be brought back to life if you wanted it to? How would you take care of it and raise it as your child? This was the basis of most of their poems that would be presented at the culmination assembly.

As the weeks went by and the work improved, the class started to show more confidence. Eventually even the reluctant ones were reading out loud in class. After the assembly we had a little pizza party in the classroom. The girl who had cried at the start came up to me and handed me a letter. She said, "Gracias, Mr. Guevara. This letter is for you." I said, "Thank you for reading. You were great!" When I got in my car that afternoon, I opened the letter. It said, "I didn't know I could write. I didn't know I could speak. I didn't know I had talent. I was never given permission to speak at home. Thank you, Mr. Guevara, thank you for letting me discover me." I was floored. I still have that letter. I treasure it.

I took the CBEST exam four times (I was never good at math) and finally passed, then worked as a substitute teacher for the Los Angeles Unified School District (LAUSD) for four harrowing years. I chose East LA as my turf, but sometimes I was sent to South Central because no one wanted to work there. I soon found out why. The school will remain nameless, but it was near Florence and Normandie, the flash point of the 1992 uprising.

I arrived, checked in at the main office where I was greeted by a staff of vacant, indifferent eyes, received my keys, and headed to the seventh-grade classroom. The teacher had left no lesson plan. As the students started to arrive, I stood by the door to greet them. I said good morning, but they barely glanced at me as they shuffled in, smirking and pushing each other—all except for a few young Latinas, who looked sympathetic. I guess they knew what I was in for.

I tried to introduce myself over the noise and finally slammed a ruler down on the desk, shattering it with a loud crack. They looked up for a second, then continued talking to each other. I gave up on the roll call. There were over thirty in the classroom. I thought back to when I was at Metro with my young boys and how tough they were. But I was with them every day and eventually earned their trust and respect. There was no way that was going to happen here. I asked them to tell me what they'd done in class the day before. A girl raised her hand, which shocked me, and told me they were reading a history book. I asked the class to pull it out. Only a few did. "Okay," I said. "If you don't stop talking, you're going have to go outside." A group of boys rushed the door and left. I called the office to let them know. "Why didn't you go after them?" they asked. "Because it's against the rules," I said.

The class finally managed to read a little, one by one, then, thank God, it was time for recess. We walked out and the boys that had run out joined the class, laughing and chasing each other. After recess I called the office and told them I needed help with the class. I was told there was no one available. So I went into automatic pilot, asking them to read out loud a paragraph at a time in their science books. Some did. Most kept talking and laughing. Finally, mercifully, lunch arrived. I sat at the desk remembering my first day at Metro and how I was shaking in my boots. A couple of very sweet girls stayed and kept me company. I was touched. They could see I was losing it. Just as I was calming down, a flurry of shots rang out nearby. I yelled at the girls to get on the floor. My heart stopped in terror. Then I saw a string of exploding firecrackers fly in. That's what it was, fucking firecrackers. The girls came over to me and consoled me—*me,* when I should have been consoling *them.* "*Así es como son, maestro.* That's just the way they are, teacher." I wanted to hug them, but that, too, was against the rules. I called the office and told them that unless they sent someone to help me, I was leaving. They said that wasn't an option, that I could lose my temporary credential if I left. I told the bored, monotone-voiced office manager that some kids had just thrown handfuls of lit firecrackers into my classroom. "Better than bullets," she said. I walked to the office and handed over the keys to the vacant-eyed manager. "I told you, you can't do that," she said. "I don't need this," I replied. "Goodbye." "Wait," she said, finally waking up. "I'll try to transfer you to a different room. I'll ask the vice principal to take over your class." I was transferred to another room, and as I was leaving the campus at the end of the day those sweet little girls waved goodbye.

A few weeks later I got a call to go to a middle school in East L.A. I had been there before and was reluctant to take the gig, but I needed the work. I arrived, checked into the office, and waited for the keys from another vacant-eyed office manager. She couldn't find them. Not a good sign. I finally arrived at the classroom, and again, no lesson plans. I bit the bullet, waiting for the worst as I stood at the door greeting the students, who only looked straight ahead. Not one looked me in the eye: not a good sign. I introduced myself to the sea of blank and bored faces. At least they weren't yelling and fighting with each other. I asked if someone wanted to take roll. Several yelled yeah. I chose one, and she proceeded. Hah! That's the secret: let *them* do some of my work. So I asked the same girl if she wanted to be the teacher for an hour. She did and she was great. The students actually paid attention to her. Good, I felt like I had a handle on it. That hour ended and a new period began, with a different batch of kids. I continued with my newfound teaching tactic, until the last period. Again they lined up and I greeted them, but no one responded as I expected. No big deal. At the end of the line was a beautiful girl who looked a lot older than she was. Long blonde streaked hair, white t-shirt, tight white jeans, and sneakers. She smiled at me. Great, I thought, someone to help me with the class. But she immediately went to the class phone on the wall and called a friend. I asked her to hang up the phone, but she ignored me, laughing and chatting away. I asked her again, and she responded by placing the phone in the crook of her neck. She then placed her the index and middle fingers in a Victory salute, but sideways up against her eyes, like a mask, then pulling them away and then back to her eyes again, saying, "Be cool, teacher, it's all cool, teacher, it's gonna be okay, be cool, it's all cool," all the while pulling her fingers out and back from her eyes. I wanted to laugh but didn't.

She finally hung up the phone and walked to her seat, asking, "What's up, teacher? What are we doing today?" The others just watched and listened. I saw that she was the star of the class, a perfect helper. I asked her to take roll, and she was doing so when suddenly a boy got up and went to the American flag, pulled it out of its stand, and started marching around the room yelling, "Fuck the teacher, fuck school, fuck the teacher, fuck school," over and over as the class joined in behind him, even the class star, my helper. It was like a scene out of *Blackboard Jungle*. It was shocking and infuriating, but I couldn't help but laugh inside. The demonstration had gone on for a few minutes when the classroom phone started ringing. "Mr. Guevara, this is the vice principal. Do you know your students are throwing books out the window at other students below?" We were on the second floor. "No, sir, I'm trying to stop a riot in my room." "Well, I'm coming up there with the school police to see who threw those books out."

The vice principal and several school police officers walked in. The students were now quietly in their seats: I could almost see the halos over their heads. "I want to know who threw the books out the window," the vice principal demanded. The room was silent. "All of you, pull out a piece of paper and write the names. Fold it and bring it up and put it in this box. Every one of you must walk up here and drop a piece of paper in the box. Got that?" No one moved. "We're going to stay until you all drop a folded piece of paper into the box." One by one they did as he asked. He then looked through the papers and found a few with names. He walked out with the cops following behind. The room erupted in cheers. Not sure why. Did one finger an enemy? Or did they just put down phony names?

I asked my helper, Miss Star, what her plans were for her future. "Oh, I'm gonna enter the Britney Spears look-a-like contest next week and win." "Oh yeah, then what?" "Well, Mister Teacher, my boyfriend is gonna marry me—

'cause I'm pregnant." "Oh, I see. Well, good luck, *m'hija.*" That was the last class I taught for LAUSD.

In all fairness, some teachers left lesson plans, but that was mostly in elementary school. That is where the success of a student will either kick off or never happen. If learning the habit of doing homework doesn't start in elementary school, it most likely won't in middle school and definitely won't in high school. The elementary school students I had were the greatest, filled with wonder, eager to learn, still respectful of adults. But I also saw a trend: Most of the students who weren't doing their homework seemed sullen and rude. Maybe they were embarrassed that they weren't doing as well as the other students. Or maybe their parents were rude at home. Whatever, parents need to work with their kids on their homework or find someone who can help them, since about 45 percent of parents in L.A.'s Latino community only speak Spanish. That's still part of the parenting job, along with the day job. It's all part of the package if you want an educated, civilized child. That's my two cents' worth.

Teaching at UCLA

I GOT A CALL IN 2004 from UCLA saying that Steve Loza had chosen me to teach his Chicano/Latino music class in the upcoming spring quarter. He was leaving to take a visiting position at another university. I jumped at it. A steady gig for a change! They also gave me another course, the development of rock. So, two courses on shit I knew. How sweet was that?!

I knew I could handle the Chicano music, and for the Latino stuff like salsa I could bring in guest speakers. Piece of cake! As for the rock class, perfectionist (or fool) that I am, I wanted to go further than the time it covered, the sixties to the nineties: I wanted to teach the entire history of rock 'n' roll, from slave songs to hip-hop, and with a social political twist. I wound up calling it "The Development of Rock: A Socio-Political History of Popular Music in the U.S." Over two hundred students signed up. Question was, how the hell was I going to teach almost two hundred years of rock history in eleven weeks? The department chair, Tim Rice, suggested Reebee Garofalo's book *Rockin' Out: Popular Music in the U.S.A.* Eleven chapters. Perfect! And so I prepared—big-time. Here was a chance to finally have a decent job teaching my love of rock 'n' roll. It was a blessing. Of sorts.

My homie Moses Mora helped me burn CDs, from the earliest field hollers and slave songs up through the blues, rhythm and blues, rock 'n' roll, soul, funk, disco, punk, and ending with Eminem. The class had listening and writing assignments based on the recordings and the readings from the Garofalo textbook. I had many late nights preparing for each twice-weekly three-hour class. It wasn't easy at 8:30 in the morning. Thank God I had two incredible teaching assistants. The quarter had two big highlights. One was my friend Brendan Mullen, impresario and founder of the punk club the Masque, coming to talk about the early L.A. punk scene and playing records from his collection. The other was when rock mogul Lou Adler graciously agreed to come and talk about the production of the 1967 Monterey Pop Festival and the making of the iconic film.

For the final meeting, I played Howlin' Wolf's "Smokestack Lightning" back to back with Nirvana's "Smells Like Teen Spirit" to illustrate that soul comes through anybody who truly feels the music. For a farewell message I said that no matter what they became in life, doctors, lawyers, whatever, they should keep the spirit of rock 'n' roll by never accepting the status quo. "Break on through to the other side," like Morrison said. "Rip it up," like Little Richard said. They took the final and wrote their evaluations. I felt like I'd won the Rose Bowl.

The Chicano class was straightforward, starting with the '40s *pachuko-boogie* of Lalo Guerrero and Don Tosti, continuing into the '50s with Little Julian Herrera and Ritchie Valens, and hitting the '60s Eastside "Golden Era" with Cannibal and the Headhunters, Thee Midniters, the Blendells, and others. I loved my large office in the brick music building, with its big desk, a great sound system, and the library. But best of all was that it was on the second floor overlooking a courtyard with flowering trees, well-kept gardens, and beautiful women studying in the shade. So this is the life of a college professor? I liked it. Maybe there'd even be a pension if I stayed long enough.

Then evaluations came in, and they were devastating. The rock history class was brutal—I was burned at the stake. I guess I wasn't as great as I thought. One said, "Why was a washed-up rock 'n' roll has-been hired to teach a college course? He was totally unqualified." I fared better with the Chicano music class. But then Professor Loza returned, and I wasn't rehired. There went my college teaching career. But hey, we rocked some mornings with Big Joe Turner, Little Richard, Muddy Waters, Albert King, Otis Redding, Sam Cooke, Sam and Dave, Jimi Hendrix, Frank Zappa, and I even played a Ruben And The Jets track or two. It was a perfect way to begin a morning after a sleepless night, with a state-of-the-art sound system and the volume cranked up. That was the payoff.

Later that year, Peter Sellars introduced me to USC professor Sasha Anawalt. She invited me to talk at a seminar she was giving, "The Latinization of Art and Culture in America." I came up with a presentation called "The Impact of Latin Music on US Pop Culture: From Ragtime to Rock 'n' Roll," which was a live webcast presentation, performance, and comparative analysis of the influence of Afro-Cuban rhythms and music in ragtime, jazz, boogie-woogie, rhythm and blues, rock 'n' roll, rockabilly, and funk. I had a distinguished audience of journalists from around the country, including Jon Pareles (*N.Y. Times*), Agustín Gurza (*L.A. Times*), among others, clapping along to the Afro-Cuban *clave* beat of Bo Diddley's "Bo Diddley," among other examples. After the presentation, Pareles suggested I write a book on the "hidden ingredients of rock 'n' roll."

Becoming a Xikano Tantrik Funk Monk

Like Icarus, I got too close to the heat. The wax melted. The feathers fell.

THROUGH A TWISTED TWIST OF FATE, I got involved with a beautiful businesswoman from Tokyo, only five years younger than me. That was quite an improvement. We met at an Isley Brothers concert at the Greek Theatre. She was in the row in front of me, a couple of seats to my right. I caught her eye when she looked around to see if anyone was watching her squirm and sigh during "Between the Sheets." Then she glanced over when "That Lady" came on, smiling on the line "Look, yeah, but don't touch." We clicked. I smiled back. We clicked again. Then as the audience rose to their feet for "Fight the Power," she was up and waving her fist in the air. On the phrase "Fight it" she glanced over and I shot her a smile while waving my fist too. Finally, a hip mature woman came into my life. Her brother owned a record store in Tokyo that specialized in American R & B. She'd grown up listening to soul music. She said it made her feel sexy and free. She loved that. She seemed to love me too, especially some of the ballads I sang on the Jets' albums. She said she had finally found a "pure heart," as pure as Donny Hathaway's voice. Nobody'd ever made that kind of comparison before, and of course I fell for her.

But after a stormy five-year on-and-mostly-off-again relationship, she said we weren't a good fit. And maybe she was right. How could a Chicano bohemian partner up with an executive? How could a well-paid professional hang with a guy who didn't have a steady job, checkbook, credit cards, or health insurance? It was just as well. In many ways it was her way or the highway, and homie don't play that. Still, I was a pile of shattered soul ashes after the final breakup, immobilized for months, comatose from daily meltdowns. It was bad, real bad—because after all . . . she was right about one thing: I didn't have my shit together.

Once the dust settled, I realized that what we had wasn't love. It was lusty loneliness. She was simply a distraction to my misery. But the dog inside was too proud to see it and admit it. At that point my sex life, as I knew it, dried up and died. I went into a torturous ten-year sex drought. That's right, *ten freakin' years!* In the past, I'd always wound up with another woman within a year after a breakup. But not this time. The drought went on, year after year, and I went into dog shock, angry and horny as a muthafuck, snarling and foaming at the mouth. Man, it was ugly.

After five years of foaming, one day I was on a peaceful meditative walk in Hollenbeck Park when out of the blue I had a realization that kicked me in the nuts. All my life, my identity as a man had been based on my sexual prowess. That's all I thought I ever had to offer a woman in a relationship. Yeah, there was intimacy, I was a nice guy, I could sing and dance, write a little, was a halfway decent dad, and all that. Yet my sum total, the bottom *linea, la pinche neta,* was that I was nothing but an ego-driven sex machine— a dog. And I didn't dig that.

Then gradually over the next few years of brutal psycho-sexual cold turkey, I emerged, butoh-like, from my ego cocoon—transformed as a man. Through painful metamorphosis I learned to accept my life as it is, all of it: the good, the bad, and the fucked-up ugly. I had no other choice but to accept it or pull the trigger, and that wasn't an option, as I said before. So I started reading books on Buddhism, simple doable stuff like Eckhart Tolle. I stopped looking to the past for my identity or to the future for my happiness. I made friends with the present, then changed what I needed to; watched the (moment-to-moment) from the inside out, became a witness to all of my shit all of the time without judging or analyzing, just watching and feeling the emotions and the pain. In time I got better at it. I started to control my ego rather than it controlling me, and in time it started to dissolve: the dog learned to listen and obey. "Sit, gotdammit!"

Through that life-altering trial by fire, I became a Xikano tantrik funk monk and created my own philosophy, the *Tao of Funkahuatl,* for the sake of my slipping sanity and self-respect. The idea was to merge all of me into a new lifestyle concept, to sculpt my spirit, sex, funk, and soul onto the path of the Beloved while living my life as a work of art. A kind of funky Xikano[1]-Asian philosophy mixing elements of *tantra,* the weaving of spirit and sex, onto the path of the Beloved—the heart of God—as in Sufism; the Sixth Dalai Lama ("Lover Lama"), a hero of mine; and *pachukismo.* Like I told the Algerian kids in Lyon, "The *pachuka* and *pachuko* don't care to make something beautiful in their lives, but rather to make *of* their lives a work of art." My life mantra then became: Be a witness to my life while living it as a work of art on the path to the Beloved. In other words, stay real with all I do, say, love, and believe in, then fuckin' live it. No compromises. No bullshit.

Being a celibate cultural funk monk wasn't so bad after all, especially after my Japanese American chiropractor gave me a book about Chinese sexual kung fu—talkin' about multiple orgasms without ejaculating (hence depleting your health, energy, and creative juices). It's amazing what you can accomplish by rechanneling your sexual energy. Don't lust, make art!

Around that time, finally, for the first time in my life, I got a place of my own, a one-bedroom bungalow in Boyle Heights. I still live there. For the first time in my life, too, I was totally independent: financially, spiritually, psychologically, and most importantly, sexually. I give thanks to Miss Tokyo for letting me go. At sixty, I was finally growing up, and I gotta give it up to the *pinche* drought. It turned the dog's rage into supernatural creative juice, enabling me to have the most productive and creative decade of my life.

Yeah, an inadvertent, celibate funk monk turning lust into love through art. The projects I describe in the next chapters were the result of that absurd, sacred alchemy.

1. A spiritualized Chicano activist.

Lust into Art:
Mexamérica and Performing at the Getty

IT WAS TIME TO GET BUSY, seriously busy, if I was going to get out and stay out of my funk, keep an eye on the dog, and do good work. It was time to sculpt and build bridges. It was time to get down—all the way down.

In 2000, together with my *tocayo,* journalist and poet Rubén Martínez, I applied to the Rockefeller Foundation's US-Mexico Fund for Culture program for a grant to coproduce a CD featuring collaborations between musicians, poets, visual artists (including my son Rubencito), and essayists from Mexico City, Tijuana, and East L.A. Here was a chance to create a unique concept album: a transnational musical collaboration between Anáhuac (Mexico) and Aztlán (the American Southwest), a bringing together of cultures in mutual celebration.[1]

The title of the CD, *Mexamérica,* came from a book I'd read in the late '80s, *The Nine Nations of North America* by Joel Garreau. He argues that North America can be divided into nine distinct regions, or "nations," based largely on economic and cultural features. It helped me to solidify my understanding that conventional national and state borders tend to be artificial, and therefore irrelevant.

I was especially interested in Mexamerica, one of Garreau's "nations," which included the southern and Central Valley portions of California as well as southern Arizona, most of New Mexico, the part of Texas bordering

---

1. Anáhuac is the ancient core of Mexico before the invasion. Aztlán is the legendary ancestral home of the Aztec. Chicano activists in the 1960s located it in the U.S. Southwest, and extending into northern Mexico, as an act of solidifying the new political movement.

on the Rio Grande, northern Mexico, and the Baja California peninsula—with my dear Los Angeles as the capital. But I wanted to go beyond the borders of Garreau's Mexamerica. I wanted to create a mythic progressive nation of cultural and political awareness that united Aztlán, the eden of the Aztec in the southwestern United States, and Anáhuac, the ancient Aztec nation that covered most of Mexico. I used an accent over the *e* in Mexamérica to distinguish my "nation" from Garreau's. The material on the collaborative CD would address issues of immigration, indigenous rights, cultural difference, feminism, and transcultural/-national unity, in the hope of breaking down what I called the Great Pocho Wall that I'd experienced back in '74 on my pilgrimage to Mexico.

The album brought Roco from Maldita Vecindad y los Hijos del Quinto Patio (Mexico City) together with Slowrider and Moses Mora (Apache-Xikano) (East L.A./Ventura). It fused the conscious hip-hop of Aztlán Underground (San Fernando Valley) with spoken Xikano-word by Funkahuatl (Boyle Heights) and punk singer Luis Güereña of ¡Tijuana No! (Tijuana). It blended the border and electronic music of the *fusionistas* in Fussible/Nortec Collective (Tijuana) with soul funksters Blues Experiment (East L.A.). Pioneer punks Mercado Negro (Tijuana) played with Los Illegals (East L.A.), with spoken word by Rubén Martínez (Los Angeles). The album included a pop/*son jarocho* duet between Claudia Morfín from Nona Delichas (Tijuana) and Martha Gonzalez of Quetzal (East L.A.). It presented Mex-punkabilly from Calavera (East L.A.) with "Poncho" Nakamura, drummer for the *punkeros* Mexican Jumpin' Frijoles (Tijuana); spoken word by Richard Montoya of the comedy troupe Culture Clash (Los Angeles); and Gerado "Border Gypsy" Navarro along with indigenous percussion by Teca from ¡Tijuana No! (Tijuana). The packaging featured work by visual artists John Valadez, Chaz Bojórquez, Nuke, and Rubén Gabriel Guevara III and was designed by Chachachatzinotl (Fritz) from Tijuana. Essays by Octavio Hernández-Díaz (Tijuana) and María Elena Fernández (Los Angeles) explained the project. The album received strong reviews. Enrique Lavin, writing in *CMJ*, called it "an emotive transfrontera manifesto," and Josh Kun, in the *L.A. Weekly*, described it as "an explosive ride." The CD was released on my label, Angelino Records.

In that same year, I was invited to a planning meeting at the Instituto Cultural Mexicano on Olvera Street to pitch the idea for a *Mexamérica* CD release concert there. They were planning a major conference, *Redescubriendo Nuestra Historia IV: Mexicans in a Multi-Ethnic Los Angeles,* on the early history of women of color in the L.A. labor movement, and the concert would be the closing event. Executive Director Leticia Quezada gave me the green light. I suggested that Rubén Martínez give the conference keynote address and that artist Diane Gamboa and scholars Josh Kun and George Lipsitz be invited as L.A. music history panelists. The concert was called *Las fronteras tiemblan / Rock the Borders*. When it took place, the plaza around the kiosko was packed. This was the first time Olvera Street's *placita* had hosted a concert featuring rock bands from both Mexico and L.A. Most of the bands and singers from the CD performed, including Roco from Mexico City's Maldita Vecindad, Claudia Morfín from Tijuana's Nona Delichas singing with Quetzal's Martha Gonzalez, and members of Ozomatli as special guests. I even got into the mix doing a spoken-word piece from the CD *Sangre de oro / Blood of Gold* with the Blues Experiment, about the spread of AIDS in Mexico from returning immigrants. The night was a blast and a half. After all, ain't that what it's ultimately all about for this sculptor/party animal/alchemist—mixing transcultural/national consciousness into rock 'n' roll cultural cocktails?

The album was coproduced, engineered, and mixed by John Avila, with the assistance of Jennifer Sánchez. Rock record moguls Lou Adler and Richard Foos made donations to help finish it, God bless 'em. The plan was to press only a few hundred copies as a cultural document of the times, but the hauntingly beautiful "Tener o ser" (Have or Be), cowritten and sung by Martha Gonzalez and Claudia Morfín, started getting a lot of college airplay, charting high on CMJ's Latin alternative charts. So I decided to release the CD nationally in 2001. I pressed and shipped a couple thousand copies to the distributor with my own money. He sent back a few unsold copies, and I never received a penny of those that did sell. Burned again, and the *pinche* beat goes on.

In 2011, there was a similar collaboration between Roco/Maldita Vecindad from Mexico City and the L.A. Xikano hip-hop group El Vuh. So eleven years later, Mexamérica lives on and the Great Pocho Wall is still slowly coming down.

My second exercise in art transmutation was *Surcos alternativos / Alternative Grooves from Mexamérica,* a site-specific performance concert for the inauguration of the Getty Museum's 2002 Summer Concert Series. *Mexamérica* had been recently released, so this concert was a perfect opportunity to promote it. It also allowed me to flex my theatrical concept muscles. The invitation came from the event curator, Sabrina Motley. We'd first met at UCLA in a performance class with the avant-opera theater director Peter Sellars. She was his teaching assistant. A new chapter in L.A.

performance theater history was about to happen thanks to the inspiration of Sellars's boldly experimental theater works.

The October afternoon weather was perfect, with a mild breeze blowing in from the west. Cuauhtémoc Danza Azteca, one hundred strong, gathered in the lush garden below the courtyard looking like an Aztec army, their tall pheasant feathers strumming the autumn air, their garments of silver and gold dazzling the eye, their ankles covered in rattles. They began with a private ceremony in the garden, burning the *copal* and blessing the four directions, the heart of the sacred *huehuetl* drum beating softly. Then the procession slowly weaved up the steps into the citadel's courtyard. The warm sun turned rust orange as it set over the distant gray-blue Pacific Ocean. I was reminded that we were on Native land, Tongva land, and my heart roared.

I stood in tearful awe (a word I never use) with my spiritual teacher and homie Moses Mora watching the troupe's grand entrance up the museum steps into the packed courtyard of mostly white spectators. I imagined that this was what it might have looked like when Moctezuma led a procession to greet and welcome Cortés and his army on the outskirts of Tenochtitlan, the Mexika/Aztec capital, in 1519. Two years later, Tenochtitlan fell.

Leading the group were small children dressed in white dresses, shirts, and pants decorated with colorful embroidery, their feet in *huaraches* (sandals), carrying woven baskets of fruit and flowers. Following them were the *danzantes* in their resplendent regalia, strong men and women, their faces solemn and focused in prayer. The *copalera* (*copal* bearer) followed, with the drummers keeping a soft steady beat, steady as a heartbeat. They marched into the center, forming a large circle, and offered another *copal* blessing to the four directions, to the audience, and to the space.

Then the drums exploded in an ear-shattering assault as if cannon were being fired. The *danzantes* leaped and spun in a flurry of power that shook the concrete. They danced, stomped, and flew around the courtyard like a giant flock of eagles, some landing on the rim of a small fountain in a determined act of *reconquista,* a symbolic reclamation of the land. It was a fierce ceremonial prayer honoring a long bloody history. I could hear the ghosts of my ancestors wail and shout their approval of sweet redemption. The flock of eagles circled round and round the courtyard in a final dance of triumph, then slowly descended the stairs in a somber procession as DJ Josh Kun began spinning a track of indigenous drumming with some hip funky grooves on top. The stunned audience didn't know what hit them. It was so good. Welcome to Xikano Aztlán, *cabrones!*

After the DJ set, the soulful sounds East L.A.'s Sabor Factory, with a guest appearance by John Avila on bass, blew out some funky grooves that got the joint jumpin'. The soul of East Los was now most def in da highbrow house of Euro-centrism. I put Fussible, an offshoot of Tijuana's Nortec Collective (who had collaborated with the Blues Experiment on *Mexamérica*), in the patio below, where they spun a set of their wild mix of *norteño, banda,* and techno drum-machine tracks along with some explosive videos. The dance floor swayed and people swooned to the cool hybrid border beats. Something new was happening in music, and it was coming from Tijuana of all places. They created a new kind of respect for my beloved TJ.

Closing out the evening back in the main-stage courtyard was one of the hippest new bands on the scene at the time, Slowrider (who were also on *Mexamérica*). They mixed slinky soulful funk and conscious hip-hop like no one else around. Led by keyboardist and former Beck sideman David W. Gomez, his rockin' crew featured the brilliant rapper Olmeca spitting out his fiery truth. They tore the house down, and the courtyard up, with Carlos Zepeda on guitar, Moises "Big Mo' Ruiz on drums, and Pat Hoed on bass. It was one of their greatest performances ever.

As the band was finishing, the *danzantes* and their *copalera* gathered the dancing audience and led them out to the museum entrance; the drummers were playing along with the band as the conch shell trumpeted out a final blast of gratitude, with the *danzantes* and their rattles kicking up a fitting closing rhythm dancing right alongside them. Members of Cuauhtémoc Danza Azteca stood on the steps holding candles and chanting farewell to the exiting audience, while the children offered fruit and flowers as they passed by.

It all seemed to work, thanks to Capitana Judith García and her *danza* group and all the gods and goddesses who helped the party-ceremony rock. We came, we got down, and we conquered. We departed the Getty in triumph, leaving an indelible symbolic stamp of *reconquista* while honoring our ancestors with Indigenous pomp and funky circumstance. Funkahuatl smiled and whispered . . . *"Con safosssss."*

The Eastside Revue: 1932–2002, A Musical Homage to Boyle Heights

MY NEXT LUST INTO ART TRANSFORMATION occurred thanks to Sojin Kim, a curator at the Japanese American National Museum (JANM) in Little Tokyo. We met at one of the *Redescrubiendo* conference planning meetings in 2000 at the Instituto Cultural Mexicano when she was in the early stages of curating the upcoming (2002) exhibition *Boyle Heights: The Power of Place* at JANM. She had read my 1984 essay "View From the Sixth Street Bridge: A History of Chicano Rock" and invited me to create a listening station on the history of East L.A. music for the exhibition. (You never know who's going to read your stuff, so make it good, *m'hijos.*)

The listening station was a musical mix of tracks spanning seventy years, ranging from '30s klezmer music, to honor the Jewish community of Boyle Heights, to '40s big band swing and *pachuko* boogie-woogie; '50s Mexican *boleros, rancheras,* doo-wop, and early rock 'n' roll; the Golden Age of the '60s Eastside Sound; Chicano rock from the '70s; punk from the '80s; and the experimental hybrids of *son jarocho, cumbia,* funk, and hip-hop of the '90s into the early 2000s. Each track had historical information for the listener posted on a chart.

After the opening, Sojin suggested I curate and produce a free concert in the courtyard plaza. I didn't want to stage just another concert. This was going to be a four-hour nonstop scripted staging—as in an opera, an experimental Xikano opera: a first, thanks again to Peter Sellars.

The Eastside Revue: 1932–2002, A Musical Homage to Boyle Heights emerged, based on the same revue format that I'd used for the shows at the Club

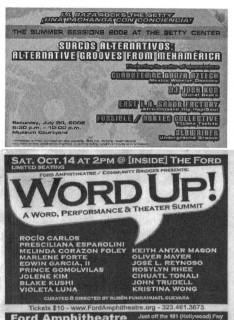

Three flyers by, and courtesy of, Joel Garcia that reflect my cross-cultural performance work: *The Eastside Revue, 1932–2002: A Musical Homage to Boyle Heights,* presented in conjunction with the exhibition *Boyle Heights: The Power of Place* at the Japanese American National Museum, Little Tokyo, Los Angeles, 2002. *Surcos Alternativos: Alternative Grooves from Mexamérica,* presented for the inauguration of the Summer Sessions, Getty Center, Los Angeles, 2002. *Word Up! A Word, Performance, and Theater Summit,* presented in the Ford Amphitheatre, Hollywood, 2007.

Lingerie in '83 and UCLA in '85. The event took place three months after the Getty concert piece. I was on a roll, and the dog was asleep.

I had the music; now I needed the cast of players. The script would come after I had a cast in place. All sets were twenty minutes long, except for Tierra's, and it all ran smoothly with my homie Willie Loya cracking the whip as stage manager. Also, a thank you to Claudia Sobral, JANM Public Programs Director at the time, who was essential in the production of the event.

I was able to secure all the major players at the time, with the exception of Ozomatli and Quetzal, who were touring. Lalo Guerrero, the godfather of Chicano music, performed his classic *pachuko* boogie-woogie '40s tunes (in a wild purple zoot suit, no less!) backed by the Skip Heller Ensemble, who also played some cool klezmer music before Lalo hit the stage. This, sadly, was Lalo's next-to-last concert before he passed. Needless to say, he rocked the house. Roosevelt High School graduate (class of 1940), poet, historian, and musician George Yoshida, who I believe was in his 80s, read a poem about his days at Roosevelt and his unjust incarceration at Manzanar backed by East L.A. Taiko, led by Maceo Hernandez, with the Reverend Brian Qualls on guitar. Reverend Qualls was a minister from 1995 to 2004 at Mt. Carmel Missionary Baptist Church, the first African American church in Boyle Heights, founded by his great-grandfather, Rev. Clem Howard, when it was known as Mt. Olive Baptist Church. Prior to becoming a minister, Reverend Qualls played guitar with '70s bands Sly, Slick, and Wicked; Brian Qualls and the Shades; and the Warriors. In our concert, he played a blistering gospel blues tune that he'd written, totally smokin' it. In the '50s and '60s segment, two of the original members of Cannibal and the Headhunters, Richard "Scar" Lopez and Robert "Rabbit" Jaramillo, performed a hair-raising set along with the group's original guitarist, Andy Tesso. The East L.A. Revue All-Stars, made up of members of the Atlantics, the East L.A. Jaguars, and the Masked Phantom Band, also covered the '50s and '60s. They brought back sweet memories of my early introduction to rock 'n' roll as a budding singer. Alice "Bag" Armendáriz, the first Chicana to lead a punk band in the late '70s, the Bags, performed with her '90s Chicana feminist acoustic folk trio, Las Tres, which was filled out by Teresa Covarrubias (the Brat) and Angela Vogel (Oddsquad). East L.A.'s unofficial poet laureate, Marisela Norte, introduced Las Tres with a poem, while *pachuko* punks Los Illegals, resplendent in zoot suits, along with the Brat later represented the '80s punk scene to a loud, enthusiastic reception. The '90s were represented by *la chula musa* folk-rock chanteuse Lysa Flores, the *jarocho*-klezmer punk of Ollín, the salsa funk hip-hop of East L.A. Sabor (they'd dropped Factory from their name), the rock funk hip-hop fusionists Slowrider, and—covering everything from the 1940s to the present—the mighty East L.A. perennials, Tierra.

Cuauhtémoc Danza Azteca once again opened the event with a four-directions ceremony, first asking permission from the Tongva ancestors. During the concert they marched down First Street protesting Columbus Day, which happened to be on that day. That was a very cool, unexpected moment. As I was closing the concert—on time—the JANM staff came up and surprised me with a beautiful birthday cake as Tierra played a funky "Happy Birthday to You" with everyone singing along. I loved it. This event was another one of my birthday presents to myself and to my city of angels. Five days later I turned sweet sixty.

L.A. Times Profile of Boyle Heights

SOMETIME IN LATE 2005, I got a call from poet Marisela Norte saying the *L.A. Times* was looking for someone to write about Boyle Heights. She suggested I take it on. I was broke and desperate at the time, as usual. So I sat down to write and came up with this:

"Ta-maaa-lehhs! Ta-maaa-lehhs!" The strolling sidewalk vendor wakes me with sweet memories of my youth as the neighborhood rooster joins in, welcoming the day. "*Dos de pollo!*" I yell out, thanking my ancestors for inventing the tamale, beautifully symbolizing the body and heart of humanity.

That's my breakfast in Boyle Heights. Afterward, I walk to the corner of Mott and Avenida César Chávez to pick up the morning paper, and I hear the pachuko boogie of Lalo Guerrero from the '40s, the Eastside Sound of Thee Midniters and Cannibal and the Headhunters from the '60s, and the punk of The Brat and Thee Undertakers from the '80s—all of them linked by mariachis serenading at quinceañeras and endless wedding dances. The Paramount Ballroom (now Casa Grande), home to these legendary performers, was, and still is, the epicenter of Eastside memories.

Heading west on Avenida César Chávez, I stop at the Bahia, a restaurant where the cooking recalls my dear grandmother's love. I hear rockin' sounds coming from the Ollín Music Conservatory as I pass a 24-hour pawnshop, a wedding chapel, a punk boutique, a tattoo parlor, a health food store, and a Chinese restaurant. At the corner of Soto and César Chávez, the heart of the Eastside, presides the mural "El Corrido de Boyle Heights" by the East Los Streetscapers. Months ago the mural was tagged beyond recognition. What disrespectful idiocy! But on this day, a miracle: painter-muralist Paul Botello is faithfully restoring it.

I used to live on Boyle Avenue, named for Andrew Boyle. In 1858, he bought a parcel of the land that had been the 1781 Mexican settlement called El Pueblo de Los Angeles, and built a home on what became this avenue.

After his death in 1871, his son-in-law, William H. Workman, subdivided the area and named it Boyle Heights.

My Boyle Avenue apartment was down the street from Mariachi Plaza, where I hired mariachis for my youngest son's first birthday party. (Easy to do, but not cheap. They don't play for beer like garage rock bands.) Also on Boyle is the International Institute, founded in 1914 to help Russians, Italians, Mexicans, Chinese, Japanese, and Jews get established. Its mission reflects the neighborhood's distinction as Los Angeles's most multiethnic community from the '20s through the '50s.

Now I live on Pennsylvania near Mott, surrounded by elegant Victorians and humble homes, some with front yards of cactus, chickens, and corn. Gentle, strong people, inspiring murals, and music mix with a turbulent social history that includes the forced "repatriation" of Mexican Americans in the '30s and the unjust incarceration of Japanese Americans in the '40s. Hail Mary's, Buddhist chants, Jewish prayers, gospel hallelujahs, oldies, hip-hop, *boleros*, *corridos*, and *rancheras*—they all lift and carry broken spirits, memories, and dreams.

My barrio speaks truth as it sings of love and betrayal. And if you listen closely to its tenacious, fragile legacy, its scarred heart touches you, and heals.

When I went to Mexico with Cheech, in 1987, for the *Born in East L.A.* film promo tour, we stopped in Ajijic, a small town by Lake Chapala in Chapala, Jalisco. We visited their small Catholic church, where I saw an altar and an encased shrine dedicated to their own local *virgencita*. Seeing that a town could have their own Blessed Virgin, I thought: why not Boyle Heights? In 2006, I wrote the following poem from the CD *The Tao of Funkahuatl* and was inspired by that visit and realization.

La Virgencita de Boyle Heights

Virgencita
Your serene sensual smile breathes eternal bliss
Carries me through streets
Of hope and despair
Of pain and *alegría*
Through broken homes and dreams

Virgencita
Your immaculate soul breathes through the sacred pores of my
　　sin-scarred skin
I can taste it in the heat of chiles and passion
In the sweet smell of fresh *masa* and lipstick
In the ecstasy of *mole poblano* and salvation

In the pure innocence of
quinceañeras
bodas
bautismos
In the stark bitter truth of death

Virgencita
I see, sense, and feel your elegant incandescent grace
Radiate and shine
Through the playful eyes and *sonrisas* of the hungry children
In the desperate tears of
los desesperados
en los ojos sabios de los abuelitos y abuelitas
In the primal soulful *grito del mariachi*
In the lurid glow of morning neon
In the perfect promise of tomorrow

Virgencita
Please watch over me
Cover me
With your benevolent luminous angel baby eyes
Follow me
With your generous divine compassion
Lead me
To the altar of your tender heart
To forgiveness
To love

Virgencita
Please never forget or leave
Boyle Heights
Land of 1000 *culturas*
Land of 1000 memories
Land of 1000 dances
Land of 1000 dreams

Virgencita preciosa de Boyle Heights
Please hear me
I belong to you
And
We belong together
Por vida
Con safos

Funkahuatl's Absurd Chronicles

A SERIES OF PERFORMANCE COLLABORATIONS followed that kept me busy and my dog at bay. They started with Josh Kun, the young journalist I'd met in San Francisco in '97 and collaborated with at UCLA in '98. Our first experiment in 2001, was a mock interview on the stage of the Mark Taper Auditorium at the Los Angeles Central Library downtown. Artist Diane Gamboa and Los Illegals were also on the bill, which was titled *El Lay: Music from the Eastside.* Josh suggested we reimagine the famous Mel Brooks and Carl Reiner comedy skit "The 2,000-Year-Old Man." But where Reiner had asked Brooks about his alleged two thousand years on the earth, Josh interviewed Funkahuatl, the unknown Aztec God of Funk, about the ancient days in Mexico all the way up to the present: a circular full-tilt-boogie music-history farce. We called the piece "Funkahuatl: The 2,001-Year-Old Man."

Josh sat all professorial on a stool and introduced me with an outrageously long and funny bio about my being discovered in a freezer at King Taco, perfectly preserved for the past few thousand years. I then entered wrapped in my weathered plastic performance bag, crawling across the stage floor in my best butoh glacial slide. I wish I could have seen the looks on the audience's faces. I reached my stool, slowly climbed up, and sat, my face covered in a mask of an eagle my son Rubencito had made in his middle school art class. Josh then asked me what it's been like the past five hundred years or so, since the invasion. I told him I saw Cortés land and saw him try to seduce Malintzin (a.k.a La Malinche), a soul singer in a local band, Los Moonlights. I then told of her getting back at Moctezuma for imprisoning her boyfriend, Funkahuatl, which led to the downfall of Tenochtitlan. He'd been locked up for rapping about the uncool practice of offering the hearts of virgins to the gods. You get the idea. It was crazy, absurdist shit, all the way to a story about being chased by the INS that very morning. That was followed by my usual lighting of the *copal* and blessing the four directions before busting into "C/S" with Los Illegals backing me up.

We revived the idea three years later with "Funkahuatl: The 2,004-Year-Old Man" in one of Walt Disney Concert Hall's performance spaces. For this performance, I didn't use the plastic bag. After being introduced with the same crazy intro, I walked out wearing shades and an enormous Aztec dancer's headdress that my homie Moses Mora let me use. The feathers almost touched the ceiling. I probably crossed the line with that one. The interview was similar to the previous one except that I talked more about how Funkahuatl helped get Chicano rock started. Folks were cracking up big-time. It felt good. I had never done comedy before. For the closer, Rubencito joined me on "C/S," with us trading off verses. We rocked the joint. Walt Disney had no idea what hit him.

The Iraq War

ON MARCH 20, 2003, THE WAR with Iraq broke out, based on the lies that Iraq was harboring weapons of mass destruction and that Saddam Hussein was responsible for 9/11. I was furious. It was nothing but a punk cowboy slapback for the humiliating 9/11 attack. I was ready to fight back against these weapons of mass deception. I quickly organized a benefit concert for Latin@s Against the War in Iraq, a coalition of students, teachers, artists, and workers led by '6os activist and Chicano Moratorium organizer Carlos Montes. Eight days after the war broke out we staged *Mexamérica por la Paz* at Self Help Graphics & Art in East L.A. I enlisted Roco (from Maldita Vecindad), now dubbed DJ Roco and His Cyber Pachukote Sound System, who presented a blistering set of antiwar tracks. With him was Video Jockey Leonardo Bondoni, providing dramatic protest footage of previous antiwar marches set to Roco's soundtrack. Suddenly it felt like the '6os and Vietnam again. East L.A. punkers Union 13 and Slowrider performed, while spoken word was provided by Mixpe from *Memories of Boyle Heights,* actress Mónica Sánchez, Yaotl from Aztlán Underground, Gerardo "Border Gypsy" Navarro, and my son Rubencito, who was a student at Los Angeles County High School for the Arts at the time. Graff pioneer Nuke created a 10' × 10' mural that served as the stage backdrop. Sound was provided by Emiliano "Meno Man" Martinez (son of John Martinez from Ruben And The Jets) and a stirring opening blessing ceremony was presented by Cuauhtémoc Danza Azteca. It was well attended. But it didn't stop the war.

Iraq was heavy on the minds of the community. We were angry that the loss of innocent lives would be for naught. The cost of fighting the war would redirect money that could be better used at home for education and the arts. But the Feds know how to manipulate fear to reach their ends: world military dominance and maintaining a foothold in an oil-rich region were their real goals. We now know it was a colossal failure, as I expected. You can't export democracy with a gun in your hand. Although we felt impotent at the time, we were determined to face it and fight it the best we could through our work.

Cross-cultural Friendships and Protests

THE FIRST TIME I COLLABORATED with Nobuko Miyamoto (founder, artistic director, and performer of Great Leap) was when she asked me to join the ensemble performance piece *Memories of Boyle Heights,* directed by Dan Kwong, in conjunction with *Boyle Heights: The Power of Place* exhibition at JANM. It opened in November of 2002 and ended in early 2003. The piece consisted of monologues by residents of Boyle Heights recounting their memories of living there. Meeting Nobuko marked the beginning of my introduction to the Little Tokyo progressive Japanese American Community that reinvigorated my activism.

Through *Memories* I also met Kathy Masaoka, an activist in the '60s who later became part of the campaign to demand reparations from the federal government for the more than 120,000 Americans of Japanese ancestry who were incarcerated during World War II. That campaign was led by the National Coalition for Redress/Reparations, later known as Nikkei for Civil Rights and Redress (NCRR), of which she was a member. They eventually got a bill passed by Congress, which provided monetary reparations and a formal apology from the government in 1988. Their dedicated perseverance paid off. Right on brothers and sisters!

In response to 9/11, NCRR activists, including Kathy, decided that they needed to get to know Muslim Americans and Arab Americans and learn more about Islam as an act of solidarity. After all, Japanese Americans were once scapegoats like Middle Easterners had now become. They called for the candlelight vigil, inviting other Little Tokyo organizations to participate, including JANM, the Japanese American Citizens League (JACL), and the Japanese American Cultural and Community Center. After the vigil, a meeting was held with folks who wanted to do more follow-up. That's when activists Mike Yanagita, Denise Uyehara, Vy Nguyen, Karen Ishizuka, and Bob Nakamura came on board to form the (later called) NCRR 9/11 Committee. Maher Hathout from the Muslim Public Affairs Council (MPAC) spoke at a forum sponsored by radio station KPCC and held at JANM, advocating dialogue between the communities. Meetings were then organized with various organizations, including South Asian Network, Arab American Anti-Discrimination Committee, Council on American-Islamic Relations, and MPAC.

When the organizations met with MPAC, Kamal al-Shamshieh, the community representative, suggested they share a meal during Ramadan, a month-long religious fast with light meals at sunrise and sundown. That was the beginning of a series of powerful annual *Breaking the Fast* observances between the two communities, organized by the NCRR 9/11 Planning Committee, the first one taking place in December of 2001. I participated in two of those observances. My first participation was during the third annual *Breaking of the Fast* in 2003. Nobuko Miyamoto and I collaborated in creating the concept and direction for the choral-poem performance *To All Relations: Sacred Moon Songs* and presented it at Senshin Buddhist Temple in South Central L.A.

The event began with Mexika Sundancer Moses Mora playing a hand drum and singing a Chumash song as a greeting to the audience arriving in the courtyard. The performance ensemble consisted of Muslim, Latino, African American, and Japanese American poets and dancers, who slowly entered the main room of the temple in a line from the back, then moved along the right wall to the front where they recited poems. They continued in slow motion to the left side of the temple, along the wall, and back to the exit. In this way, the performers created a large circle within the temple. The most dramatic and chilling moment occurred at the end when Nobuko's son, Kamau, a Japanese American–African American Muslim, sang the call to prayer, signaling that the day's fast had ended—probably the first time *that* had ever happened in a Buddhist Temple.

A light buffet had been set up in the social hall, where everyone ate. I was reminded that during WWII some Japanese Americans hid their belongings in the back rooms of the hall while they were held in concentration camps. After the meal, there was more poetry and music. MPAC offered their gratitude. The audience then gathered in the courtyard for a solemn closing candlelight ceremony, with everyone walking slowly in a circle singing a song of solidarity. It was quite moving.

In 2004, after my teaching debacle at UCLA, Nobuko Miyamoto invited me to collaborate on a new cross-cultural full-theater-production performance work, a revision of *Sacred Moon Songs* for her Great Leap performance art group. I codirected the piece and cowrote the lyrics for the title song. My ambition to create a theater piece to follow *Who Are the People?* was finally realized, over thirty years later. It was way overdue.

The cast was made up of nonprofessional actors, including a few from the *Memories of Boyle Heights* cast. I was thrilled that one of L.A.'s finest poets, Kamau Daáood, would also participate. We had performed together on a fundraising bill for radio station KPFK (Pete Seeger headlined), and I was dazzled by his raw poetic power.

The revised piece focused on the similarities between Muslim and Buddhist prayer beads, the Iraq war, the WWII Japanese American concentration camps, the history of Mexican deportation and immigration in the United States, and the Guantánamo Bay prison. A small band of musicians accompanied the work, including legendary singer "Atomic" Nancy Matoba and pianist and arranger Derek Nakamoto. The production ran for four nights at East-West Players in Little Tokyo and is without a doubt my greatest theater accomplishment so far. In it, I presented a poem I wrote about the first Latino killed in the Iraq War.

Tree of Life
(For Marine Lance Corporal Jesús Suárez del Solar, his father, widow, and son)

March 27, 2004
The bloodstained Iraqi earth where
Cpl. *Jesús Suárez del Solar* died
Cries deep and trembles
Bleeding with terror

The ancient ravaged earth
Chokes on tears, bits of flesh, blood, and bone
While destiny dances a death dream

Screams of men, women, and children
Have blurred and charred the sun's rays
Turning the sky into a howling black hell hole

The stars have burned out
The gods and angels are hiding
Only the moon remains

Alone
Waiting for a miracle

February 14, 2004
A small group gathered
In Escondido, California
Led by *Jesús's* father
To plant a pepper tree in his honor

Iraqi, Tijuana, and California soil embraced
As Aztec dancers consecrated the breathing earth
With prayers
Danza
Offering burning sage to
Mother Earth
To help heal her shattered heart

Suddenly a song is heard from the
Sacred ground as the pepper tree is planted

A flock of doves are released

Sing Mother Earth
Let your sacred song
Smash and swallow the madness and horror of war

Let your sacred song bless
Jesús
And all fallen soldiers and civilians

Bless their wasted blood and tears and
Let them nourish this humble
Pepper Tree of Life and Peace
So we can breathe its spirit
Its medicine
Its power
So we can breathe the miracle
So we can breathe the Creator

The same year I was asked by the 9/11 Planning Committee and MPAC to
help organize the cultural component for the fourth annual Ramadan
observance, *An Angelino Gathering for Ramadan* at Higashi Honganji
Buddhist Temple along with Centenary United Methodist Church in Little
Tokyo. I suggested we have an interfaith panel discussing their particular

points of view regarding the war and the turbulence between religious communities in the country at large.

Calling the panel "Communities under Siege, Keeping the Faith," we recruited Imam Saadiq Saafir of Masjid Ibaadillah, Reverend Nori Ito of Higashi Honganji Buddhist Temple, Father Michael Kennedy of the Dolores Mission, Rabbi Naomi Levy of Nashuva, Mexika Sundancer Moses Mora, and Reverend Mark Nakagawa of Centenary United Methodist Church. Over three hundred attended at Higashi. The altar, radiating with glowing gold religious objects, presented a dramatic backdrop to the long table of panelists dressed in their various religious garments. I'd never seen anything like that before.

The panel discussion and Q & A were lively, candid, and inspiring. At the end of the meeting, the Muslim call to prayer rang through the temple signaling the break of the fast. Man, it was too much. We later crossed the street to Centenary United Methodist church, where a potluck dinner of delicacies from around the world was served. Then the intercultural performance began, featuring the Chikara Daiko Taiko Group, the Dolores Mission Youth Poetry Collective (my Arts 4 City Youth poetry students), the Avaz International Dance Theatre with Brandy Maya Healy, and Great Leap with Nobuko Miyamoto. What a day—an L.A. interfaith, intercultural exchange embracing the possibilities of Angelinohood.

. . .

I continued my artistic and activist collaborations with the NCRR 9/11 Committee, and in 2006 we organized a march in support of Japanese American Lt. Ehren "Erin" Watada. He was facing a court-martial for refusing to deploy to Iraq, on the grounds that he believed the war to be illegal—the first commissioned officer to do so. He contended that under the doctrine of command responsibility, participation would make him a party to war crimes. I was deeply impressed with this guy. Finally, someone standing up to the illegal war *and* the U.S. Army. What courage!

We gathered, some four hundred strong, at the Friendship Knot peace statue on the corner of Second and San Pedro in Little Tokyo. The group marched east on Second, turned left through Japanese Village Plaza (waking up the tranquil patrons) onto First Street, then right on Central and south to Third, chanting "Free Erin Watada!" Drums were beating and prayer symbols clanging as Lt. Watada's mother, Carolyn Ho, and members of NCRR walked in front, carrying a large protest banner with his picture on it. My job was to monitor and direct the marchers to Higashi Honganji on Third and Central, for a rally in the social hall. It was one of the most powerfully emotional marches I had ever been in: marching through Little Tokyo with a group of folks many of whom had family members who had been incarcerated in the concentration camps during WWII but went on to survive and thrive with dignity and honor. They were now marching and fighting to preserve for others the rights that had previously been denied to them. Now, that's democracy, courage, and honor in action.

I also helped to organize the cultural component of the rally. Quetzal performed a rousing set. A smokin' hip-hop duet featuring Olmeca, together with poet and activist traci kato-kiriyama, rounded out the night. Erin's mother gave a stirring and loving speech in praise of her son's courage in standing up for his principles. She offered her immense gratitude for everyone's support.

In 2007, the court-martial of Lt. Watada ended in a mistrial. His defense team brilliantly outperformed the court, which couldn't argue against Erin's position. He was discharged in 2009. The truth won out. It was a rare victory for the people.

To illustrate the historical solidarity between L.A.'s Mexican American/ Chicano and Japanese American communities, NCRR asked me to help organize a screening at the new location of Self Help Graphics & Art in Boyle Heights of the film *Stand Up for Justice: The Ralph Lazo Story*. The film was about a Belmont High School Mexican American–Irish American teenager who snuck into Manzanar to be with his incarcerated homies. Talk about brotherhood in action! In 1944, he was elected Manzanar High School student body president. That August, ironically, he was drafted into the army, and later he was awarded the Bronze Star for heroism in combat.

The documentary film *Maceo: Demon Drummer from East L.A.*, produced and directed by John Esaki, was also screened. It tells the incredible story of Maceo Hernandez (who was in *Memories of Boyle Heights*), a Chicano from East L.A. who learned to play *taiko* drums at a Buddhist temple in Montebello. He eventually was recruited to perform with the internationally famous Ondekoza *taiko* group from Japan, who saw him perform while on tour in the United States. He moved to Japan to begin the arduous physical training required by the ensemble. While running one day on a workout, however, he was struck in the leg by a steel pipe that accidentally rolled off the back of a truck. The leg had to be amputated. That didn't stop him: he trained harder than ever. Eventually he came back to East L.A., and later he finished the New York Marathon (twice) with a prosthetic leg. He now performs with his band East L.A. Taiko blending traditional *taiko* drumming with jazz and rock. Maceo is an extraordinary soul survivor and a true hero of mine.

. . .

In 2012, Nobuko and the band Quetzal began a collaborative series of cross-cultural performances at Japanese American Cultural and Community Center, called FandangObon. It is a celebration with Mexican *son jarocho* (music with African roots), African music and dance, and also observing Obon, the Japanese day of honoring the ancestors. I was asked to write and read poems at these events. The following poem was presented in 2015.

FandangObon: An Informal Xikano Haiku

OBON

Boom! Boom! Kapow! Boom!
Kapow! Pow! Pow! Kapow! Boom!
Japanese *taiko*

Obon has arrived!
Drums calling ancestors home
Time to reconnect

Obon lifts the skies
Ritual ceremony
Drums dream new dances

Boom! Boom! Kapow! Boom!
Kapow! Pow! Pow! Kapow! Boom!
Boom! Boom! Kapow! Boom!

FANDANGO

Fandango Indio
African, Mexican roots
Sacred synthesis

All night rituals
Music, poetry, and dance
Social catharsis

Touching ancestors
Songs and poems of honor
Humanity sings

Life rites of passage
Weddings, births and funerals
Procession of love

FANDANGOBON

Mexico, Japan
Africa Diaspora
Alchemy of soul

Drums, rhythms, heart beats
Blood pushing our souls to dance
Life compels movement

Welcome to the dance
Hold my hand dear ancestor
Dance! Dance! Laugh! Spin! Rise!

Boom! Boom! Pa! Pa! Boom!
Para bailar la Bamba
With a little grace

Pa! Pa! Pa! Pa! Pa!
Orisha, Yoruba, sing!
Heal histories' wounds

Fandango Obon
Poly-cultural remix
Jammin' a prayer

Angelino souls
Transforming ethnic borders
Birthing a new world

Manzanar Pilgrimage

IN 2008, MIKE YANAGITA, not only an organizer with NCRR but also a performer in the theatrical version of *Sacred Moon Songs,* invited me to participate in the annual Manzanar Pilgrimage. The event began in 1969 as a way of honoring the Americans of Japanese ancestry who were incarcerated there during WWII, and continues to take place every year on the last Saturday in April. Mike and his homeboys Victor Shibata, Steve Nagano, and Michael Akhtab had been going up to Manzanar for years. The site of the former concentration camp is about 250 miles north of L.A., in the Owens Valley. They usually camp out nearby the night before (the eastern Sierra and Mt. Whitney overlook the site), attend the Saturday ceremony, and return home on Sunday. I accepted the invitation as an act of solidarity, although I had never camped out before. I'm a serious city slicker and can't stand being cold.

We pitched camp in the Upper Grays Meadow campground, on land that was once Paiute country, land that had been inhabited by Native Americans for over ten thousand years. A small creek ran alongside our camp, where Mike cast his fishing line. I felt serene and peaceful watching him by the stream. A strong sense of freedom came over me that only the outdoors can give. Then I thought of those who were incarcerated only a few miles below our campsite, imprisoned below the majestic High Sierra. What a cruel paradox! One reason the guys camp out is to endure the cold nights in commemoration of what incarcerees suffered. We built a big fire and grilled corn wrapped in tin foil, vegetables, fish, and various meats. Steve cooked up some mean *saba* mackerel that floored me with its buttery flavor. I used chopsticks for the tamales I'd brought to share; although I could have used a fork, I prefer the sticks because you eat slower and the food tastes better. We sat around the campfire feasting away, talking about life, work, and what we would do in retirement. "Retirement?" I said. "That's what white people do." We all cracked up.

Mike let me borrow his sleeping bag and I found a flat spot by the fire. Everybody turned in, but I stayed up with a cup of wine and some hash watching the fire burn down like an opera of mortality. Slowly the glowing embers would die, only to be revived with a breath of air and valiantly fight and gasp for their lives. Now glowing, catching fire, reaching up to the sky, then grasping, gasping, fading, fading, to black; but then another sudden breath of air and they would light up, glow, catch fire, and reach for the sky again, burn, burn, burning alive as I cheered them on. I sat mesmerized, watching the death of the fire. Embers are fierce and subtle spirits. They don't die easy. They reminded me of those who were incarcerated at Manzanar, and of my many brushes with fire and my defiant determination to stay alive.

I kept my clothes and tennis shoes on and wrapped myself in my *tío* Lolo's heavy leather jacket. I zipped up the sleeping bag, lay back, and bam! I saw the stars shining like polished diamonds against the onyx black sky. Man, it was better than the Griffith Park Observatory space show. You don't see stars like that in L.A. I thought of the Aztecs and remembered that they worshiped the stars with human sacrifices. Since human blood is the most precious of liquids, they believed that sacrificing their blood would appease the gods, who in gratitude would lubricate the movement of the stars—a kind of a cosmic WD-40. They believed if the stars stopped moving, their time would be up. It kind of makes sense.

I drank and smoked some more to fall asleep in the cold night air, then flew into incredible dreamtime. I dreamed of my history classes back at Berendo Junior High when I first learned about World War II, looking at the dramatic, harsh black-and-white photos of the atrocities in the German death camps. There was no mention of Manzanar. Then somehow my teacher's beautiful legs appeared in my dreams.

The following morning we ate scrambled eggs, ham, bacon, potatoes, and any leftovers we could find, washing it all down with coffee and tea. There's something about hot food cooking in the wilderness that brings out the primal. We cleaned up and set out for Manzanar.

Driving down from the mountain campsite, we could see the Owens Valley stretched out below, between the Sierra Nevada behind us to the west and the Inyo Mountains to the east. It is a dry, desolate desert covered in sagebrush, with trees only along creeks and patches of small yellow springtime flowers only where the soil has been disturbed. How poetic. The summers are scorching, often over 100 degrees; the winters are windy and freezing. It is an unforgiving, hostile, yet beautiful landscape, overlooked by the towering snow-capped Sierra Nevada sawing through the ice blue sky—a surreal, cruel juxtaposition. Only about twenty minutes from Grays Meadow, a preserved gun tower greets as you drive onto the grounds, a stark reminder of what conditions were like there. Living under armed guard having committed no crime would have driven me crazy.

We gathered at the cemetery, on the western edge of the camp. It is marked by a monument built by Ryozo Kado in 1943. An inscription on the front reads 慰霊塔 (Soul Consoling Tower); on the back are the words "Erected by the Manzanar Japanese" on the left and "August 1943" on the right. Survivors and other visitors leave offerings of personal items as mementos to honor the dead. On the morning we visited, an interfaith prayer ceremony was held to memorialize those who had died there, conducted by Buddhist, Christian, and Muslim clergy. No shouting, no anger, no rancor: only poised grace.

That year, NCRR invited a large contingent of Muslim Americans from MPAC to attend as guests. They wanted to learn the history of the Japanese American incarceration experience and about the abuses of an unpredictable federal government. What a noble joint effort and act of Angileno brother-sisterhood. The tradition continues.

After the interfaith prayer ceremony, there was a program with *taiko* drumming, *ondo* dancing, and speeches honoring individuals past and present. Mary Nomura, a former incarceree known as "The Songbird of Manzanar," performed. She was in her eighties, but her voice was still strong. The drama of the Manzanar saga hit me hard while she sang "I Can't Give You Anything but Love, Baby." After all, that's all they had. I felt a heart-breaking surge of sentiment that cemented my love and respect for their heroic emotional stamina. Talk about soul, baby.

A week before we were scheduled to leave for the 2012 pilgrimage, home-boy Victor Hujio Shibata suddenly passed away. With typical Japanese humility, he had never told me about his illustrious history of activism in the JA community. He was a founding member in 1969 of the Yellow Brotherhood, which reached out to drug-addicted gang youth in his tough Crenshaw district neighborhood. He was also one of the inspirations for, and a cofounder of, the Manzanar Pilgrimage. He never mentioned any of this. I only learned about it at his memorial service. The Crenshaw district in south-west Los Angeles was made up primarily of African Americans, Japanese Americans, and some whites. Victor spoke in a hip Black street accent, and

Manzanar cemetery monument built by Ryozo Kado, Owens Valley, California, 1943. Photo by Rubén Funkahuatl Guevara, 2009. Courtesy of the Funkahuatl family archive.

we got along very well. Mike left a photo of him on the cemetery monument on our last pilgrimage.

As we were about to leave the monument, a group of runners arrived led by veteran JA activist Mo Nishida. The annual 250-mile run from Little Tokyo to Manzanar known as the 50/500 (it was first run on the fiftieth anniversary of the incarceration). It began as a spiritual unity and prayer run inspired by the Native American transcontinental Peace and Dignity run. Mo and Victor were the originators of the Manzanar run. We told Mo the sad news, then the runners, Mo, Mike, and I lined up in front of the monument. We each stepped forward and said a few words about Victor. Mo was the last to speak. He waved burning sage and moaned in grief for his fallen brother, even though they had had bitter disagreements in the past and had not spoken in years. Mike said he had never seen Mo cry before.

·   ·   ·

After that visit I wrote a short story, "Yuriko and Carlos," as a way of honoring those who were incarcerated. It's about two teenagers from L.A.'s Roosevelt High School, a Mexican American boy and a Japanese American girl, who fall in love right before the war. It took second place in the first annual Little Tokyo Historical Society's short story contest and was later published in the Japanese American newspaper *Rafu Shimpo*. It was my first piece of fiction. Here is an excerpt:

> After a long workout, I headed to the Ebisu to see my girl. It was a warm and sunny day in December, and I was feeling all fine and *firme*. Then, while I was enjoying some miso soup, the radio blared out, "Japan has attacked Pearl Harbor!" Everyone in the restaurant froze in dead silence. It felt like the world had come to an end. I grabbed Yuriko's hand and squeezed it tight. We just stared into each other's eyes. We couldn't talk. Nobody could. It was a very sad Christmas that year.
>
> In February, the following year, President Roosevelt signed Executive Order 9066 that said all Japanese Americans were to evacuate their homes and property and were to go to what they called "internment camps," but actually were prisons. Doña Casillas graciously offered to store most of Yuriko's things. Yuriko wasn't able to attend her, nor my, graduation, nor my championship fight, which I lost. And finally, my father passed away from drinking. I was alone for the first time in my life, facing the biggest challenge of my life—being apart from Yuriko.
>
> Glenn Miller's romantic "Moonlight Serenade," Yuriko's favorite, was playing on the radio as I wrote her this letter. She taught me how to write Japanese haiku poetry before she left.
>
> *Mi Querida,* Yuriko:
>
> This poem is about the last time I saw you at your temple as you and your parents got on the bus with all the others. *Ojalá que te guste.* I hope you like it.

"*Goodbye*"

The sun couldn't shine
Air choking with emotion
Destiny breathing

Five busses pulled up
Lined up ready to fill up
Straight to Manzanar

Needed a strong heart
Strong as a samurai sword
Fierce as a *Yaqui*

Melted when you smiled
Arms wrapped in desperation
Our tears fell in grace

"This ain't right," I said
"Relatives in Tijuana
Let's get out of here!"

"Can't leave family
Can't leave my duty behind
It's my cross to bear"

Watched you with parents
Sitting in meditation
Honor, crown of thorns

Busses pulled away
Almost refusing to go
As the stunned crowd waved

Winds started to moan
Dark clouds spun a sad rainbow
Angels sang the blues

Sayonara, babe
Cuidate bien, mi reina
Adiós Yuriko

Te amo,

Carlos

She wrote back.

Mi Querido, Carlos:

Thanks for the beautiful haiku. You have become a great poet! Here is
my reply, also an informal haiku.

"Manzanar"

Camp is heartbreaking
But this is our destiny
Make the most of it

Guards in gun towers
Watching us like criminals
Wrapped in cold barbed wire

The skies are ice blue
Jagged peaks covered in snow
Desert dust storms choke

Cold nights this winter
Bitter wind blows through wall cracks
Our love keeps me warm

Obon this summer
Keeping traditions alive
Ancestors will dance

Our love will endure
Meditation keeps me calm
Your love is my strength

I miss my garden
I miss Little Tokyo
I miss you, sweetheart

Te amo,

Yuriko

Yellow Pearl Remix

EARLY IN 2012, NOBUKO INVITED me to perform in her new Great Leap performance piece, *Yellow Pearl Remix,* directed by Dan Kwong. Great Leap is the only L.A. performance group that does intergenerational, intercultural, and interfaith community building through the arts. The cast of performers was astounding. Heading the list was the legendary "Atomic" Nancy Matoba, who was once a waitress at her parents' legendary Little Tokyo restaurant, the Atomic Café, which was *thee* afterhours hang for noodles with the best jukebox in town, a magnet for the early L.A. punk scene and downtown art denizens. It was rumored that David Bowie and Andy Warhol once ate there, but Atomic Nancy was the draw: she was the best show in town, serving food in her outrageous costumes and makeup, sometimes even on roller skates. She later sang with Hiroshima, one of the first fusion bands mixing jazz, R & B, and traditional Japanese instruments. She was my hero in the late '70s, and here she was thirty years later and I was on the same bill with her. I was thrilled.

We went on with only one rehearsal with the band, musicians Benny Yee, Danny Yamamoto, and Charles Kim, and no sound check. The performance started with rare footage of the Black, Chicano, Asian American, and Native American social justice movements compiled by the director Dan Kwong. The opening few minutes tore me up with the combined fury and commitment to these causes. That by itself could have been the show, it was so powerfully moving. But then Tatsuo Hirano spoke about a contingent from L.A. (many from Boyle Heights) who had been invited by the American Indian Movement to participate in the Wounded Knee protests in 1973. They were part of the Rainbow Warriors, a collective embracing the cause for self-determination. This was news to me and to most of the people I spoke with later. "Tats" exuded the energy field of a samurai shaman as he recounted being there, further mesmerizing the audience.

He was followed by Atomic Nancy, who brought the house down with a soul-stirring song about peace and unity. She had kept up her chops by singing in a gospel choir for the past nineteen and was dynamite Aretha lethal! I was glued to my chair, drenched in tears, when I realized that I was on next. I read some haiku I'd written, then sang a duet with Nobuko and the killer band. We rocked. Poet-activist Kathy Masaoka spoke about her early organizing days, and poet-activist traci kato-kiriyama read a heartbreaking, loving tribute to her mentor, Nobuko. The house went nuts after the closing number. That was one performance event I will never forget. Thank you, Nobuko, for inviting me.

This is the haiku I read that night:

As Long as There's Love
(A haiku for my JA homies)

Buddhahead brothers
Loyal, always had your back
¡Órale, Kenbo!

Clarence Matsui
Spoke better Spanish than me
Monster sax player

Buddhahead sisters
Smart, poised, deep and beautiful
All Nisei Week Queens

Sweet Helen Funai
Berendo Junior High crush
My broken heart cried

We danced to oldies
Lowered our cars to the ground
"Hey, where's the party?"

Saint Mary's Bazaar
Pompadour hair styles combed high
JA *pachukos*

Mago's on Sawtelle
Teriyaki burritos
JA-Mex cuisine

Apollos car club
Haroa, Stan Imoto
Homeboys to the core

History calls me
World War II brought hate attacks
Mexicans and "Japs"

What democracy?
Felt the blows of racism
Zoot Riots, Poston

Brothers in combat
Serving an unjust nation
Heroes died in vain

Back on the home front
Chicano in Manzanar
Brother Ralph Lazo

Vietnam explodes
Black, Brown, and Yellow fodder
Moratorium

Yellow Pearl, touched us
Santana, Hiroshima
Dancing in the streets

We read Malcolm X
Brown Berets and Black Panthers
Power to the peeps!

Chicanos, JA's
Boyle Heights on the Eastside
One heart *por vida*

Ancestors calling
Obon and Day of the Dead
Heard them say, "Stay strong"

Love and soul power
A law of the universe
An eternal song

Siempre en lucha
Standing for justice and truth
Standing push come shove

Brothers and sisters
Chicanos and Buddhaheads
As long as there's love

Saving the Toypurina Monument

I GOT A RANDOM EMAIL IN 2005, from a *tocayo,* Rubén Mendoza, asking if I'd be interested in participating in a protest performance piece against the anti-immigrant hate group the Minutemen. They were demanding that a public art monument created by pioneer Chicana artist Judy Baca in Baldwin Park in the San Gabriel Valley be torn down because it honored the heroic deeds of a woman Tongva leader, Toypurina, who some say led a successful revolt against the Spanish at the San Gabriel Mission in 1785. Mendoza's idea was to have a protest-parade-happening-concert-theater piece—something right up my alley. He wanted to invite a lowrider car club, the guerilla theater group Teatro Callejero, and a performance group that he'd organized at SPARC. I invited hip-hop groups Aztlán Underground, the all-women Cihuatl Tonali, and the duo Mezklah. We had to scratch the parade component because we couldn't get a car club to participate, although that would have been the bomb.

At the demo-performance itself, a skirmish broke out with some throwing of plastic water bottles. The armed and shielded police in riot gear marched into the performance area to break things up, but then, surprisingly, they were ordered to retreat. The demo-performance went on as planned, and Baca's monument was eventually saved. I wrote and performed this poem (introducing it with Nahuatl and Spanish verses from the original text *The Last Mandate of Our Venerable Kuauhtemok*), wearing a placard hanging over my body that read "500+ Years of *Joda*" (i.e., being fucked with):

The Last Eagle and Jaguar Warrior Dance

Tenochtitlan-Mexiko
Yei Kalli
Tlaxochimako
Matlaktli Iuan Yei Kuetzpallin

México-Tenochtitlan
Año Tres Casa
Ofrenda de Flores
Día Trece Lagartija
12 de Agosto de 1521

México-Tenochtitlan
Year Three House
Flower Offering
Day Thirteen Lizard
August 12, 1521

Even the sun, the moon, and the stars were covered with blood
Tenochtitlan and Tlatelolco covered with horror, defiance, tears,
    and honor

A civilization lay bleeding,
Sangre sagrada
Sangre de vida
Sangre de lagrimas
Singing its last song
As Eagle and Jaguar warriors fell
Mexika and Tlatelolka women and children
Picked up their weapons and fought
Singing their last song
Knowing that life and death is a dance of destiny

Kuauhtemok spoke:
There will be darkness for many ages
But the sun will shine again when we open our hearts
We will be powerful again
Not by the sword
But by the heart
True power

He said, The seeds of life and happiness are within
The treasure that Cortés was looking for will never be found
Because it is where the seeds are hidden
In our hearts

Now is the time to wake up to our true power
To our *flor y canto*
The poetry of the heart

The source of life
The source of love
The source of wisdom

He said, All things in life are connected
Listen to its song
Its wisdom
It lives in our seeds

The revolution toward change and consciousness
Begins in our hearts
Begins with our actions
Begins with compassion
Begins with love

Not talking about romance
Talking about grace

We are now in the Sixth Sun/Age
A time of light
A time of action
A time of conscious resistance
A time of fighting for peace
A time to be a warrior of the heart

Rock 'n' Rights for the Mentally Disabled

ONE DAY IN 2005 I received an email out of the blue from a group looking for a facilitator for an eight-week summer youth program. It was a welcome miracle, since I was broke as usual. I went to the interview confident that I had the experience to take on the position.

I was hired to work with ten teenagers who were bused to the youth center every weekday for eight weeks. They were taught the principles of democracy from a study guide, and then they had to decide on a final project that would illustrate democracy in action. The students were a multicultural mix of white, Black, Latino, and Asian boys and girls, a very smart and eager group, ready to jump in. No flakes here.

During one session the program's director, Miss V., a beautiful young woman with a sweet, melodious voice, told the class how she came to America. Her mother, a Vietnamese refugee, had left with only the clothes on her back, a few coins, and pregnant with Miss V. One freezing night after her arrival in the States, she was in a homeless camp. It was so cold that when she relieved herself, the urine froze on the ground. As I was hearing this, I couldn't help but think of the nightmare ordeal she endured, and the relentless drive it must have taken to come to this country, this so-called "democratic" country, especially after it practically destroyed hers.

The class decided to produce a free concert for the homeless of Skid Row. It was called *Rock 'n' Rights for the Mentally Disabled* and was presented in the center's courtyard plaza. To attend, you had to bring cans of food and new or barely used clothing. Over 150 people showed up. The students contacted the LAMP Community homeless shelter on Skid Row, arranged transportation for the homeless guests, wrote and sent out press releases, and painted a huge banner that they hung on the front of the center announcing the show. One of the students invited a councilman to come and speak. He applauded the students for organizing the event and for shining the light of humanity on the guests, and presented them with an award for doing so. Ollín played at the concert, but the show was stolen by their protégé youth band, Old Souls, who got the audience up on their feet and dancing to a soulful medley of Motown hits. It was a heartwarming event and overall an inspiring experience. If you give youth a chance to show what they got, they will blow your mind.

Resistance and Respect: Los Angeles
Muralism and Graff Art

A MURAL PAINTED BY MY HOMIES the East Los Streetscapers has sat for many years on the corner of César Chávez (formerly Brooklyn Avenue) and Soto in my Boyle Heights neighborhood. *El Corrido de Boyle Heights* is a monumental memory piece about life in the barrio and was an inspiration for many of my poems. One day, while out on a stroll, I stopped in my tracks, frozen in disbelief. The mural had been brutally tagged beyond recognition. I was outraged and saddened that someone had so little respect for their culture and art that they felt compelled to desecrate a beloved cultural landmark. Maybe the community needed to be educated on the history of Chicano muralism. Maybe that could help stop the mindless spray can terrorists. I decided to organize a series of community forums to address the issue.

Los Angeles has long been a hotbed of resistance mural art-making, ever since 1932 when visiting Mexican painter/muralist David Alvafo Siqueiros created three masterpieces here: *Mitin Obrero* (Workers' Meeting), at the Chouinard Art Institute in the Westlake district (now buried under layers of paint and cement, it is a possible candidate for restoration); *Portrait of Mexico Today, 1932*, originally painted on the wall of the Pacific Palisades home of filmmaker Dudley Murphy (today housed at the Santa Barbara Art Museum); and the prototype of Chicano muralism, *América Tropical* on Olvera Street. The last mural outraged the Los Angeles City Council so much that they ordered it whitewashed because of its highly charged, subversive content. The controversy rages on up to today over what can and cannot be painted on L.A.'s walls. Several new Graff art murals were recently removed from the Arroyo Seco Channel, even though permits had been secured.

I thought that censorship and the tagging of traditional murals would be good issues for discussion. I contacted two art organizations (East Los Streetscapers and the Social and Public Art Resource Center [SPARC]) and individual artists to present two free public forums, with funding by Rhino Records president Richard Foos.

The first, called *Resistance and Respect: Los Angeles Muralism and Graff Art, 1932–2007*, was held in 2007, presented by Arts 4 City Youth. The panel discussion included a slideshow of selected pictorial history of Los Angeles muralism and Graff art, held at the Crewest Gallery, the first Graff art gallery in downtown L.A. Graff artists Rage One, Oscar Magallanes, and Olmeca spoke about their efforts in creating Resistance Graff. Students of Xela and Mixpe (two emerging Xikana poets) presented spoken-word performances. The landmark 1971 PBS documentary *América Tropical* by Chicano filmmaker Jesús Salvador Treviño was screened, showing the creation and early attempts at restoring Siqueiros's iconic mural. I was fortunate to secure a panel consisting of Deborah Padilla (SPARC), Wayne Alaniz Healy (East Los Streetscapers), Yreina Cervántez (California State University Northridge), Chaz Bojórquez (pioneer Graff artist), and Noni Olabisi (muralist). Man One served as moderator.

The second forum, *Resistance and Respect II: Current Issues*, was presented in 2009, by a coalition of community arts advocates, including Arts 4 City Youth, Crewest Gallery, Teocintli, Tía Chucha's Centro Cultural, and Rage One. It also provided a historical overview of Los Angeles muralism and Graff art from 1932 to the present. We once again screened the documentary *América Tropical*. This time Treviño was present, and he gave a talk on the making of the documentary. Following the screening, panels convened to address major issues facing traditional muralists and Graff artists today. The forum's goal was to give voice to L.A. inner-city youth by giving them an opportunity to state their concerns, needs, and artistic visions. Many students from Roosevelt High School attended and participated in a heated Q & A session arguing the difference between tagging and Graff art, the conclusion being that tagging is strictly guerilla gang writing, with art not being a consideration or goal. I hope the panels and open discussions generated awareness, unity, and respect among the community, the youth, and the two schools of muralism(traditional and Graff)inspiring them to continue contributing to the form's illustrious seventy-seven-year legacy, and that the youth got the message and will pass that legacy on to their friends.

Miss Bogotá and the X Festival Ibéroamericano del Teatro

IN 2006, I WORKED AS THE LATINO and Asian audience development dude at the Ford Amphitheatre. As part of the job, they sent me to the X Festival Ibéroamericano del Teatro de Bogotá, Colombia, to act as a talent scout for possible future Latino bookings at the Ford. The festival invited theater and dance companies from all over the world to participate in the month-long series of performances. There was something going on practically twenty-four hours a day in streets, parks, art galleries, vacant lots, and conventional theaters all over the city, including musical concerts, street theater, and circus performances. I was there for two weeks and experienced enough concerts to last several lifetimes. I became a living concert myself, attending, breathing, dreaming, and living the arts. It was exhilarating and inspiring, to say the least. I barely slept.

One theatrical experience left an unforgettable, indelible impression on me of the power of theater. It was by the local company Proyecto Pirámide. The piece was *La procesión va por dentro / The Procession Goes Inside,* directed by José Domingo Garzón. It took place in an old abandoned house in the Candelaria neighborhood in the lush hills above the city. A group of seven to ten audience members went from bedroom to bedroom to experience brief performances, none longer than fifteen minutes. In one small, dimly lit bedroom we sat in silence for maybe ten minutes watching a woman sitting on her bed looking despondent and heartbroken. We were only about ten feet away from her. She didn't say a word, but the tension in the small room built to an intensity that was deafening. Suddenly the door opened and a man walked in, sat down, looked at her, then down at the floor, twisting a ring on his finger without speaking. They continued looking at each other, or at the floor, in silence for what seemed an eternity, until slowly he got up, pulled off the ring, and placed it on the dresser. He sat down again, and they resumed their awkward silence. Finally he got up and walked to the door, looked back at her for a moment, and left, gently closing the door behind him. It was gut-wrenching, in your face, living theater without a word spoken.

We proceeded to another small, dimly lit room. A white ceramic basin of water rested on the floor about five feet away from me. A young woman, bare-foot in a flimsy gown, stood like a statue, a sad blank stare on her pristine face. After a long period of thick silence, a young priest walked in. The room felt like it was about to explode. She softly told him she was pregnant. She was a nun.

Stepping into the basin of water, she began repeatedly pushing an object up between her legs as if performing an abortion. As she recounted the night he'd seduced her in a long poetic, heartbreaking monologue, streams of blood appeared running down her legs into the basin of water as she slowly kept pushing up into her. The priest sobbed and pleaded for forgiveness. She did not forgive him. She then stepped out of the bloody water and walked past the sobbing priest out of the room. He got up and left as well.

In the next room a woman lay curled up in an open trunk only a few feet away from the spectators. When the door closed and the lights went out, the woman turned on a flashlight, shining it on her face as she launched into a monologue in Spanish on the oppression of feminine beauty in a male-dom-inated society and the feeling of being trapped by her own beauty. It could have been written by Pablo Neruda—lush, sensual, deep, and powerful.

She was unbelievably beautiful, with her long, ink-black hair pulled back into a bun, her eyes dark, warm, and penetrating, her mouth red and seduc-tive, her skin satin bronze. Her tone of voice was neither bitter nor angry, but sorrowful, eloquent, elegant, and compelling, without self-pity. I was so grate-ful to understand most of it. I was taken back to my early childhood when I only spoke Spanish. The Spanish language is pure poetry. There is a certain intimate sonority and lyricism that touches the listener like music, like love.

She turned off her flashlight. In total darkness she asked the audience to pick up the flashlights that were on the floor by the benches. She asked that we shine the light on her as she sat up on the trunk. "Touch me and love me with your light and promise to remember this moment." I slowly covered every inch of her hair, face, neck, and shoulders. I've never made love to a woman like that before. What sublime eroticism. Of course I fell in love with her, and so did the dog. Then she said, simply, "Good night," and the audience stood up, stunned, and without applause filed out of the room. I stayed. When we were alone, I said, "Bravo." She stared at me, startled, as I turned and walked away. I couldn't say anything else.

Sankai Juko, the Japanese butoh dance company I'd experienced at UCLA back in '93, was there. I was curious how Colombians would respond to their form of dance-theater. It was another epic performance with their silent, slow, anguished movement that could be interpreted in a million ways: truly a theater of the subconscious. Surprisingly, the audience went wild. I sat in my balcony seat watching the company take their elegant bows one by one, still in performance mode, as the audience cheered them on and on. I don't know why I was moved to tears, but I was. Maybe it was because as an audience you have a collective experience of sharing the subconscious together. That is very intimate and potent at once.

Finally I stood and headed for the stairway. As I drifted down the stairs I saw the beauty from the flashlight piece walking up toward me. I didn't know whether to follow her and introduce myself or just let it go, since my Spanish isn't that great. But no, I had to try. I caught up to her and clumsily introduced myself as the guy that had said "bravo." She remembered and said, "*Que lindo*—how beautiful." I was telling her that I was there from L.A. representing a theater when it occurred to me that I should try to bring her company to the Ford. Of course I had ulterior motives, but I told her I would try. She was very gracious and polite and sincerely grateful for my appreciation. I later spoke to one of the festival hosts and asked about her. He said she used to be one of the most popular and highest-paid Telenovela actresses in Colombia but had left it behind for experimental agit-prop theater. She now lives very simply and out of the limelight. Unfortunately, I couldn't convince the Ford to bring the company to L.A. Still, I think of her often and am reminded of the purpose of performance and theater: to touch deep into the soul and like an alchemist transform ordinary existence into sacred knowing.

The flight home was with a mix of inspiration and great sadness as I entered the Panama City airport for my transfer flight back to L.A. I was in the country where my father had passed the previous month. I couldn't attend his funeral because I didn't have the money, yet now here I was. It cut deep, and I'm still bleeding.

Word Up! *A Word, Performance, and Theater Summit*

WHILE AT THE FORD, I suggested that they stage a performance art, theater, and spoken-word summit, since no such thing had ever been held in L.A. before. *Word Up!* was conceived and presented in 2006 in conjunction with the conference "Cultivating Audiences in a Poly-Cultural, Post–New World," organized by me and the Ford's Community Bridges staff. Among the artists were Native American poet-activist John Trudell, award-winning playwright Oliver Mayer, performance art pioneer Keith Antar Mason, the bold and hilarious Kristina Wong, and the sublimely powerful Violeta Luna.

I had first worked with Kristina when she presented her one-woman show *Wong Flew over the Cuckoo's Nest,* about the high rates of depression and suicide among Asian American women. This was for the Asian Pacific American play-reading series that I initiated for the Ford's Community Bridges program. Kristina left a deep impression, presenting the freshest and best of what performance art had evolved into: a way to speak about the unspeakable with bold humor and heart. She later performed in one of Tía Chucha's benefits that I helped organize at the amphitheater, where she conducted a hilarious ICE raid on the mostly Latino audience. How bold is that? Naturally, I fell in love with her and her art.

John Trudell came out with all guns blazing, a nonstop barrage of poetic thunder and lightning in a stream of white-heat primal consciousness that recounted the turbulent history of the United States' betrayals of Native Americans. Violeta Luna came down from San Francisco, and my experience with her was an awakening that compelled me once again to have to control my dog lust. While waiting for her turn to close the concert, we were alone in the dark dressing room next to the stage. She was topless, wearing only a white floor-length peasant skirt. She handed me a marker and asked me to write "Not for Sale" on her immaculate bare back. With one hand, I held the corner of her bare shoulder to write. It had been four years since I'd touched the naked skin of a beautiful woman. It was sensual, yet at the same time serious. Her skin was as smooth as obsidian. For an instant I wanted to continue the caress ... but no. She turned to me and said, "Thank you," then walked onto the stage and performed an astonishing piece about the mistreatment of women in Mexico. The other performers stood in a circle around her, at times heckling her and at times becoming a rousing army. She was explosive, dangerous, inspiring, and liberating. As she came off stage, the audience roared its approval. She looked heroic. As I congratulated her for her courage and artistry, embracing her wet shoulders and back, she started to cry quietly in my arms. I will never forget it: a true, sacred moment of love and respect.

That next summer I volunteered to organize a benefit at the Ford Amphitheatre for the nonprofit community arts center Tía Chucha's Centro Cultural, cofounded by my homie the poet Luis J. Rodriguez. This was an opportunity to continue my multicultural work of bringing together L.A.'s communities of color to experience one another's music, theater, poetry, and dance—to savor what I call Angelino culture, a fusion of many semi-autonomous cultures.

The benefit included the rebellious Chicano comedy troupe Culture Clash, with Richard Montoya, Ric Salinas, and Herbert Siguenza; East L.A. musical titans Tierra with the Salas Brothers; and John Densmore of the Doors performing a spoken-word piece with African drummers. I felt it was important to give new, emerging artists an opportunity to do their thing, so conscious hip-hop artists Xela and El Vuh were brought onboard, along with Eastside punksters Ollín, while Tía Chucha's resident *danza* group, Temachtia Quetzalcoatl Danza Mexika, offered opening-ceremony blessings. I asked the car club Old Memories (South L.A.) to bring in some "bomb" cars, and we put a couple of them on stage as backdrop props. Before the show there was a *danzante* ceremonial blessing of the cars, which were lined up in the parking lot. That was a trip. The evening was hosted by comedian Ernie G. We called it "A Celebration of Community and Culture *¡Sí Se Puede!*" Man, lemme tell you, it was one helluva celebration!

I was later hired as the Centro's development dude (grant writing and fundraising). We continued with three more summer benefit concerts, the first of which included my homie, the irrepressible Cheech Marin, who sang "Born in East L.A." for a rousing closer. We also featured L.A. funk pioneer Charles Wright and the Watts 103rd Street Rhythm Band; veteran singer-performer-activist and homegirl Nobuko Miyamoto singing a special blessing; and homie Luis J. Rodríguez reading his inspiring works.[1] Thanks to my homies, I had gone from being solely a Chicano culture sculptor to being a Chicano Angelino culture sculptor.[2]

1. Other benefit concerts included the outrageous comedy of OPM (Opening People's Minds); stirring conscious hip-hop by Olmeca; ska upstarts Upground; host Herbert Siguenza (Culture Clash); *vallenato* bad boys Very Be Careful; *son jarocho* by zocaloZüe; alternative Latin fusionists La Santa Cecilia, featuring the soulful voice of Marisoul; traditional Filipino music by Kayamana Ng Lahi. Our last show, "Fire and Soul: L.A. Women Unite for Tía Chucha's," featured songstress Perla Batalla; L.A. blues woman and unofficial poet laureate of Los Angeles Wanda Coleman (her last public performance before she passed away); once again the incomparable Kristina Wong (I can't get enough of her); smokin' Latin alt-rock by Ceci Bastida; and the hilarious Xikana political comedians Las Ramonas. Temachtia Quetzalcoatl Danza Mexika opened all shows with their ceremonial blessings. A special shout-out to Walter Little, who assisted me, and to the rest of Tía Chucha's committed and tireless staff.

2. A project that summed up my community arts activism was *Rushing Waters, Rising Dreams: How the Arts Are Transforming a Community,* a documentary film by John Cantú, that shows the cultural and economic impact Tía Chucha's has made in the northeast San Fernando Valley. I worked on getting the grant from the L.A. County Arts Commission, wrote an essay on the pop music history of the region for the accompanying book (focused on Ritchie Valens), and supervised the soundtrack along with Cantú.

Meeting My Brothers from the Westbank
First Nation, British Columbia

SOMETIME IN EARLY 2007 I received a mysterious voicemail: "If your father was Rubén Ladrón de Guevara, please call me back." I did, and the person was the mother-in-law of a man who claimed to be my father's son. She gave me his email and we started to correspond. My father did tell me that he had a new family in Seattle when I called him about my sister Bonita's tragic death in 1970. So it wasn't a complete surprise for me to hear from them. Miguel (Mike) said that he would be coming to L.A. soon with his younger brother Rafael (Raf), and I agreed to meet with them. I immediately recognized my father's eyes in Miguel. The brothers were both in tears and smiling from ear to ear. Then the saddest story I'd ever heard unraveled, thankfully with no anger toward me.

One day my dad took the three boys, ages five, six, and seven, to a clothing store where he bought them all new suits, then he took them to get some ice cream. When they got home, he said goodbye—and never came back. Their mother had a drinking problem and not much later mysteriously disappeared. The boys were sent separately to foster homes. Because their mother was First Nation Okanagan, they eventually were sent to live on the Westbank First Nation reserve near Kelowna, British Columbia, where they were raised. Mike may have been named after Miguel Aceves Mejía, and Raf after Rafael Méndez, the classical trumpet player and a boyhood friend of my dad's. The oldest, Mariano (Mar), was probably named after dad's father, also Mariano. Mike and Raf eventually became leaders in the tribal council and helped develop the reserve (as reservations are called in Canada). The two had come to Los Angeles to do some research on Indian casinos, since they were considering building one on their reserve. I tried to dissuade them from doing so, saying casinos kill culture. Fortunately, the tribal council decided to build a hospital instead. Mike and Raf, along with the council, have created what I understand to be the most successfully self-sustained reserve in Canada.

I was shocked and felt deep disgust for my father after hearing their heart-breaking story. I couldn't possibly defend him. But what I found most interesting was how important it was for my brothers to get in touch with me. They had never met anyone who knew our dad, with the exception of one uncle. Close family ties are essential to indigenous identity and collective psychic unity. By finally meeting me they had found a family link that erased a lot of ambiguity, shame, and sorrow. They told me that they now felt more real, more human, more whole. What struck me most of all was their humble demeanor. There was no rancor or anger over what had happened. They were just a couple of sincere, warm-hearted guys. They felt like brothers to me . . . and they were. They even offered me a place to live if I ever wanted to retire. That is something I think about often.

A few years later, Raf and his wife, Buffy (named after the First Nation Cree singer Buffy Sainte-Marie), invited me to come and stay with them for a few days to attend their daughter Fawn's high school graduation. I had already met Fawn and her sister Summer when they had come to L.A. for a visit. This time I got to meet Mike's daughter, Reba, a brilliant young woman devoted to preserving and teaching Okanagan culture. I enjoyed talking with her when we attended Fawn's "Grad Walk," a ceremony in which the graduating students parade in formal attire through a park as family and guests look on. I asked Reba what she'd worn for her walk the previous year. "My First Nation regalia and my favorite moccasins," she replied. Her gentle fire filled me with deep respect. She was interning for the summer at the tribal museum and repository on the reserve before returning to the University of British Columbia.

Later that night as I was processing the day's events, it occurred to me that Reba, Fawn, and Summer are my father's granddaughters. It tore me up that he never knew them, yet I also felt a strange sense of gratitude.

When I was leaving, Mike presented me with a sacred eagle feather, which Reba handed to me. His son, Dustin, is also a fine young man, learning the ways of the rodeo, a favorite pastime of Mike's. Mar's son, Ronald, also blew my mind with his uncanny resemblance to my dad in his youth, and to my youngest son, Rubencito. His wisdom for an eighteen-year-old was astonishing. My father would be so proud of his beautiful grandchildren.

Two cherished family portraits. *Top:* My reunion with my Okanagan brothers. *Left to right:* Mariano "Mar," me, Rafael "Raf," and Miguel "Mike" Ladrón de Guevara. Bear Creek, British Colombia, Canada, 2015. (Photo by Buffy Eli DeGuevara.) *Bottom:* My mom and I, with my sisters. *Left to right:* my sister Linda, my mom, and my baby sister Loretta. Lancaster, California, ca. 1990. Courtesy of the Funkahuatl family archive.

Mar is a burly bear of a man with a hearty laugh and a gentle heart. On the second night of my visit, we finally had the talk he had been waiting for all of his life. We were outside at Raf's recently built home on the reserve overlooking the magnificent Okanagan Lake. To view the lake is like dreaming a prayer. I watched as Raf and Mar built a roaring fire that licked the sky, speaking a language of its own. Mar and I stood facing each other, and I knew what was coming. As the oldest brother, he was the hardest hit by the abandonment. He remembered things the other boys did not. He'd found solace through drugs and a runaway lifestyle. He needed healing the most. I knew I'd lived with our father longer than he and his brothers did, and I felt guilty about that. Yet I was not in a position to defend him; I couldn't. I felt like I was between the proverbial rock and a hard place. But I had to stand my ground and eat my shame, and my father's too. It was my brotherly duty. We cried, we hugged, we howled forgiveness with the fire roaring behind us, and promised to stay in each other's lives.

Haiku for Mariano

Brotherhood by fire
Blood lines crisscrossed with life pain
Flames licking deep wounds

Embers breathing fate
Gasping for breaths of fresh air
Stoking destiny

Will you stay in touch?
As our name is Guevara
As our blood sings true

Will you stay in touch?
As cosmic dust is our home
As wisdom is fire

Will you stay in touch?
As the night time follows day
As love follows me

Epiphany at Joshua Tree

AS A RETREAT FROM THE CITY, I started making a pilgrimage to Joshua Tree every New Year's Day in a ritual of gratitude, to pray for redemption and direction. On my first New Year's Day hike in 2008, about two miles from the road, I came across a giant boulder perched high on a cliff. I called it Rubén's Rock. Every New Year's Day I would test my endurance by climbing it. It became my sanctuary and my temple.

That first year, standing on top of my rock, I asked myself, "Why am I here? What's my next move? What should I do?" I would turn sixty-six in October. Time was slipping away. Suddenly the Hindu saying that I wrote in a poem for my *tío* Lolo flashed through my mind: "God respects me when I work, but He loves me when I sing." Of course! I'm a singer! I was born a singer, I'll die a singer. That's what I should be doing!

But wait—I haven't sung in almost thirty years. Who in their right mind makes a comeback at sixty-six years of age?

That's when I made the pact with the Great Spirit, the Source, the Tao. "Creator, I wanna write and sing about my new way of life, my Tao of Funkahuatl. Maybe men will become less dogs and better lovers, better husbands, better fathers, better men. But I need to know you've got my back for my comeback. I need your power behind me. Creator, do you hear me?"

Silence.

"Great Spirit, do you hear me?"

Silence.

"The Source of All That Is—does anybody hear me!?"

A raven flew by with a piercing caw that cut through my skin and skull. "Am I all alone in this!?" I fell to my hands and knees crying and trembling.

A lizard ran over my tears as they merged with the rocks, the sand, the flowers, insects, sky.

Then it hit me: there's stardust in my DNA! We all come from the same source—the sand, the lizard, the raven, the sky. Me. We *are* interconnected, like the Buddhists and Native Americans say: "To all relations."

I slowly got up, licking my salty tears, and looked around at all the beauty that surrounded me—and suddenly I felt as solid and strong as my rock. I was as high as the sky and my aim was as sure as a shaman's. I was ready. I was ready to come back. Ready to rock 'n' fuckin' roll.

A series of miracles happened shortly thereafter, confirming that the Creator did have my back. Both previous Ruben and the Jets albums were re-released digitally (now rendered as Ruben And The Jets), and the reviews were spectacular. My bittersweet past reputation gave me newfound confidence and a reason to live. The second miracle occurred before our first gig. *L.A. Weekly* music journalist Jonny Whiteside wrote us up as a "pick," calling attention to my revival. I had never met the cat before, but he happened to be an old Ruben And The Jets fan. He followed that up with a profile for the "Best of L.A. People 2009" issue celebrating L.A. artists. My comeback was launched.

Miss Altar in the Sky

THAT FOLLOWING SUMMER, I went to Joel "Rage" Garcia's thirtieth birthday party, attended mostly by East L.A. Zapatista and indigenous rights activists, an assortment of artists, and some of his homies from the Maravilla housing projects. Gomez Comes Alive was the DJ, and he was laying it down. There weren't many others my age to hang with, so I was about to leave—and then she walked in and sat down close by. She glanced over and smiled at me as if she knew me. I'd never seen her before. I smiled back but nothing more. She looked too young for me. Yeah, she was beautiful, very beautiful, and I let it go at that. Why waste my time? Why play with matches? Why suffer? I pulled the dog's chain.

Just before she arrived, someone had sat down next to me and pulled out a pipe and I took a hit. It was good. Nice buzz. Then he got up and left, and out of the blue she got up from her chair, walked over, and sat down next to me; she turned and gave me another friendly smile, not flirty at all. I was thrown for a loop, trying like a muthafuckuh to control myself—and my high. She was unbelievably gorgeous up close. "I saw you at the Self Help Graphics community meeting a while back," she said. "I took a picture of you talking to Ernie de la Loza. I once painted a mural with him." I was taken aback. We talked briefly about the meeting and the future of Self Help Graphics & Art, which had recently closed its doors.

Her voice was low, silky, clear, and calm. "What's your name?" I asked. "Alternative sky," she said—or that's what I thought she said. That tripped me out. Alternative sky. Wow. How beautiful is that? "Man, if I was only younger," I blurted, not thinking about how lame that sounded. "What do you mean?" she asked. "Well, I would swoop you up from here like Superman and take you away." "What do you mean?" "I would take you to an alternative sky, a parallel universe, and . . ." I couldn't finish. "And what?" she asked. "And . . . and take care of you." Though of course I wanted to say, "And make love to you."

She told me about her jewelry work and her relationship with certain stones and how she used their energies to help heal people. "So you're living your life as a healer?" "Yes," she said, smiling. That's when I fell in love with her. I felt compelled to bring up the "age difference" thing again, feeling I had to be honest with her on all levels. Then, like a fool, I tried to guess her age. "I'm thinking you're about twenty-five, twenty-eight." "Oh no, I have a twenty-year-old daughter!" "What? Did you have her when you were ten?" She laughed. I realized she was around my daughter's age. I looked into her *ojos cósmicos,* put my hands on her shoulders, and said, "This is no coincidence. We were meant to meet." She just stared at me with those cosmic eyes and smiled a killer smile.

When Gomez put on some Al Green, she got up and started dancing. I moved a chair out of the way, and she said, "Getting ready to bust some moves?" That cracked me up. We danced facing each other, digging the music, and it felt good . . . real good. She later invited me to stop by her jewelry table in the Caracol Marketplace at Proyecto Jardín, a community garden behind White Memorial Hospital in Boyle Heights. I said sure. She gave me her card. I gave her mine. We politely embraced, saying good night and how great it was to meet. I mustered up the courage to ask if she would be interested in going out for dinner or a concert sometime, and she surprisingly said yes.

I immediately looked up her website, then sent an email saying that meeting her was a gift, a sacred gift. She responded by first correcting me on her name, saying it was "altar in the sky," not "alternative sky." Even more beautiful. She went on to say, "I'm glad there has been a spark ignited. It's moments like last night that make our souls happy. When souls recognize each other a spark ignites creating a healing vibration throughout our being and emanating out into the universe, making the stars feel their shine is not in vain." She closed by saying, "Namaste—I bow to the light within you—may you continue to be blessed with love, creativity, and compassion." After reading that, I fell in love with her all over again. How could I not? It felt like the sixties redux. A second shot of cosmic love.

"Yeah, our souls danced and evaporated together, if only for a few moments, then returned to their source," I wrote. "I'm sure we made the stars happy last night."

I felt like a kid again. But what the hell was I doing? This could never go anywhere. She was too young for me. She was my daughter's age, for chrissake!

Or was she? What's too young, anyway? After all, she raised a daughter, now twenty, by herself. She was a *woman!*

So I decided to go for it and see what would happen.

Walking up the steps of Proyecto Jardín, I remembered being there five years earlier at the groundbreaking ceremony. I read a poem, Nobuko Miyamoto sang a song. The councilman and future mayor Antonio Villaraigosa said a few words. I walked over to the food stand and watched as she paid the cook. She hadn't seen me yet. She looked like an earth mother goddess straight out of a sixties Love-In at the Griffith Park merry-go-round. Her shiny long black hair was pulled back, and she was wearing a wraparound sarong. Her tanned skin looked like olive satin velvet, silky smooth. She turned then, saw me, and we embraced. She told me she was a fan of Frank Zappa's music and also said she liked Ruben And The Jets, which threw me for another cosmic loony loop. It tripped me out that she'd taken the time to Google me.

I bought a few pieces of jewelry for future gifts. As I was leaving she said, "Call me. Let's have that dinner." I was flattered that she was still interested, although it added to my dilemma on how to proceed.

A few days later I woke up in a deep funk depressed that she hadn't answered my emails. Here I was almost sixty-six and feeling like a heartbroken teenager. Crazy. I didn't know they'd all gone into my junk mail.

Another few days went by. I was waiting in a library for my car to be fixed when I remembered an article I'd read—which became part of my emerging philosophy, the Tao of Funkahuatl—about accepting the present and not needing to look to the past for identity nor having expectations that the future will bring happiness. With that in mind I started to write her a haiku—and all of a sudden an earthquake hit and we had to evacuate the building. Was it some kind of omen? Her signals were confusing and frustrating, but I ignored them. Or rather, my ego-dog ignored them and proceeded like a moth to a flame.

The day of our dinner date arrived. My car still wasn't running too good, so I rented one, a brand-new bronze Chevy HHR. Johnny Midnite would've dug it. I called her and she answered in her sexy raspy low voice: "Hey. I'm hungry." "Hey, I'm about ten minutes away." "Okay, I'll be ready."

I couldn't get over how familiar and intimate she sounded—like a girlfriend. No chitchat, no "How are you?" etc. It warmed my heart, although it was racing like a caged dog about to be cut loose. I drove up Scott in Echo Park to the top of the hill and looked for the address. It was a big blue ornate

Victorian house. She came running out and down the stairs dressed very casually, jeans and a blouse with a jean jacket, hair pulled back. We greeted each other with a polite *abrazo*. At El Cochinito, a Cuban restaurant down on Sunset, I opened the car door for her. It felt good doing that; I hadn't done it in a hundred light years. On the one hand, it was a date with a friend, and on the other it was also a date with a possible lover—if it wasn't for the "age thing." I was walking a fine, slippery line, skating on thin ice, and trying not to feel self-conscious about how we might look to others. I tried not to think that we were a couple, just two friends having dinner. The waitress led us to our table and kindly gave us the menus and asked with no noticeable attitude what we wanted to drink. The paranoia was all in my head.

She was very relaxed. I tried to be the same, although my heart was hammering. She looked beautiful, with simple makeup, and every now and then that killer smile would break through. She ordered black beans and rice, *yucca* with *ajo* (garlic), avocado salad, and fried bananas. I had roasted garlic chicken, black beans, and rice. It was a feast. We shared our dishes. Conversation flowed easily and smoothly. I kept reminding myself to stay in tune with her, and detached from expectations of an outcome. It wasn't easy. Still, I watched her closely and fantasized kissing her, making love to her. How could I not?

"I saw on your website that you're having a birthday next Saturday," I said. "Yeah, do you wanna come? I'll put you on the guest list. I hope you like to boogie." "Say what? Do I like to boogie? *Boogie* is my middle name, and getting down is my claim to fame," I joked.

After dinner, as we drove east on Sunset, she reminisced about walking the sidewalks there when her daughter was a child. We stopped at the Tribal Café, but it was closed, so I headed downtown to the Banquette Café on 3rd and Main. She ordered a green tea and I had a double espresso. I was relaxed—except for my heart choking for air. I talked about my marriage and divorce. "I've been single for the past ten years. It turned me into an independent man, financially, spiritually, psychologically, and sexually." She smiled at the last word. Our conversation led to my daughter and the adoption custody battle I'd lost. She looked intently at me, not blinking, as I recounted the story. I was mesmerized by her stare, by her eyes, wet pools of love. She looked celestial, extraterrestrial. It was like looking into the eyes of God. Then she raised her cup, looked deeper into my eyes, and offered a toast: "Here's to your daughter." I took a deep breath and cracked a sad smile.

Later, I wrote "The Eyes of God" based on that moment. I broke down several times while writing it. The pain of missing my daughter and the fact that my youth was quickly fading cut deep. I knew I could never have her because of my age. It tore me apart, because I don't feel my age, and some say I don't look it, but the fact is, I was nearly thirty years older than her.

After our coffee and tea we drove north on Main. The radio was on Art Laboe and he was making a dedication. I told her that I'd been listening to him since the mid-fifties, not caring that saying that would date me. "I used to make dedications on his show," I was saying, just as Little Anthony and the Imperials came on with "Tears on my Pillow." She started singing along, and I joined her. I had never sung an oldie with someone that young before. I was fuckin' charmed beyond belief. As the tune ended she said "Gee, those songs are so romantic and heartbreaking at the same time." I said, "Yeah, wouldn't it have been better if the words were a little more like "Baby, please love me with your love light shining, like in the song 'Turn on Your Love Light'?" She smiled.

She directed me home via back streets, up through Chinatown and into Elysian Park past the Police Academy: the same streets the sailors marched down the night the Zoot Suit Riots broke out back in '43. She told me about one of her first loves, an older kid who used to spend all his time indoors ironing his pants and shirts, making sure the creases were just right. She would wait and wait for him to come out, but he never did. She could see him inside ironing away, "all cute with his hair all gangster. I'm a little OG," she admitted. That charmed the shit out of me.

We arrived at her Victorian castle, and I gave her a polite hug goodbye. As she walked away she said, "Call me sometime. Stay in touch." "Sure," I said, as a hurricane tore up my heart. Was this a blessing or a curse for being a *pinche* poet, romanticizing more than there is?

The next day I went to Yaohan Plaza in Little Tokyo and bought her an iron teapot and some green tea for her birthday. Man, it felt good to be able to afford it. I called and we made plans to meet at the party. "It's at Zen Sushi," she said. "It starts at ten and goes until four A.M.," she said. That cracked me up. Going to a gorgeous lady's birthday party at a disco in Silver Lake that will last until four in the morning! How old am I? Who cares! Age ain't nothing but a fuckin' number!

But still, I struggled with whether or not to go. I started feeling like this was all nothing but a crazy ego trip, a big fuckin' mistake. Why subject myself to the torture? I'd look stupid dancing, like a crazy old man trying to look young. She was just being polite inviting me.

Then I thought, hell, fuck it, just go and have a good time. Just be a friend and drop all this romantic bullshit drama.

I put on my Brazilian leopard dancing shoes with the wild striped Bali jacket that Miss Tokyo had bought me ten years ago. I was ready to boogie down, all the way down. I swallowed my ego, took a hit, chained the dog, and off we went.

I walked in all bad, went to the bar and looked around. Everyone was younger than me, way younger, but I didn't give a fuck. The dance room was almost pitch black, and the DJ was playing some cool Afro-Beat. The place was rockin' and I was ready to bust some serious moves. I finally spotted her and danced my way over. We locked. I did a little groovy funky circling number around her, very smooth, and she smiled. I felt ageless. My body didn't ache at all. We continued dancing for a minute, then she faded away, dancing with her friends. So I got deeper into my own ageless world as Fela came on. Fuck age!

When the party started to wind down around 3:30, I was still dancin', still prancin', but it was time to say goodnight. Her soft back was wet with sweat as I gave her a friendly hug. Good gawd, it felt good. "Thanks for the pitchers of margaritas," she said. "That was sweet of you." "It was my pleasure. How about dinner next week so I can give you your birthday present?" "Sure, call me." I floated out into the early morning.

I was so fired up I couldn't sleep, so I took off for the coast. I drove to Dockweiler Beach and walked awhile, then headed up PCH for Ventura where I ran on the beach like an unbridled resurrected wild stallion, the freshly risen sun burning my pale, hungry body, my heart stirring like a busted hornet's nest. It had been six long years since Miss Tokyo. Six long years since I'd made love. Six long years of fate-imposed celibacy. Six long years of beating the dog. Six long years of shedding dead skin.

But . . . there was no sign from her that she was feeling the way I was. All I was getting was mixed signals. Maybe we *were* only meant to meet as a reminder for me to stay on track, to stay on the soul path, nothing more, nothing less. It was a bittersweet, heart-crushing realization, since I knew I could've loved her to death—and beyond. But instead, I ate some more bitter ego pie, trying to figure out how I could love her. I had to love her. I needed to love her, like fish need water, like fire needs air, like the moon needs the sun to shine.

That's when I decided I would do it through art. After all, that's what I had to offer. My sixty-sixth birthday was coming up, and I wanted to create a performance piece with her and the new band, the Eastside Luvers. I wanted to publicly put my age on the sacrificial stone while confessing my love for the goddess. Now, *that* would be a party—a performance party.

I finally worked up the guts to ask if she would perform with me and the band, and she said yes. I admired her courage and trust in me, since we wouldn't have a rehearsal. I don't like working with a net.

The night arrived. I started by telling the packed tiny Eastside Luv bar, "I had a dream last night about my hero, the Sixth Dalai Lama, also known as the 'Playboy Rebel Lama' because of his love of wine, women, and poetry. He asked me to read a poem tonight, a poem he'd written for his last girlfriend, a barmaid at the local Lhasa bar. Someone had followed his footprints in the snow from the palace to the bar one night. He was busted and eventually exiled. So last night he asked that I read it to her tonight. She'd be here. She'd be listening."

The band started with some dreamy atmospheric freeform sounds as I started to read the poem, a poem that was actually written for Miss Altar in the Sky. On cue, she appeared, as if an apparition, standing on the bar that faced the bandstand about fifty feet away. She was wearing an embroidered Middle Eastern floor-length gown with a red shawl over her head cascading down past her shoulders. She looked like a living dream, a goddess from another dimension. I stood awestruck for a few seconds, looking at what I had unknowingly created, as she glided toward me down the bar in slow butoh-like strides. The audience was dumbstruck. Nobody talked. Nobody drank.

Altar de Luz / Altar of Light

You looked at me with your obsidian jet-black hair on fire
Shining like a raven's wet breast

I watched the opening of your heart
Along with every smile
Along with every uttered truth of light

I watched the opening of your heart like the cactus at my doorstep
Blooming in the womb of the warm night air
Surrendering its moist white velvet petal lips to my world

Oh, *querida altar de luz*
Let your love light shine beyond flesh and time
Let it melt and burn my foolish ego
Let it carry me to you
Let it carry us home
To the Tao: the sacred source of all beginnings

I paced my reading to finish by the time she reached me. I dropped to my knees. She took off her shawl and placed it around my neck as in a blessing. She turned in slow motion and, gliding back down the bar, descended and vanished as I stayed on my knees, my eyes wet, the band still blowing improvised spirit music. It was a miracle moment. It was what I live for.

I then slowly rose with all my might as the band started playing "When I Was Young," my swan song to my youth. I took off in soul flight as I danced down the bar, throwing red roses to the women à la Al Green. I stopped and handed one to Miss Altar in the Sky, who smiled demurely. I then went back to the stage to hover and burn for the rest of the tantrik funk miracle set like a funk monk on fire.

"Thank you for blowing my mind," I said to her, trying to catch my breath after the set. "I hope it was what you wanted," she said. I smiled and hugged her as my birthday cake was brought out and placed on the bar. The audience started singing "Las Mañanitas," the first time that ever happened to me. She was standing next to me, singing her heart out, and I broke apart with emotion.

I walked her to her car, complimented her again on her incandescent performance, and she said, "Thanks. It was fun." I waited, my heart hammering, hoping that she would say something about the poem so I could tell her it was written for her, but she didn't mention it. Maybe she couldn't hear the words. Or maybe it was all just too heavy. I gave her a long hug, holding back the dog, as she softly said, "Good night. See you later."

The next thing I heard, she'd taken off to Burning Man (how fuckin' ironic), then got engaged, but it didn't work out. Then she hooked up again with somebody else, and I lost track of her and went into a deep funk—in the worst sense of the word. If I was going to come out of it, I knew I had to get over her or else bleed a slow painful death.

While stroking my shattered heart I realized I had to go beyond my dog lust in order to have her, in order to love her. It was that simple. It was that difficult. There was no other way. I imagined the many ways I could love her. I could love her in dreamtime, in every breath, in every song I sing. They call it "platonic"— an intimate nonsexual love affair. Sounded like a fuckin' contradiction at first, but then eventually I got it. After sniffing, licking, and pawing your dog lust, take it higher with shared loving care into the love light of your soul . . . and breathe it. Unconditional love: immutable, sacred. Then, live it.

That was the beginning, the ordination, the consecration of my tantrik funk monkhood. Yeah, she was my main muse all right, *mi mera musa,* and meeting her was a sacred gift after all. The following song lyrics were inspired by our meeting, and were part of the metamorphic process of leaving my cocoon from dog to man. "Crawlin' in Lust, Love, and Light" was a song I wrote while in my pre-enlightenment period, when I was sorting out my feelings between lust, love, and light. They wound up on my comeback album, *The Tao of Funkahuatl.*

The Eyes of God

The room was dimly lit
A downtown café
You made a toast to a daughter
I lost along the way

You looked at me with eyes
That could melt a stone
Eyes wet with compassion
Soothed my scarred soul

Oh, sacred beauty
Oh, sacred love
When I looked into your eyes sweet darlin'
Was like looking into the eyes of God

I've learned true love is sacred
It only comes to those that see
That love is God's music
When you sing it, it sets you free

Oh, sacred beauty
Oh, sacred love
When I looked into your eyes sweet darlin'
Was like looking into the eyes of God

No man is too old to love
No man is too old to cry
Even though there are many years between us
I'm gonna love you girl . . . till I die

Even though we may never be lovers
Still, there are many ways to love
I will love you in all my dreamtime
In every heartbeat, breath, and song

Oh, sacred beauty
Oh, sacred love
When I looked into your eyes sweet angel
Was like looking into the eyes of God

When I Was Young

There was a time
When love was just a plaything
When I was young
Love was nothing but a game

Oh lots of pretty women
Were always around me
When I was young
Thought it'd always stay the same

There was a time
When making love was easy
When I was young
Love was nothing but cheap thrills

But I got older
An' all those pretty women aren't around no mo'
My hair turned grey, some teeth fell out
An' my smile no longer kills

Hey, it's not about
How many women I can take home
It's not about
How many women I can taste

It's not about
How many women love my candy
It's not about
How many hearts I can break

No it's not about
That sweet sweet honey
It's not about
A playboy macho role

I've come to learn
If you want a love to last forever

You gotta love her
With all your heart and soul

So, go 'head an' love your woman
Not just with your body
Go 'head an' love your woman
With all your heart and soul

Smash your foolish ego
And love her with your naked soul
Gotta love your woman
With a whole lotta soul

Crawlin' in Lust, Love, and Light

I don't wanna fall in love with you like a stray dog in heat, bow wow,
    woof woof
I don't wanna fall in love with you like a hot pimp on the street, oh
    no, that's not enough
I don't wanna mesmerize you with my bullshit ego, oh no, no, no

I just wanna be your lover before we get down with the flow
So, c'mon baby let's go

Gonna crawl in lust, then love, into the light
Gonna take it slow 'n' easy, it's gonna be alright
We gonna crawl in lust, then love, into the light
Gonna take you slow an' easy with all my might

Just wanna take you higher than you've ever gone before
I wanna take you to a place girl, where you've never been before
An' I just wanna touch you, where you've never been touched before
An' I wanna kiss you, where you've never been kissed before

So, can I touch it?
Can I pinch it?
Can I squeeze it?
Can I kiss it?

Talkin' about your soul, girl
When's the last time your soul been kissed?
Talkin' about your soul, girl
When's the last time your soul been blissed?

When our lips kiss
Our souls will hiss and sizzle
If our hearts explode
Our bliss will never fizzle

When our bodies touch
Our souls will blush and flutter
When our thighs melt
Good gawd, talkin' about body butter

Gonna crawl in lust, then love, into the light
Gonna take it slow 'n' easy, it's gonna be alright
We gonna crawl in lust, then love, into the light
Gonna take you slow an' easy with all my might

So, can I touch it?
Can I pinch it?
Can I squeeze it?
Can I kiss it?

Talkin' about your soul, girl
When's the last time your soul been kissed?
Talkin' about your soul, girl
When's the last time your soul been blissed?

We'll crawl in lust
Then in love
Into the light
Into the light

I wanna touch your tasty body first
Lick your tasty body first
Then I'll work my way up to your soul
Then into the light

Flesh and Bone

She's like a cactus flower
Blooming in the moonlight
Velvet petal lips
Then she's outta' sight

Up, up and away
She took me for a ride
Beyond space and time
Nowhere to hide

Oh, she's a pure spirit
I'm a rollin' stone
She's born a sweet child of God
I'm born of flesh and bone

I said I want you forever
She said don't be a fool
All there is, is this moment
An eternal rule

She said listen baby
No need to look back
The future is now
So get on track

Don't tell yo' mama
How old I am
Just tell yo' mama
I'm a good lovin' man

Don't tell yo' papa
How bold I am
Just tell yo' papa
I'm a soul medicine man

The Eastside Luvers

I WAS SET ON PUTTING together an all-star killer band with musicians I had known and respected over the years: Ramón Banda, who played drums in Con Safos in the early '80s; monster tenor sax man Steve Alaniz (who played with George Duke, Stanley Clarke, and Lalo Guerrero, and who played at the Whisky benefit in '99 with John Martinez and I); the "Bass Beast" John Avila (Oingo Boingo, and coproducer of *Mexamérica*); and guitar god Bob Robles (Thee Midniters, Jackson Browne). This was going to be a Chicano Cream dream come true.

We played our first date on September 18, 2008, at the Eastside Luv, the new hip underground wine bar located in Boyle Heights. I'd talked the owner, Guillermo "Willie" Uribe, into letting me work out my new material while breaking in the band and developing a following. It was the perfect woodshed, and I decided to name the band the Eastside Luvers in gratitude for the opportunity. I wanted to bring my performance and theater chops into the mix with a new band—as well as making musical art sense out of my history with women. The concept included bringing back Funkahuatl, only this time cast as the neo-Aztek deity of tantrik funk. I saw it as a neo-*pachuko* Xikano funk performance art band. It was a high, groovy concept, maybe too high, and only a few adventurers came to our debut, including my son Ben and his girl, Didi. I wound up $200 in the red, but it was a start, albeit a shaky start, on a long and arduous comeback trail.

The Eastside Luv wine bar had opened in 2006, and it radically changed the Eastside's social and cultural landscape. It suddenly became hip for downtowners to go to Boyle Heights. Uribe booked and nurtured local talent, including Ecléctica's cool DJs Reyes Rodríguez and Glenn Red, who played funk with world beat flavors, music some Eastsiders had never heard before. Then Willie made mariachi music hip by showcasing Trio Ellas, a group of very beautiful and very talented Latinas, and the young dashing Los Toros. What a trip to see young, trim mariachi dudes dancing with beautiful Latinas between sets, with Al Green on the house speakers. Not only is that one of the hippest things I've ever seen, it's one of the most revolutionary—a true *hip* lesson for the so-called downtown "hipsters."

In 2009 I decided to celebrate my birthday there in a roundabout way by calling it Funkahuatl's hundredth birthday celebration. It was my sixty-seventh. I was thrilled that both of my sons were there, along with many of my homies, including photographer George Rodriguez. Plus Miss Altar in the Sky made it too. I was ready to smoke, and we did.

The band was becoming a tightly knit funk juggernaut and they kicked my ass into a higher sphere, just what I had prayed for. The highlight, though, was making a wish before I blew out the candles for the continued happiness of my sons. Damn, I love those guys. Then, the capper, everyone sang *"Las Mañanitas,"* and my heart sang right along with them. There ain't nothing quite like it, a sweet reminder that I'm a Mexican and fuckin' proud of it.

I was feeling a strong thirst and drank a Bohemia down in one gulp, then walked out side with some friends to smoke a little something. I took a couple of hits from a pipe and, still feeling thirsty, went back in and ordered a bottle of water at the bar. Next thing I knew, I was looking up at a circle of people looking down at me in shock—Chaz Bojórquez and his wife Christina, John Avila, Richard and Consuelo Montoya, Raúl Pacheco, Freedo Ortiz, Willie the owner, and Alán the manager, who was asking how many fingers he was holding up. I didn't feel any fear, surprise, or worry, just serenely at peace. It was surreal for reals. I counted five fingers, and Alán pulled me up from the floor asking over and over if I was okay. "Yeah, I'm cool." I looked around for my sons and the goddess, but thankfully they'd missed the stupid drama. I went to the bar and ordered another bottle of water. Next thing I knew, I was looking up at the same astonished circle! Again I counted the fingers on Alán's hand and slowly got up and walked to the bar for *another* bottle of water and some cheese and crackers. "Whatever happens in the Eastside Luv stays in the Eastside Luv," I muttered to the shocked bunch, who chuckled. I sat down on a bench to drink and eat. A young lady nearby leaned over and said, "Hey man, that was cool." "What, do you mean?" I asked. "The way you went down—twice—so slow and smooth like in slow motion, like in a dream. That was so cool." I thanked her and bought her and her friend a glass of wine, then joined them.

I went to the doctor a few days later and got a checkup—treadmill, the works. I passed everything with flying colors. Doc said I was probably just dehydrated and weak from no food. He was right. I didn't drink any water and had only eaten a banana that day. It was a lucky wake-up call, reminding me that I wasn't thirty anymore, even though I felt like I was. But yeah, the reality was that I was pushing seventy. How the fuck did that happen?

And by the way, if fainting is like dying, then death is a piece of cake. No big thing.

The Tao of Funkahuatl

A COUPLE OF YEARS GO BY and I finally finish my solo album, *The Tao of Funkahuatl*. It only took me sixty-seven years. I'm happy with it, although a few imperfections got by. I dedicated the album to my dad and gave shout-outs to my platonic garden, which can be seen as either pathetic or thoughtful. The album is another cultural document, only this time a more personal look into the soul of a Xikano artist.

I'd hurt my leg doing some of my crazy dance moves and it was painful walking from the bus to the recording sessions at John Avila's studio in San Gabriel, plus it was a very hot summer. I was depressed because deep inside I knew I wasn't going to recoup my expenses—over $15,000—and I was living as usual on the edge of homelessness. But there were highlights, especially Steve Alaniz's soulful sax solo in "When I Was Young." His entrance into the solo is one of the most exciting I've ever heard on wax. It made it all worthwhile.

The sessions went well overall. John Avila was a pleasure to work with, as always, and Ramón Banda and Bob Robles were very generous with their time and help with some of the arrangements, as was Steve. The bulk of the cost went into the mixing process, since I tend to be a perfectionist. I wanted the album to be a musical audio mural/novel soundtrack and also a conceptual work of art: a vinyl music-art piece. I asked my homie John Valadez to draw an ink illustration of a couple in a tantric embrace for the cover, a fine-art litho-print of which was inserted into each of the 150 limited-edition vinyl albums. My homie Francesco X. Siqueiros pressed and pulled the prints at his El Nopal Press in downtown L.A., where he's been since 1992. Joel "Rage" Garcia, a former mural student of Paul Botello at the Maravilla housing projects (with my Arts 4 City Youth program), was the graphic designer for the album. He was also very generous with his time and talent—a solid soul brother. Yeah, it was a painful labor of love, as all my projects are.

The Tao of Funkahuatl

He's a conduit, a messenger
A tantrik medicine man
Spreadin' the Tao, spreadin' the way
Spreadin' the Funkahuatl Plan

It's about makin' love, with your life
Your spirit, and your soul
So hook 'em up, with your heart
Down salvation road

Talkin' about the Tao of Funkahuatl
The Tao of Funkahuatl will feed your hungry heart
You know the Tao, of Funkahuatl
The Tao of Funkahuatl is living as a work of art

Let's go to my place and make some tantrik music
Let's go to my place and make a whole lotta love
Let's take it to a place where sex is sacred
Let's take it to a place where love is God

You know Marvin Gaye advised an' you know he pleaded
We gotta get down an' share some sexual healing
So let's mix our spirit with our sex an' soul
Gonna take our love higher, higher to a new plateau

Talkin' about the Tao of Funkahuatl
The Tao of Funkahuatl will feed your hungry heart
You know the Tao, of Funkahuatl
The Tao of Funkahuatl is living as a work of art

You know the Tao, of Funkahuatl
Yeah, the Tao, of Funkahuatl will soothe your sexy soul
Yeah, the Tao, of Funkahuatl
The Tao, of Funkahuatl will never get ol'

Release of The Tao of Funkahuatl
CD in L.A. and Japan

MY FRIEND FROM JAPAN, Shin Miyata, contacted me saying he wanted to release *The Tao of Funkahuatl* as a CD in Japan on his Barrio Gold Records label. What a fantastic break! It made sense, since there already was an interest there with Ruben And The Jets. But *Tao* isn't a typical Chicano album. Gotta give credit to Shin for saying that that was okay, that it was time to show Japanese youth the evolution of Chicano music and culture—at least in my case. Here is an excerpt of a letter I wrote to him explaining the concept behind the album:

Dear Shin,

I use the term and spelling "Xikano" to identify myself and my music. It doesn't just mean Chicano, a politicized Mexican American that wants to educate, enrich, and empower his community and people. I also see it as a person who lives with spiritual awareness in their life and actions, pushing the envelope in human relationships and even stepping out of the culture to bring in other philosophies like Buddhism, Tantra, and Sufism. I have done that with *The Tao of Funkahuatl*. That's why I call it "Xikano tantrik funk."

The Los Angeles CD release party at Tropico de Nopal was a mix of highs and lows. A heavy rainstorm hit, keeping attendance down. The highlight was a collaboration with performance artist Liliflor, who dressed up all fine as a *pachuka* version of the Virgen de Guadalupe, only she was the Virgen de Boyle Heights. I read the song poem "La Virgencita de Boyle Heights" from my new album, with the band playing an oldie doo-wop riff as she threw rose petals to the audience while walking to the stage. It was perfect *pachuk@* performance art.

Then disaster struck. On the day the CD was to be shipped to Japan, March 11, the devastating earthquake and tsunami hit. I was reminded of the Albert King lyric, "If it wasn't for bad luck, I wouldn't have no luck at all." Fortunately, Shin and his family were okay. But the country and its economy were in shambles. The shipment sat on the runway at LAX for a few days. But Shin, bless his heart, decided not to cancel the order. He could have canceled, and I would have completely understood. That is true *carnalismo* brotherhood in action.

The album was reviewed favorably in two major Japanese record magazines. One store owner, Nobutaka of Q-Vo records, became a fan and even tattooed *Funkahuatl* on his arm, together with a geisha holding a 45 RPM record with *C/S* printed on it. It was the ultimate compliment. You just never know who's paying attention. Gotta love my Japanese brothers and sisters.

But what exactly is going on with the fascination with cholo culture? Japan has one of the highest youth suicide rates in the world. Maybe the emotionally repressive culture and the extreme expectations of material success drive kids to kill themselves. So they adopt the renegade culture of the *chol@*—a symbol of radical freedom and recklessness. Maybe that's their way of saying "fuck you" to society, their *con safos*.

MEX/LA

I WAS INVITED BY VISUAL artist and independent curator Rubén Ortiz-Torres to create a listening station on the history of Los Angeles Chicano rock 'n' roll (covering the years 1948 to 1985) for the landmark exhibition *MEX/LA: "Mexican" Modernism(s) in Los Angeles, 1930–1985* at the Museum of Latin American Art. This would become my greatest lifetime achievement: to sculpt the history of Chicano popular music in Los Angeles and see it presented alongside such Mexican visual art titans as Rivera, Orozco, Siqueiros et al. It was also the first time this museum showcased Mexican American/Chicano and Chicana artists—the rule having been to show only Latin American art. Many of those artists are personal friends, including Barbara Carrasco, John Valadez, Harry Gamboa Jr., and Chaz Bojórquez, whom I have seen grow and emerge as giants themselves. I was humbled and blown away big time to be a part of this milestone event at the intersection of Mexican and Chicano/Mexican American art history.

I wrote the "The Present-Day Pachuco Refuses to Die!"[1] for the listening station, but then was asked to rewrite it: the piece needed to be shorter and more to the point, since it was going to be posted on the wall and read next to the listening station. I didn't know that it would also be printed in the catalogue when I agreed to rewrite it. If I had known, I wouldn't have rewritten it. Below is the original and the final essay combined.

---

1. Two L.A. avant-rock icons were deeply influenced by pachuco/Chicano/Mexican American culture: Frank Zappa's motto was "The present-day Pachuco refuses to die," written in the liner notes of his Mothers of Invention *Cruising with Ruben & the Jets* album (1968), an homage to a Mexican American doo-wop garage band, while his sometime collaborator Captain Beefheart composed the classic mind-bending "Pachuco Cadaver" for his 1969 masterpiece *Trout Mask Replica*. (Pachuco is spelled with a *c* here to reflect Zappa's original spelling.)

Mexican Americans have had a love-hate relationship with the City of Angels throughout its history. Considered non-Americans in the puritanical WASP sense, we have endured generations of abuse, disrespect, and racist brutality. But we have survived and flourished because of tight family ties, tenacious hard work, blood, sweat, and tears, and—the arts.

We were inspired by Mexican muralists to paint truth. We were inspired by Mexican musicians to sing truth. We were inspired by Mexican poets to write truth. And actors were inspired by Mexican *carpas* (tent shows) to be truth. What is that truth? Love: The love for our *familias* that have journeyed north since the Mexican revolution overcoming life-and-death obstacles; the love for our children and wanting to give them a better life in the face of fierce hardship; the love for our loyal friends who support our struggle to succeed; and love for a city that became our cherished home—in spite of not accepting us.

Our musical sensibilities merged with those of African Americans of the 1940s who were also struggling for acceptance. Los Angeles Mexican American musicians Lalo Guerrero and Don Tosti created *pachuco* boogie-woogie in the 1940s, a hybrid musical genre influenced by many L.A. swing/jump blues musicians, including African Americans Roy Milton and Joe Liggins and Greek American Johnny Otis, among others. This prophetic, pulsating mix laid the foundation for Chicano rock and an emerging cultural and political Mexican American identity.

We wore the flamboyant Zoot Suit made popular by the Mexican actor-comedian Tin Tan and which became a suave, stylistic symbol of defiant self-identity, cultural pride, and self-determination. We created our own street hipster slang, *caló*, which was celebrated in the music, lyrics, and our social life. Chicano poet Alurista defined the *pachuco* and *pachuca* as "someone who didn't care to make something beautiful in their lives, but rather to make of their lives—a work of art." Many 1940s L.A. Mexican American musicians and their followers were the essential embodiment of that poetic declaration.

In the 1960s, we embraced the controversial term "Chicano" (recast as a politicized Mexican American) as a new cultural and civil rights movement was taking hold, starting with the unionization of farm workers led by Dolores Huerta and César Chávez and later with the East L.A. student walkouts, or "Blowouts," of 1968, all culminating in the Chicano Moratorium of 1970 where over 30,000 protested the disproportionate deaths of Chicanos in the Vietnam War and the poor quality of education and social services on the East Side of Los Angeles. Rubén Salazar, an *L.A. Times* journalist, and two others perished on that fateful day.

While this turmoil was boiling, Chicano and Chicana musicians once again merged musical sensibilities inspired by their African American brothers and sisters. The Motown Sound made a strong impression on Cannibal &

the Headhunters, a rhythm & blues vocal group from the Ramona Gardens housing projects in Boyle Heights who went on to chart nationally and opened for the Beatles' 1965 national tour. The Premiers also charted nationally with a tune by an L.A. African American duo, Don & Dewey, and later went on to open for the Rolling Stones. L.A. Chicano rock was finally emerging as a vital force in American popular music with many recording artists achieving national and international success, beginning with Little Julian Herrera and Ritchie Valens in the fifties; Thee Midniters, Little Ray, the Salas Brothers, the Romancers, and the Blendells in the sixties; El Chicano, Yaqui, the Bags, and Ruben And The Jets in the seventies; Tierra, the Plugz, the Brat, Los Illegals, and Con Safos in the eighties; Aztlán Underground, Ozomatli, Quetzal, and Rage Against the Machine in the nineties; and the longtime standard-bearers, Los Lobos.

Let's not forget that the popular music coming out of Mexican Los Angeles from the thirties to the mid-eighties—*boleros, rancheras, corridos, pachuko* boogie-woogie, swing, jump blues, jazz, rhythm & blues, rock 'n' roll, punk, funk, hip hop, and salsa—was not just party music, nor was it merely background music for the Chicano civil rights movement. The music helped shape, sculpt, and define an evolving cultural and political identity and future consciousness—*chicanismo:* a commitment for social change through political engagement as well as cultural and spiritual regeneration and responsibility through the arts. Without the artists—the musicians, painters, photographers, filmmakers, *danzantes,* writers, poets, playwrights, and actors—we couldn't have danced to the music of the struggle.

Now in 2011, we are still dancing. We are still singing. We are still making our lives into works of art in this mythical Mexican city of angels and demons. We endure. *¡No nos rajamos!* And, this present-day *pachuko*—refuses to die. *Con safos.*

Thanks again to my *tocayo,* Rubén Ortiz-Torres, for offering this opportunity. It was another milestone landmark achievement and one of my greatest cultural sculpture pieces so far.

Rockin' the House of Dues and Grand Performances

IN LATE 2010, LOUIE PÉREZ of Los Lobos contacted me about opening for his band at the House of Blues. What a break! I worked out, slept right, ate right, did all I could do right to get ready for the big comeback show. The Great Spirit was watching my back after all. But unfortunately, and true to form, two weeks before the show I came down with a nasty cold. I couldn't shake it. The weird thing was, I hadn't had a cold in years. Then my right leg got tight and sore again. I went to a physical therapist for a workout routine. I wound up overdoing what he prescribed, and my leg got worse. I couldn't sleep, talk, or walk. I got scared, and started praying and meditating big-time. The night before the gig, I couldn't sleep. The biggest show of my musical rebirth, and I couldn't even say my name let alone sing it.

The day arrived. I did some deep breathing, stretched a little, meditated, and drove to the gig, stopping along the way to buy a dozen red roses to throw out to the audience. The gig fee was a lot less than what I'd negotiated with Los Lobos' manager, but this would be a great platform to relaunch my career. It turned out Los Lobos were going to pay us from their share of the gig. Now that's *carnalismo*/brotherhood in action.

When I got to the club, Walter Little, our road manager, greeted me with the news that we had to put up a credit card to cover the people that came in over the guest list limit, a tidy sum of $750. He went on to say the band couldn't play until the card was given to the box office. I tried to remember my teachings, to breathe deep and accept the moment and let the drama flow through me. I gave them my debit card with only about $200 in the bank, not really caring because it was just all too fuckin' crazy. Rock 'n' roll, you gotta love it.

This wasn't supposed to happen. The Creator was supposed to have my back. That was the pact we made at Joshua Tree. What the fuck?!

Limping up to the dressing room was depressing. My throat hadn't improved, so I could barely talk, never mind sing. We had about ten minutes for what passed as a sound check—no vocal mic check, just amps and drums. Then I'm told our set is cut from forty minutes to thirty. What a welcome. What a fuckin' nightmare. Creator, are you sure you're with me?

My younger son, Rubencito, showed up in my dressing room and that helped me snap out of it a bit. He told me that Ben was also there. Damn! Both my sons. They were here for me, even though I haven't always been there for them. Thanks to my homies John Valadez and Francesco Siqueiros for giving up their tickets to my sons when they saw they couldn't get in. Seeing Rubencito and Ben really lifted my spirits. I felt it was important to share the event with them, to show them a man at sixty-eight can still craft his art against all odds.

I put on my Tibetan quilt pants, a vintage Chaz Bojórquez graffiti t-shirt, my coat from Bali, my Brazilian canvas leopard-skin shoes, my rust-colored Panama straw hat, my faux leopard-skin floor-length bathrobe, and shades. Superman and Funkahuatl never looked so good. I was ready for action. I was ready to die on stage, if necessary.

I went over the set list with Steve and Bob. It was time. Funkahuatl was at another moment of truth, *"el momento de verdad"*—the most dangerous moment of a bullfight when the matador finally kills the bull, or gets killed. Both are exhausted and wounded, and one wrong move and either one can go down, usually the man.

The curtain was down as I hobbled across the stage to check the microphone. I thought I'd at least get that. I yelled, "Checking," and a sound technician told me that they were ready. "Yeah, but I'm not!" I yelled. As the curtain started going up I heard cheering from the audience. It surprised me. There was a rainstorm going on and I thought the place would be empty, at least for the opening act. The curtain was halfway up when I saw it was a full house. Stunned, I instinctively swung into professional mode. We started with "At the Eastside Luv." Not the best opener, but it was a good way to place the band (as being from East L.A.) and set up a jazzy blues-rock vibe in the room. The band was on and was sounding great. Unfortunately, there were no drums in my monitors. Still, we received a decent response. A few die-hard fans from the Eastside Luv showed up, and that was encouraging. I still felt disconnected from the band because of the drums missing in my monitor. But I moved forward, totally on instinct, like a blind and deaf migrating bird singing and flying through a lightning storm.

The Eastside Luvers opening for Los Lobos at the House of Blues, Hollywood, 2010. *Left to right*: Bob Robles (guitar), John Avila (bass), Ramón Banda (drums), Funkahuatl (vocals), Steve Alaniz (tenor sax). Photo by, and courtesy of, George Rodriguez.

With my handsome sons (Rubén III on the left, Ben on the right) celebrating my sixty-sixth birthday, Eastside Luv, Boyle Heights, California, 2008. Photo by, and courtesy of, George Rodriguez.

I invited John Densmore from the Doors to join us on the spoken-word piece "C/S." He performed it with us on a *djembe,* an African hand drum. We had been performing it together over the past couple of years as a duo at community fundraisers. There was a roar from the crowd as he walked out. We got into it as best we could, neither of us able to hear the drums. I was exhausted from dancing and shouting, but I felt we were finally really connecting with the audience as I danced across the stage throwing out roses to the crowd. I ended the piece with "Won't you listen to what the walls have to say, L.A.? All they are saying is: *¡Que viva Los Angeles! ¡Que viva Yangna! ¡Que viva mi tierra! ¡Que viva Aztlán!* Hey . . . long live L.A.!"

We didn't have a solid ending for the tune, so it ended kind of suddenly and anticlimactically. It felt like a dud. Plus, I wasn't sure how the house sound mix was. But we got some solid feedback that we did a killer show. Evidently, it *was* great. Even Lobo David Hidalgo dug it. And the band *did* play their asses off. I was starting to feel better. Then I remembered the $750 door tab, but I decided not to let it faze me. Fuck the tab. Densmore heard about my predicament and offered to cover half. The band agreed not to get paid, and their small fee went to the tab. Now, that's professionalism and brotherhood to the max.

Was it worth it? It was worth Hidalgo's compliment, and Louie said he wanted to do it again. But was it *worth* it? Well, there were a few moments, a few sparks of fire-lightning that lit up and tore up the nightmare. And after all, that's what I live for: To hotwire rock 'n' roll, to live or die in a song. But the most meaningful part of the evening was having my two sons there. They are my true legacy. They reminded me that what's really valuable in life can't be measured by achievements, no matter how great. And I wanted to remind them that age is just a number and that they too should follow their own dreams, even late in life. A rock 'n' roll career is a footnote in history at best. But your kids? They're forever.

Another career-affirming moment occurred at California Plaza for the Grand Performances concert series. It was a tribute to the Phillips music store, a former landmark in Boyle Heights. Reed Johnson of the *L.A. Times* wrote a nice "Calendar" cover piece on it before the show.

Ramón Banda and Bob Robles were previously booked and couldn't do the gig, so I asked Andee Avila, John's nephew, to sing and play drums and my *tocayo* Rubén Guaderrama from the Blazers to cover the guitar and vocals. As they supplied doo-wop vocal harmonies, I read the spoken-word piece "La Virgencita de Boyle Heights." It was glorious. Then we busted into "C/S," and it smoked. At the end of the song-poem—". . . what's that strange writing on the walls?"—I felt a deep surge of emotion that made my voice crack. Looking out at the crowd, over five thousand strong—the largest we'd ever played for—the towering skyscrapers sitting on top of Bunker Hill, the band cookin' deep in the pocket, and singing about my city, my people's history, and me, my life and the struggle I've gone through getting to that moment, was a solid reminder why I sing and why I came back: to feel my words and music surge through me with intense truth, love, and humility.

Fifty Years in Show Biz

IT WAS JUNE 1, 2011, and I went to bed feeling grateful: Adolfo Guzmán López from KPCC had interviewed me earlier in the day about my fifty years as a musician. Yeah, it had been fifty years since the Apollo Brothers' first single, "My Beloved One," hit the airwaves. I had no idea the interview was going to wind up on the radio the very next morning! When the clock-radio alarm went off, I woke up hearing host Madeleine Brand introducing me as "Not exactly a household name." That cracked me up. It was sick and surreal at the same time, being on National Public Radio when I can barely pay the rent. What a trip. What a heartbreaker. But you just gotta keep rockin' 'n' rollin' with the punches and let life keep the beat.

Later that day, I opened my email and saw an article from *Milenio,* a Mexico City newspaper (thanks to Rubén Martínez), with a review of *The Tao of Funkahuatl* and some background on me. It was sweet payback from the country that in '74 had derided me and my culture. But what tripped me out was that I was giving Mexico some new imagery and iconography: "Funkahuatl, the neo Aztek deity of tantrik funk," as opposed to "*Matón* (Killer)" or other stereotypical gangsterisms. Now they were saying "*The Tao of Funkahuatl* is the *tao* of neo-*pachukismo,* a creative spiritual/sexual life-style." ¡*Órale Mexicanos cabrones! ¡Y que!*

It was now time for my big fiftieth-anniversary concert at the Eastside Luv. My energy level was high and I was ready for the challenge. The Luvers and I were still buzzing from the tight Museum of Latin American Art concert a week earlier, and we were ready to burn the house down. I decided to put the cover at a reasonable $8—eight lousy bucks to be a witness to a fifty-year career of surviving rock 'n' fuckin' roll. How could I lose? I was sure that would fill the house. Besides, wouldn't the Universe have my back even if it was on an off-night Wednesday? Sadly, it turned out to be one of the coldest days on record, close to freezing. Plus, there was a major accident on the 60 freeway that closed the traffic in both directions. "If it wasn't for bad luck . . ."

I wanted to give the show a theatrical element to honor my performance art work over the years. So I invited endy trece, a *danzante* and also a former butoh student with Sankai Juko, who wore a traditional Afghani dress and performed a mesmerizing opening ceremony combining butoh movement with Aztec/Mexika *danza* elements. She wore conch shells on her ankles and danced a slow whirling-dervish piece, turning fifty times, one for every year of my career. I was awestruck, especially since I hadn't known what she was going to do. Then another performer, José L. Reynoso, whom I had booked for the performance summit *Word Up!* at the Ford, jumped on the bar and began a crazy spoken-word dance piece wearing a Buddhist monk's robe and waving boxing gloves with wild disco music playing. He looked like a Mongolian boogie-priest go-go boy honoring my past fifty with perfect out-of-this-world reverence. They both were spellbinding. It was mysterious and powerfully beautiful. The bar had never been that quiet. The audience didn't know what hit them.

I was fired up. We went on and everything clicked. We got into the magic-zone pocket where it's all musical telepathy. We even did a blues tune for the first time. I made up the words. After three years of sporadic performances, we were one single breath of funk and soul, and I sang as if my life depended on it, pushing my voice into new terrain. I must say I got down . . . and didn't fall down. It was the best show of my life, for reals, and got several encores. I looked into the audience and saw my homie and longtime collaborator John Valadez. It made me feel good that he was there even though the house was empty and I knew I was in trouble financially. I wanted him to see me really do my thing. He'd been there at Eastside Luv the first night of my comeback too. It was a sloppy performance that night. But now, I felt good that he was finally seeing my art in action.

The final count was that ten people paid the $8 cover. We sold two CDs. After I paid the band, I was $150 in the hole. Some things just never change. Burned again. What up, Great Spirit? I thought you had my back. Then suddenly out of nowhere, a beautiful young blonde wearing a fancy evening gown—she could've been a New York high fashion model—walked up to me and said, "Can I hug you? I love your energy." Am I a loser or a hero? I don't know, maybe both. So ultimately, it's not about how many people pay to see your work. It's about doing good work . . . at whatever the price. Like Zappa used to say, "Just shut up and play yer guitar."

Yeah, I wrote this song, "Rock 'n' Roll with the Punches," to convey that sentiment:

> You gotta rock 'n' roll with the punches, let life keep the beat
> Slip and slide with your hunches, don't ever think about retreat
> I was born to boogie woogie, I was born to jump and shout
> I was born to make my dreams come true
> Yeah, that's what it's all about
>
> I'll never have a million dollars
> I'll never have a PhD
> Just wanted to sing that sweet soul music
> 'Cause it's the only thing that matters to me

Miss Beijing

I MET A LOVELY LADY from China when I was teaching the boys at Metropolitan State Hospital. She was working in the administration office while she finished a master's degree. She'd been a gynecologist in Beijing but couldn't practice here because she lacked the necessary credentials. One day our paths crossed while I was walking my class to the playground. We smiled at each other in a collegial sort of way, and I just said hi. But there was something there. Something in her eyes and smile that seemed to imply a respect for what I was doing—working there as a teacher with those difficult boys. I felt it, and it touched me. We became friends and eventually started going out to lunch together. She asked about my work with the boys and how it was going. She had a sweet accent. I was so grateful that somebody would care to ask me those questions. She was a Godsend, and naturally, being the love-starved fool that I was, I fell for her. (This was during the time I was in the on–and-mostly-off relationship with Miss Tokyo.) One day at lunch, just before Christmas vacation, she dropped a bomb: She was going on vacation to Greece with her boyfriend to meet his parents. Boyfriend? Why didn't she ever tell me about a boyfriend? I bit the bullet, hid my heartbreak, and wished her well.

After the depressing holidays, I was walking through the administration building and saw someone's shadow walking, and then running, toward me. It was her. She looked happy to see me—very happy. I was baffled, and thought maybe she'd broken up with her boyfriend. I asked her to lunch and she accepted. While describing her trip she handed me a necklace of beads that were thought to be from Atlantis. Then came another bomb: her boyfriend had proposed marriage. Again I bit the bullet, smiling but with a knife in my heart. The knife sunk deeper when she asked me to write and read a poem at their wedding reception. What's a dogged love warrior to do? I accepted.

The chapel was filled with Asians, Greeks, and assorted friends. I was the only Latino there. I sat in the back. I was wearing my tux and feeling okay. This was a stone trip, a real test of character—or stone fuckin' madness. The organ started playing and everyone turned around to watch the bride enter. I was afraid to look. How much more could I take? She glided by me on her father's arm with a sheer white veil partially covering her face, her gown trailing behind. My heart sank as she walked past me. She looked glorious. After a long ceremony they were pronounced husband and wife, kissed, and started up the aisle arm in arm. They looked beautiful. I forced a smile as they walked by.

I stood in a long line outside waiting to congratulate them, wondering how that would go. When I finally reached her, I gave her a polite cheek-to-cheek kiss and waited to be introduced to her husband. It didn't happen. I waited. It didn't happen. She introduced me to her parents instead, while he looked at me with a puzzled look on his face. Feeling nervous, I blurted out my name and said that I'd been asked to read a poem at the reception. He just stared at me, bewildered. It was very awkward.

The hall was packed. The wedding party was on the stage, with the newlyweds in the middle. Members of the family made toasts and read testimonials to the couple. I listened and waited to be introduced. When it looked like no one was going to introduce me, I took the mic from the last speaker and introduced myself, saying that the bride and I were coworkers at Metro and that she'd asked me to write and present a wedding poem. Her husband turned and stared at me, I'm sure wondering, "Who the fuck is this guy?!" There was silence. I read a haiku about the sanctity of love and marriage, finished to more silence, then, slowly, came polite applause—another very awkward moment. I made my way to my seat and waited for the cake, then quickly left, waving goodbye to the bride and groom, mouthing "congratulations" as I went. Shortly thereafter, she moved away.

Seven years later on frickin' Facebook, I got a friend request. It was her. She'd had a son and her marriage had collapsed: the dude wanted out. I wondered if my poem had anything to do with it. We set a date to meet for dinner, to celebrate our birthdays. She was also a Libra. I rented a car, bought some new clothes; I also bought an orchid plant, a bouquet of roses, and chocolates for her and some books for her son. I was ready to rock.

As I sat on a bench outside the restaurant waiting for them to arrive, I wondered what she would look like after all these years. Was she still sweet and beautiful or sour and haggard? It didn't matter. Either way, I was eager to see her again. Then she appeared, walking toward me holding her son's hand. She was more beautiful than on her wedding day. My heart leaped into my throat as we hugged. She introduced me to her son, a very well-mannered five-year-old, and complimented me on my cool Nehru jacket, noting that I was still trim. I said thanks and told her she was more beautiful than I had imagined she'd be. She blushed and said thank you. She didn't bring up the failed marriage, instead talking about her new job and the demanding role of motherhood. The dinner was grand, with fish, salads, and desserts. When the check came, she insisted on paying half. I eventually said okay, although I was a bit embarrassed. She drove me to my rental car and I pulled out the gifts and proudly gave them to her. She smiled and said, "Oh my, thank you so much!" She still had that adorable accent. We planned another dinner, but it never happened.

A few years later, she surprised the hell out of me when she came up to me as I was talking with Little Willie G. backstage after the *MEX/LA* concert. Man, I was thrilled to see her, but wary that anything would develop, since her life was about raising her son. She sincerely complimented me on the performance, saying that the poem "La Virgencita de Boyle Heights" was her favorite moment. That touched my heart. We promised to meet again, but it never happened. Just as well. What could I have offered her? Where could it have gone? Sometimes, love simply isn't enough.

Miss Monterey Park

AFTER THREE LONG YEARS and countless dinners at the restaurant in Monterey Park, she finally looked at me. She was preparing to get off work, standing in front of a mirror by the lockers. She stared at me in the mirror. It was very odd, especially for a Chinese woman. They are generally super discreet, never making eye contact, especially with a non-Asian dude. But she stared a long time. I tried not to pay attention, but our eyes met for a few seconds and it tripped me out.

Several months went by before I went there again. When I walked in, this time she didn't look at me at all. She was as distant as China and as cold as ice. I decided to forget about her. Why waste my time? Yet I was fascinated with her unbelievable beauty and that enigmatic stare, which seemed to say, "Who the fuck are you and why are you looking at me"? I couldn't get her out of my mind. Eventually I worked up the courage to go see her again. This time she was serving the buffet. She was frozen stone solid with that icy stare. As I ordered, my eyes got sucked into her gaze, into her beauty, and for a split second our eyes locked. I could only point to the food I wanted, and even with that, I stammered.

I watched her work while I ate. She never stopped moving. The hardest-working waitress I'd ever seen. I wondered why she was there. She was beautiful enough to have any man that wanted her. If she could be an empress for some rich fat cat, why was she slaving as a waitress? And what the fuck did I have to offer? Still, I wasn't going to give up. When she came by my table, I pointed to her name tag, Angel, and jokingly asked if she was an angel or a devil. She stared at me, said nothing, just kept moving. Then I realized: she didn't speak English! So if I was going to seduce her, it would have to be a soul-to-soul thing. What a trip.

After a few months and yet another breakup with Miss Tokyo, I went back. I saw that they served smoothies. When she finally looked my way I said very slowly and clearly, "Can...I...have...an...Angel...smoothie?" while pointing to the menu on the wall. She stared at me with that glacial glare, then, slowly, flashed a tiny smile for a brief instant. Damn! I'd finally cracked the Great freakin' Wall of China! Now whenever I entered the restaurant the other waitresses would yell out, "Angel smoothie, Angel smoothie," and giggle. She slowly started to melt and we became friendlier as time went by. I bought her gifts, including hand lotion for her rough hands. Then one night she miraculously gave me her phone number. But when I'd call she would only sing to me, since she couldn't speak English. It was weird but beautiful. And man, she had an unbelievably lovely voice. It charmed the hell out of the dog. We would be on the phone for hours into the early morning and she would sing in Mandarin, song after song. "That was so beautiful," I would say after each one. "Beautiful. For you"—that's all she would say. I'd never communicated with a woman like that. Maybe she *was* an angel.

One night a few months later she was on a break and studying for her citizenship test. I offered to help. Trust was being built, and we eventually went out for birthday dinners (both of us were also Libras), to a Chinese buffet place in San Gabriel where you load a plate with raw food and cook it at your table. She scooped crab, fish, sliced beef, pork, chicken, and vegetables onto my plate. As she was cooking up the feast I imagined her as my wife. But then reality sunk in: I couldn't afford her. No money, no honey.

After dinner I walked her to her car, determined to finally give her a kiss. As she sat in her car looking forward, I leaned down from outside and softly kissed her cheek. She didn't move; she just froze, then, still looking forward, drove off. I stood there dazed and could only say, "What the fuck?!" Maybe it was what my homie Francesco said, too much moisture in the kiss. Or maybe I'd crossed some kind of cultural line. Whatever—she disappeared and I never saw her again.

When all is said and done, if all that can ever come out of these hapless romantic escapades is a poem or two, that's good enough for me. It has to be. Plus, it keeps the dog karma down.

Haiku for Xia

Xia, *la chinita*
Ojos de luz y noche
Toca mi alma

Xia, China in flesh
Eyes of light and endless night
Touch my hungry soul

¿Hablarte? ¿Cómo?
Solamente con amor
Lenguaje de luz

We speak foreign tongues
Only hearts and souls can know
A language of Light

Nee how ma, chula?
(How are you, gorgeous?)
Wor syung gern nee zai ee chee
(I want to make love to you)
Beyond flesh and time

Of Lust, Love, and Light
(For Xia)

Looking up at her, as she stood above me in the tub ready to join
me, I savored her Mandarin beauty with every inch of my
starved, shredded senses. Years had passed since I gazed at the
naked body of a beautiful woman.
The candlelight reflected golden shards of desire off her small
breasts and the long, onyx-black hair that partly covered them.
The glow resonated with *la virgencita*'s muted Mona Lisa smile
shining through the candle votives as if saying, "*M'hijito,* my
dear child, know the sacred mystery of love from the flesh and
beyond. Let it take you higher. Let it take you to heaven. Let it
take you to God."
I knew that moment would find me someday as I passed the stylish
transsexual hookers on Towne Street with their ambiguous
seductive smiles while fighting my lusty dog for fast-food sex.
But releasing into a prostitute would be too easy, empty. Has
nothing to do with religion or morality. It's about the positive
and negative flow of energy. Ultimately, we are nothing but

energy and our destiny is determined by how we choose to use it or—abuse it. In the end, it's like the Yaqui shaman Don Juan said to Castañeda in summarizing life: "We come from light, we return to light." So the sooner we realize that, the sooner we'll return. I clearly remembered those words as I cupped her perfect peaches, her erect nipples softly pressing against the palm of my hand, firm and smooth as small, fresh-picked grapes.

Move tenderly, let the body simmer. Carefully will the sacred current with reciprocal intention. Feel it flow through your body—and hers. Connect. Feel. Listen. Respond with a focused mind. Savor the surges, the subtle orgasms with every twitch of the body. Gradually turn the heat up. Relish the rise.

I put my hand around her neck and tenderly pulled her down to me. I didn't want to rush the kiss. Needed to move slow. Slow as a birth. Slow as a sunset.

Our mouths met. I moved my tongue around her inner lips gracefully, then slid deeper into her. Her tongue was shy but eventually came alive. She pulled away, sighing my name over and over, part English, part Spanish, part Mandarin.

I had to contain the energy and mindfully proceed. What pleasure in that containment! (Is that what a Buddhist Tantric master experiences, multiple orgasms without ejecting seed?)

Our mouths met again as I moved to a faster rhythm, taking us deeper and higher into the light source. Our bodies locked, sweating in sync with very slow, butoh-like movement.

We became one. One current surged through us, locked in the cosmic pulse, the cosmic heartbeat, the cosmic dance of temporal immortal pleasure. Seconds, lifetimes rushed through us. Only the intensity of a supernatural power, breathing beyond the body, beyond thought, existed. A primal, pristine consciousness: Ecstasy.

The rush of blood to both of my heads felt like breaking the sound barrier. Breaking through reality's membrane into a parallel universe, a supra reality, moving at the speed of light. Moving at the speed of love. Interesting how time stops while making love. Only skin and sweat, breath and pulse, exist. Another dimension takes over, suspending time and space where one is temporarily a god.

The room suddenly glowed as in an apparition, and as we became one with it *la virgencita* smiled and winked her approval, as we floated above the water . . . steam still rising off our backs.

End of the Ten-Year Sex Drought

Love doesn't need the distraction of intercourse.

GABRIEL GARCÍA MÁRQUEZ

AS I TRIED TO CLIMB my rock at Joshua Tree on another New Year's Day ritual of thanksgiving, I wondered if the beautiful woman I had just met was the one who would break my ten-year dry spell. My leg was tight and sore, it was painful to climb, and I couldn't reach the top. Over two years had passed since I'd pulled another muscle doing my crazy dance moves, and it had never healed. Fuck, I *was* getting old. I felt my time was running out.

I decided to call the woman, and we met the following week.

And . . . we rocked 'til the fuses blew. It was electric and atomic.

We met a couple more times, but the dog was having trouble keeping his mojo working, so I finally broke down and got some Viagra. Man! Never thought I'd ever have to do that. But hey, seventy was staring me in the face. I had to accept it.

I saw her a few more times, but something was missing—love, not from her, from me. I didn't want to take advantage of her, so I ended it. I may be a dog, but I'm a dog with a conscience . . . and a heart.

True love is not carnal, although it can be sexual, sensual, and spiritual, as in tantra. True love is a deeper energy that is exchanged through trust, empathy, and compassion, rather than passion, which is only the spark. Then after many years of commitment to mutual spiritual growth, true love appears, like a flower through mud.

I would love to love someone unconditionally in another intimate, romantic relationship before I leave the planet. That's what ultimately makes a human, human. After all, isn't love the music of God? Aren't I a singer? As I've said before, it's a reciprocal thing, a give-and-take thing, a promise to support the flowering of each other's spirit and a promise to live in its sacred funk, *por vida*. That's what a true lover *and* revolutionary must do. Like my *tocayo* Che Guevara said, "You can't have a revolution without love."

Seventy and Still Running

I STARTED A TRADITION WHEN I turned forty of putting together a kick-ass concept concert every decade that doubled as a birthday party blow-out present to myself and a cultural event, starting with *The Eastside Revue* in '83. But I was stumped about what to do for my seventieth. I just wasn't feeling it.

I kicked that number around, back and forth, struggling with it for weeks. I had a real hard time accepting it. Seventy—fuck, that's old! *Old!* I hate that fucking word! Why should I broadcast that I'm now obsolete, irrelevant, and as disposable as last night's condom? It's fucking absurd!

But wait a minute: that's exactly what my life has been—one long, unraveling, absurd joke. It's right in line. So, I got in line. When I started inviting my friends, it blew my mind how many I had: a lot. So what the fuck, man, get over it! I have family and friends, and I'm healthy for an old warrior dog. What more did I want? So, what the fuck! Fuck society! Fuck conformity! Let's partaaay, whachusaaaay?!

My homie Reyes Rodríguez generously offered his art gallery for my *funk-changa* birf-day blowout. I invited the band, who offered to play as a gift. That blew me away. God bless professional musicians. The guest list exploded with over 150 close friends and family, including my painter homies John Valadez, Wayne Alaniz Healy, Chaz Bojórquez, Francesco X. Siqueiros, David Botello, Willie Herrón III, and Tito Delgado; performance artists María Elena Fernández, endy, and pioneer performance artist and director Dan Kwong; guest musicians Freedo Ortíz (Beastie Boys), singer Tamara Vasquez, Raúl Pacheco (Ozomatli), and Guillermo "Willie" Uribe, owner of the Eastside Luv, with manager Alán Rangel. My dear friends Lily and Mike Yanagita, Kathy Masaoka, and Kay Sera were also present. My son Ben with his beautiful partner, Didi Lody, and my dear sister Bonita's son, Samuel, whom I hadn't seen in years, were there, along with his dad, Sam Mavros, and stepmom, Marilyn: that made the night complete. (Rubencito was living in New York and couldn't make it, and neither did my nephew Tony Mavros.)

I made it a potluck thing and we had a Mexican, Japanese, Indian, and Korean feast fit for a seventy-year-old spunky funky monkey soul survivor. Homie Willie Loya's *chile verde* was the bomb supreme. My dear friend KPCC radio broadcast journalist Adolfo Guzmán López read a moving poem about my crazy life journey, and Richard Montoya (Culture Clash) also read a poem. Xiuy Velo, bass player for Los Illegals, introduced me. I walked up to the mic and thanked everyone for coming, then said I had a confession to make. "Tonight, I'm coming out of the closet . . ." There was a gasp of silence. ". . . The age closet. I am seventy mother-fucking years old today, *¡y que cabrones!*" It felt good to get it off my chest, and finally say it: "*Se-ven-ty.* So let's fuckin' get cray-zy!" The band started playing a hard Latin funky groove and we took off. We hadn't performed together all year, and we smoked, tearing the roof off. I sang and moved like I was back on *Shindig!* At least, it felt that way.

The next day I drove out to Point Mugu, north of Malibu. I had to fulfill a promise I made at my fiftieth birthday, of running full-tilt-boogie on the beach on my seventieth. I smoked some incredible hash and drove up the coast on Highway 1, remembering the drives up the same coast to Oxnard with my beloved *tata* as a kid. Nothing had changed: it was the same rugged-smooth mountains along the highway cutting and kissing the Chumash sky, the cobalt blue-green ocean crashing and smashing its fierce love against the rocks below. It was a perfect day, in the high seventies and sunny, no clouds, very unusual for mid-October.

When I reached my destination, the dog was ready to run. It was sunset, and the beach was deserted. It was all mine. I started at a slow pace along the shore, splashing my feet as I ran. The water was mild. My right leg felt good, so I picked up the pace. Little by little I started to run faster, then bam! I broke into a full sprint and took off running like a stallion, a bolt of lightning, licking and kicking up the white foamy water. My tears mixing with salt, running, running, running through my past, running through my burns, running through the terrors, the fears, running through my heartbreaks, running through my loves, running like a track star, running like a rock star, running like a man on fire, running to the end of the world. I fell, rolled in the sweet, baptismal water, rolled back up, cut the dog loose, and kept on running, running, laughing my ass off into the sunset.

Platonic Homegirls

THAT NIGHT I DREAMT I was in a mystical garden surrounded by my platonic homegirls. They were flowers from their feet to their waist, their legs like flower stems rising from the ground, and from the waist up, human, like planted flower sirens. They were all smiling at me in a golden light that lit the psychedelic night sky: Miss Blue Eyes; the Enchantress; Miss Beijing; Miss Monterey Park; Miss V.; Miss traci kato-kiriyama; Miss Bogotá; Miss Altar in the Sky; Tlahuiyolotzín the *danzante;* endy trece; Mixpe, Kristina Wong; Danile Shimada; Tamara Vasquez; and Ixya, the Goddess of Song.

Suddenly my daughter appeared from the shimmering amber light and said in a soft, melodious voice, "Father, these women, these sisters, these homegirls, were dream vessels of my love to you, a way of sharing my heart with you. Thank you for honoring my love by not being the dog that you are, with them." We laughed.

In the dream, my daughter reminded me that platonic love is dispassionate, nonsexual, and most importantly, spiritual. "Thank you *m'hija.* I love you."

She embraced me, looking straight into and through my eyes, and tenderly said, "I love you, father, I have always loved you." She kissed my cheek, stepped back into the love light, smiled, and waved as she slowly evaporated into my heart while my platonic homegirls soulfully sang:

"Remember, and honor what your daughter said.

Remember her eternal truth.

Remember her eternal love.

Remember.

Remember."

Joseph Trotter

I LIKE TAKING THE NEW Gold Line train to Little Tokyo from my place in Boyle Heights. It's about ten minutes away. (My car died a few years ago and I had to choose between another car or recording the new album.) I go to Little Tokyo often for dinner, to Suehiro Cafe on First Street. This Christmas Eve will be twenty years since the night Junko gave me the change that I had forgotten, the night I had only enough for a bowl of *miso* soup and some rice, newly separated and alone without my wife and son.

I befriended a homeless cat who panhandles there, holding on to an old, bent walker next to his shopping cart filled with his life possessions. He's a very intelligent, soft-spoken African American gentleman. We're the same age. I've known him for about seven years now, and have given him money, clothes, and blankets over that time. He's also a well-read cat. We recently discussed Richard Wright's *Native Son,* one of his favorites. We talked about the end of the book, when Bigger Thomas tells his attorney before his execution that he wished he "would've lived right so he could die right." Remembering and repeating that line struck a raw nerve in both of us.

One night we talked about the tsunami that had hit Japan the year before and how people lost everything. Then I finally asked him, "So what happened, bro'? How did you wind up on the street?" "I'm a strong man," he said, "but I lost my grip when *my* bad-luck tsunami hit. I lost everything—my job, my family. My life. But I got through it . . . still am getting through." Tears welled up in his eyes, and for a second I saw all my fears and pain in those shattered eyes, fears I've had all my life, of winding up broke and homeless on the streets of my beloved Los Angeles. He said, "But you know what, man, what I do have, and what is most important, is your friendship. You talk to me. Nobody else does. Most don't even look at me. Kindness, bro', that's the greatest treasure of all. Our conversations are my riches . . . my real estate."

I said thanks and handed him a couple of bucks and my CD. "Here, man. Merry Christmas." "Can you please sign it?" he asked, a big toothless grin lighting up his life-and-weather-beaten face. I wrote, "To Joseph, stay strong, my brother. Live right, so you can die right." He bowed his head and said, "Thank you. Thank you for remembering my name." I said good night and shook his hand, a gentle, sun-baked, leather-hard hand as strong as his broken life.

Joseph passed away in 2015, and the news hit me hard. I had lost a true friend.

A Boyle Heights Cultural Treasure

BY A GENTLE TWIST OF FATE, in 2012 I was named a Boyle Heights cultural treasure. I'm sure they scraped the bottom of the barrel to come up with me. Nevertheless, this is the acceptance speech I wrote, though I wasn't able to give it at the ceremony due to time restrictions.

I love history. I love to write about it, sing about it, and I love being a part of it. History is not fixed except for dates and events. It is fluid like culture and can be shaped like clay into . . . sculpture. So, I kind of think of myself as a culture sculptor: creating art works that reflect a time, a place, a people, and their history.

Los Angeles, Boyle Heights, and East L.A. have been the focus of my work for the past fifty years: as a record producer documenting the neglected contributions that our Mexican American musicians have made to the recorded body of rock 'n' roll; and as a singer, musician, composer, songwriter, poet, author, and theater artist reflecting my love of culture and community, and my intolerance for social injustice.

I am inspired by our youth and their drive to succeed if given an opportunity. That's what motivated me to found Arts 4 City Youth in 1993, a free arts program serving over nine thousand Eastside and downtown kids for nearly two decades.

I hope that my free arts program can serve as a model for the continued growth of our youth and our community. I also hope our political leaders will continue to include the residents at the negotiating table when it comes to commercial development and keeping a handle on impending gentrification. Our voices must never be rumors or whispers.

A strong and healthy community is one that is economically, culturally, spiritually, and politically independent and self-sustainable, a place where residents and families are in touch with each other through the arts, politics, and commerce, where youth have a positive sense of belonging and can share their success leading to an optimistic hope for their future. This creates a healthy community with imagination and cohesion between youth and their parents and the community.

Now, in the second half of my life, I can say I finally have roots in a community. My seed was planted here in Boyle Heights at White Memorial Hospital seven decades ago. I have been back for over thirty years now and am proud to live and work here, to make history here: to be part of the proud and strong multicultural legacy of Boyle Heights and of its cultural future.

Thank you for considering me a Boyle Heights cultural treasure. That honor is not taken lightly. But the real treasure lies in the accomplishments of a community grounded in respect, love, education, spirituality, social justice, and the arts. Let's fill up that treasure chest by living our lives as works of art. Let's keep on making history. *¡Que viva Boyle Heights! Tlazocahmati. Gracias.* Thank you.

Boyle Heights Por Vida

BOYLE HEIGHTS IS GOING THROUGH some gentrification challenges with its newfound popularity. In 2009, I was one of many eastside artists who helped form Artists Revitalizing the Eastside (ARTES). We would sometimes meet in my neighborhood at Otomisan (founded in 1956), one of the last Japanese restaurants of Boyle Heights, having (so far) survived the onslaught of colonial displacement. ARTES eventually stopped the First Street Arts Corridor city initiative, intended to funnel revitalization funds into First Street between Anderson Avenue and Chicago Street.

Although at first the initiative seemed like a good idea, ARTES soon realized that it could also cause alienation by outside interests that do not have the community's economic, social, and cultural realities at heart. Through our research and networks it became clear that this was a global issue. In Boyle Heights, mariachis were being displaced due to exorbitant rent increases, and the housing crisis was placing some of our members in danger of losing their homes. In Los Angeles, artists of the original Arts District in Little Tokyo and then later the new Downtown Arts District were seeing their creative use of space being usurped as development surged, causing displacement of residents (including the artists themselves). ARTES became aware of a devious strategy used by real estate developers, which is to label a community an "Arts District" in order to erase the current community and then create a "new and hip" community in its place.

Although there is still a lot of tension around displacement and development in Boyle Heights, the First Street strip (between Anderson Avenue and Chicago Street) still houses mariachi groups; the Eastside Luv Wine Bar; the M Bar; two community theatres, Casa 0101 and Little Casa (founded by Boyle Heights native Josefina López); the community arts center Corazón del

Pueblo (now closed); the Primera Taza café; Espacio 1839, an internet radio station and record, book, and original clothing boutique; independent bookstore Libros Schmibros; and the weekly farmers markets and concerts at the new Mariachi Plaza.

One night in late 2012, I experienced a cultural landscape shift that possibly foreshadowed the future of Boyle Heights. I had just performed a spoken-word set (with Quetzal Flores on guitar and Martha Gonzalez on *cajón*) for a benefit for Liliflor at Little Casa and Corazón del Pueblo, and decided to stop by the Eastside Luv for a glass of wine. Then I went across the street to the M Bar to say hi to a friend, before moving on to the Salón de la Plaza on First and State for a concert by a new buzz band, Chicano Batman. I expected to see the usual Eastside denizens but was surprised to see the place packed with mostly downtown wannabes, mostly white hipsters having the time of their lives. I felt mixed emotions. Although I was glad to see a successful turnout for new talent, I wasn't so sure what it would mean for the future of my neighborhood.

The pseudo-hipsters (we called them yuppies in the '80s) have discovered the cool action and are starting to move into Boyle Heights. Downtown L.A. Art Walk "entrepreneurs" have opened an international hostel across the street from Mariachi Plaza, with other developments pending. There are two major battles going on: one is to prevent the destruction of Mariachi Plaza's longtime mom-and-pop businesses, and the other is to preserve the historic Wyvernwood Apartments from becoming a new high-rise condo complex. The community has unified to protect the Mariachi Plaza businesses, yet is split on the Wyvenwood matter, resulting in some bitter accusations among dear friends.

I was getting so burned out, heartbroken, and frustrated by the discord that I was thinking about moving to an artist colony in Tijuana, but at the last minute I changed my mind. I belong in L.A. and need to help fight off the invasion of the gentrifiers in Boyle Heights and East L.A. I've suggested that one way to deal with the interlopers will be to have them sign off on a Code of Ethics and Expectations to ensure that longtime residents and businesses are not displaced and to enrich the legacy of Boyle Heights. "They will be held accountable, by all means necessary." The truly hip will understand and sign off. Those that don't will be forced to get the fuck out.

Communities, like culture, aren't static. They are alive, fluid, always finding new ways to evolve, to transform, to meld into a kind of magical organic urban alchemy: to sing in a new language; to dance to a foreign beat; to love in a new skin.

Around 1993, *Time* magazine had a picture of an incredibly beautiful woman on its cover. She was a computerized composite of the new American: a blending of all races and cultures. I recently saw the real thing at Reyes's Ecléctica, a world music DJ night at Eastside Luv. She confidently walked up to me and asked me to dance. I took her lovely hand and I felt the soul of the neighborhood rush through me, its deep inner music and stories pulsating, throbbing, as she spun me around the dance floor like a happy bride at a wedding reception. Yeah, the face and soul of Boyle Heights has always been beautiful . . . always will be. *¡A huevo!*

¡Angelin@s Presente!

IN 2015, I HELPED ORGANIZE *¡Angelin@s Presente!,* a fundraiser for Tía Chucha's Centro Cultural in conjunction with a celebration of the cofounder, Luis J. Rodriguez being appointed the new Poet Laureate of Los Angeles. I was in charge of curating the art auction, a poetry reading, and the concert. It turned out to be my most rewarding piece of Chicanx-Angelinx[1] culture sculpture to date. It was presented on June 28 at the historic Pico House (Casa de Pico) on the site of the birthplace of Los Angeles (1781), built as a hotel by businessman Pio Jesús Pico, the last Mexican governor of Alta California before it was annexed by the U.S. in 1846 following the Mexican-American War. When the Pico House opened in 1870, it was considered the most luxurious hotel in Southern California. A tumultuous history sings and screams through those haunted, hallowed walls.

The art auction included most of the Chicanx visual artists and photographers that I have championed over the past thirty years, along with new emerging Angelinx artists, thirty-seven in total. It was one of the largest auctions of Chicanx art I've ever seen. The best part of curating an art auction is visiting my old friends and checking out their new work and catching up, as well as making friends with emerging artists and giving their careers a boost.[2]

---

1. It is a new socio/cultural/political trend to use an *x* instead of an *o* or *a* for greater inclusivity of all genders and identities.

2. The artists in the art auction were José Antonio Aguirre, Carlos Almaraz, José Alpuche, Raul Paulino Baltazar, Chaz Bojórquez, David Botello, Rafael Cardenas, Barbara Carrasco, Richard Duardo, Ofelia Esparza, Emilia García, Margaret Garcia, Daniel Gonzalez, Wayne Alaniz Healy, Judithe Hernández, Willie F. Herrón III, José Lozano, Gilbert "Magu" Luján, Vicente Mercado, Mike Murase, Man One, Nuke One, Rick Ortega,

The poetry reading included a wide spectrum of singular Angelino poets, including Luis J. Rodriguez, Luivette Resto, traci kato-kiriyama, Mike Sonksen and Peter J. Harris.

The powerhouse mix of Angelinx performing artists began with Nobuko Miyamoto entering the interior patio with her shamanic presence singing "To All Relations" while she rubbed a small mallet along the rim of a Tibetan singing bowl, creating a beautiful harmonic sound. Then the rest of her singing group, the Generations, sang solo pieces a cappella: "Atomic" Nancy Matoba shook the walls with "Lands"; Carla Vega sang a very moving jazz tune; then Nobuko's beautiful granddaughter Asiyah Ayubbi sang a Sufi devotional song before the transfixed crowd. Finally, the group performed an inspiring new song, "Black Lives Matter," with June "Jumakae" Kaewsith on keyboards and background vocals. Their presentation reminded me of Sweet Honey in the Rock.

Next up was ten-year-old prodigy Sandino Gonzalez-Flores, son of Quetzal Flores and Martha Gonzalez (both of the band Quetzal), who brought the house down with a couple of stirring *son jarocho* songs. He is destined for greatness. Martha followed with a new song dedicated to the memory of forty-three students from Ayotzinapa, Mexico, who had been disappeared by the local and federal authorities the previous year. Gilberto Gutierrez, *son jarocho* maestro from Vera Cruz, Xochi Flores and César Castro (Cambalache), and special guest Mellow Man Ace further electrified the crowd. Sound was provided by Emiliano "Menoman" Martinez.

I once again performed my song-poem to L.A. "C/S," with John Densmore on *djembe* (African hand drum), Maceo Hernandez on *taiko* drums, George Abe on *shakuhachi* (Japanese flute), and Sean Miura and on *shamisen* (Japanese guitar), which resonated nicely in the open patio, the building's stormy history singing along, harmonizing, and echoing off the resilient, battered walls. Atomic Nancy and I, along with the entire cast, closed the event with an uplifting rendition of "Stand by Me." I know the ancestors and spirits of L.A. were singing and dancing right along with us.

Wenceslao Quiroz, Lili Ramirez, George Rodriguez, Sandy Rodriguez, Sonia Romero, Shizu Saldamando, Herbert Siguenza, Francesco X. Siqueiros, Eloy Torrez, Mario Trillo, Arturo Urista, John Valadez, Jaime "Germs" Zacarias, and Gabriela Malinalxochitl Zapata.

Sara Casillas-Gutiérrez Guevara,
1923–2016

I WENT TO VISIT MY MOTHER for her ninety-second birthday on December 19, 2015. She was in a convalescent home in Hemet, where she had been living for the past several years with my sister Linda as her caregiver and my youngest sister Loretta also watching over her, bless their hearts. Fortunately, I was able to spend time with her, giving Linda a break that allowed her to go visit her children. I knew the end was coming, but we had cheerful conversations. It was so good to hear her laughter. I asked her if she was afraid of dying, and without missing a beat she said no.

When I first saw her, she was sitting in a wheelchair staring out into space. She had been in declining health, suffering from dementia, for the past several years, so I braced myself for a possible meltdown as I approached, a bouquet of red roses in my hand. "Hi, Mom," I said as I handed her the flowers. She turned to look at me, but I could see that she didn't recognize me. I repeated, "Hi, Mom. I've brought you some roses. It's your birthday. Happy birthday, Mom!" She took the roses and placed them in her lap, staring at them. Suddenly her eyes became moist—maybe she was remembering what a birthday was or why people give flowers. I stood watching in silence, my heart shattered into a million tears. It was the most heartbreaking moment since my sister Bonita's tragic death forty-six years before.

It was time for dinner, so I wheeled her to a table and helped her eat. She gently placed the roses on the table, still looking at them silently with tears in her eyes. I spoke with her in a normal voice, trying to make easy conversation like everything was okay, although I was choking inside. I helped her eat her food, remembering that she'd once fed me as an infant—and I saw my life unfold in 3-D: walking hand-in-hand to the *Jamaica* when I was four, then watching her dance like the wind; flying through the front glass door of my *nana's* house, freaking them both out; my fifth birthday party, the happiest day of my youth; marching in the parade with the school band as she and dad cheered me on. I forced myself to speak in a cheery voice, saying "Happy birthday, Mom" over and over, though it was clear I wasn't connecting. She just stared straight ahead, eating, her eyes still wet. My mortality once again stared me in the face as I recalled seeing my father for the last time. I forced myself to maintain.

I wheeled her back to her room and handed the roses to the nurse. She put them into a vase, then I helped her get mom into bed. I held her hand for a while, trying to keep my emotions in check, then kissed her forehead and once again wished her a happy birthday. She just stared at the ceiling.

As I walked out I said to the nurse, "You take good care of my mom. She once was a movie star." At that moment, she turned to me and a faint smile appeared on her still-beautiful face.

She peacefully crossed over in her sleep five months later, on Mexican Mother's Day, May 10, 2016. May her spirit dance forever.

Staged Confessions

IN DECEMBER 2015, DAVID REYES invited me to give a talk on the history of Chicano doo-wop before a performance of a play he was involved in, along with Tom Waldman, at Casa 0101 Theater in Boyle Heights. It was about the eastside rock scene of the sixties and called "Eastside Heartbeats." I accepted, but since I would be presenting in a theater, I decided rather than a talk, I would make it a reading-performance and read excerpts from this book, accompanied by my *Shindig!* video, vintage band photos, and some of my recordings from the past fifty-five years.

Confessions of a Radical Chicano Doo-Wop Singer, a solo, multimedia reading-performance, was first presented at Casa 0101 on January 24, 2016. It was a super treat to be working in a theater again, and with an outstanding tech crew and staff. I gotta give it up to Josefina López and Emmanuel Deleange for having the courage and commitment to bring theater to the Eastside. Emmanuel was a classmate of mine at UCLA, though I did not know him at the time. Ten years later he spotted me at Union Station and came up to me and said, "I saw your performance final at UCLA. It blew my mind. I'm building a theater in Boyle Heights, and I'd like to work with you someday." *Confessions* took place ten years later—twenty years after he saw my performance at UCLA. So again I'll say: whatever you do, do it good chil'ren. You never know who's watching.

Casa 0101 is the only theater on the Eastside offering classes in theater arts for all ages, and is a fertile training ground for aspiring Latinx actors and playwrights. Too cool. Boyle Heights has gotten its theater game on full-tilt boogie and it's looking good, thanks to Casa 0101.

The multimedia reading-performance got a surprisingly strong response from the audience, who were up on their feet and cheering at the end. I was startled, since I had never gotten a standing ovation for a solo performance before. Consequently, Emmanuel wanted to do a full theatrical staging. I said, "Hell yeah, let's find some dough and do it!" We applied for and received a grant from the Eastside Arts Initiative, which allowed us to stage it with a killer full-on set, light, and sound design, directed by my collaborator and close friend the mighty Dan Kwong. It ran for nine performances the last three weeks of the following July. And I don't mind saying it again: standing ovations every night. At seventy-three, I guess I still had some juice left. Interestingly, *Who Are the People?* debuted exactly forty-five years before (July 30–31, 1971) the last two nights of the run.

Opening night was more challenging than the House of Dues gig six years earlier. We'd done a preview the night before that took all I had to deliver. I couldn't sleep that night, just tossed and turned like a drunk cement mixer. It got worse as the sun came up. I stretched, prayed my ass off, stretched some more, and ate some breakfast, all in a scary blur. When the stage manager, Chloe Diaz, arrived to drive me to the gig, I was still in a panic, trying not to show my nervousness. Walking to my dressing room, I couldn't believe that I was about to do ninety minutes. I desperately asked my vocal coach, Corky Dominguez, what I could do to get some energy. He said, "Slap your arms, body, and legs to get the blood flowing." I replied, "What blood, man?!"

The house was close to capacity. I did my vocal warm-ups with Corky, got into wardrobe, and waited for my entrance cue, the opening bars of "To Be Loved" by me and the Jets, my best doo-wop recording by far. Once the music started, I went into automatic pilot and just strolled out into the music. The music: it has certain powers. I took another Carlos Castañeda leap and dove into my life story, leaving my ego panic behind.

Dan did a genius job of streamlining my script, and created some hilarious moments that brought out the comedian in me. I dug it. But it was also a nightmare. Here I was seventy-three, doing three weekends in a row, when I had never performed more than two nights in a row in my life. I was not exactly in shape. But by the second weekend I was getting into the groove, even though I still couldn't sleep at night and my leg was bad. Superman came to the rescue.

On the second weekend, my Berendo classmate crush Helen Funai came to see the show. Turned out she was a friend of Steve Nagano, one of my Manzanar pilgrimage brothers. What were the odds of that happening? Almost sixty years had passed. She looked beautiful, full of grace and charm, still a beauty queen (1963 Nisei Week). We exchanged email addresses and promised to stay in touch. Life sure is a trip.

The show did decent at the box office—a miracle, considering I'm not exactly a young hot item. It was heartwarming to see so many longtime friends show up and offer their cheers.

On October 15, 2017, *Confessions* was restaged at the downtown L.A. Central Library's Mark Taper Auditorium, with Dan Kwong directing again. It was the most challenging and strongest performance of my career. I turned seventy-five two days later and kept my promise to run on the beach, although I limped a bit along with my dog. My rock 'n' roll leg was telling me I was no longer Aztec Watts.

There is interest to take the show on tour to various universities in conjunction with the release of this book. You just never know how the story is going to end. That's why I keep on going, even though there are times I want to throw in the towel. But like the song says, "You gotta rock 'n' roll with the punches, let life keep the beat."

The Fall

WHILE CALLING AN ART AUCTION for the first time, I was once again reminded that I'm not thirty years old anymore. It was at Tía Chucha's 15th anniversary *quinceañera* gala at LA Plaza de Cultura y Artes, across from the Pico House, on October 8, 2016. I was finally hitting my stride after a nervous start: I could talk and sell the art and the artist just fine, since most were my old friends, but I'd never worked at taking bids. But then I got on a hot roll, selling left and right—until I got to number eleven of twelve, "Echo Park 4," a classic serigraph by Carlos Almaraz. As I was taking the bids, I felt like someone had stuck an invisible vacuum cleaner hose into my back and was sucking the life out of me in slow motion. Then I faded to black in front of three hundred people. I went down, and my head slammed back onto the concrete stage, getting a good crack. I was bleeding when I came to and saw a circle of shocked friends looking down at me. There I was again, like the time I passed out at the Eastside Luv seven years before. But that time, the club was empty except for a few friends. This time I was busted, big-time.

As people helped me up onto the gurney, I realized that my ex-wife Cristina was walking along with me to the ambulance. We got in and were swept away to the hospital. Seeing the concerned look on her face as we spoke about what had just happened touched my heart. Actually, it broke it a little. I was wheeled into the emergency room at L.A. County General, a first, and she stood by my side as I got three staples in my skull, x-rays, brain scan, and heart and blood checked. The verdict was exhaustion. Of course, no sleep, water, or food equals disaster, especially on the eve of a seventy-fourth birthday.

They wanted to keep me for observation, so as she was leaving she said to call if I needed a ride home. I squeezed her hand in gratitude. She looked beautiful as ever. When they finally released me it was late and I didn't want to disturb her, so I called my friend Eréndira, who came by at 3 A.M. and took me home.

Cristina didn't have to ride to the hospital with me. Man, now *that's* love in action. I finally learned what true love is and that it lasts through life's trials by fire, the heartbreaks and disappointments.

A few months later I met Jaclyn Bernstein who was at the gala and saw me fall. She reassured me not to feel embarrassed. She said she saw sparks of light flying out of me as I was calling the auction, and then a large flash as I fell. What the hell? Were the sparks from my Chicano commitment and essence at work? Did she see my soul spark?

Take Me Higher, Mi Reina

WHEN I LIVED ON CATALINA STREET in the mid-fifties, it was just one block from John Fante's apartment on Berendo where he wrote the classic L.A. novel *Ask the Dust,* based on the time he'd lived on Bunker Hill in downtown L.A. in the mid-thirties. Fante's Los Angeles was looked on by a heartless sun that baked his sense of humor, serving up promises wrapped in dust dreams. My L.A. sun kissed me at birth, promising me miracles wrapped in fire, music, and love.

I know Fante's L.A. streets. I still walk them. I know the New Follies on 5th and Main, where I saw my first burlesque show at fifteen years of age (ah Tempest Storm!); the May Company department store on 8th and Broadway with its elaborate Christmas display, a toy electric train chugging around the first floor, a fake Santa with kids on his knee. I know the Grand Central Market on 3rd and Broadway, where I'd shop with my mother for the day's produce for the Mexican restaurant we once owned. I know the Million Dollar Theatre next door, where my parents met and fell in love, and the Paramount Theatre on 6th and Broadway, where I saw Johnny Otis tear it up with the Hollywood Flames and the Three Tons of Joy. I know Olvera Street, where I tasted my first *taquitos* at Cielito Lindo with my father after the war; the Placita church across the street, where Fante's alter ego, Arturo Bandini, prayed for his salvation and where Rubencito was baptized. I know Westlake Park, where I paddled across the lake one night, sensing penny wishes and drowning tears. I know Union Station, that grand cathedral of trapped ghosts of ripped hearts and laughter, where the *pinche* Manifest Destiny Railroad connected east and west on the blistered, busted backs of human beasts of burden. I know 8th and Alameda, where Tongva men, women, and children and other indigenous people were corralled like cattle, left to howl and pray to the moon in honor and in shame. I know Chinatown, where a serene Buddha sits by a clear pond meditating on the reflection of crushed spirits in opium dens and dangling from trees. I know 5th and Broadway, where I saw an exquisite beauty drop a couple of bucks into a tin cup held up by a man-beast with half a face. I know Skid Row, where the Great Depression never left, where I once saw a sign scrawled on a wall saying, "Why is God hiding?"

I know Hollywood, which surgically cuts and carves out live innocent hearts and feeds them to gluttonous executive cannibals. I know the San Fernando Valley, its rich orchards turned into a spiritual wasteland by toxic film studios. I know South Central L.A., where the smoldering embers from the Watts Riots still threaten to ignite as Brown and Black people continue to experience police brutality. I know the warehouses in Southeast L.A. where I unloaded box cars and almost lost my face to sulphuric acid, where the stench of the slaughterhouses grip and rip your gut.

East of the L.A. River with its concrete banks cemented with Angelino apartheid lies *mi querido* Boyle Heights, where murals sing *corrido*-doo-wop–hip-hop epiphanies, where street vendors sell tacos of tongues, ears, brains, and intestines wrapped in corn tortillas with *frijoles, arroz,* and *chiles,* sustenance from over millennia supporting a better dream for a better death. The Evergreen Cemetery crematorium is a couple of blocks from my Boyle Heights bungalow. The dust in my place isn't brown or gray; it's black: each speck a lifetime, each speck a minute, each speck a pregnant dream, each speck a love promised, *por vida.*

And to the west, my beloved Santa Monica. My barrio La Veinte is gone, but the pier still stands, the carousel still turns, the ocean still licks the shore with love, still caresses the memory of Bandini's sweetheart, Camilla López, frolicking free as a shimmering bronze dolphin through the moonlit midnight waves, where sea gulls still squawk cries of hunger, where L.A. cools down on a scorched, homicidal summer night while the San Andreas fault sleeps conjuring an apocalypse.

Fante's doomed heroine, Camilla López, was the indigenous soul of L.A. I don't think he knew that. She was the desert, the sun, the sea, the mountains, the *nopales,* the wildflowers, the wildfires—a beauty Bandini could never understand or have, but only desire. He, like so many immigrants from the Midwest and East, came to a place that promised fast women and sunshine wrapped in skintight gold lamé. They didn't expect the dust, the dirt, the shit, the piss, the vomit, the stepped-on shattered dreams on shiny slick, quicksand sidewalks.

And with all due respect, Mr. Fante, it wasn't marijuana that killed Camilla. It was the color of her skin, a constant reminder that she was Mexican in a town and country that despised her. This was her ancestral land, yet her soul was dishonored serving cheap beer with forced smiles to insatiable transient losers. It was the oppression of dreams and hope that killed her, like it almost killed me.

Yeah, I know you, L.A., and I know you know me. You saw the birth and death of my dreams, and the fears, doubts, and guilt that almost killed me too. So the next time I crash and burn, take me in your arms and wrap me in satin wings of fallen angels, broken promises, unanswered prayers, songs never heard, and the tortured hearts of poets, priests, pimps, and prostitutes.

Now, lets jump on Angel's Flight and soar high above City Hall's pyramid crown, where you breathe with the moon seducing the sunset, where hawks and spirits fly through lightning, where gods and goddesses make love, where angels dance the Pachuko Hop with demons and dogs, where broken hearts search for the soul of your music.

Then hold me tight, L.A.

Tighter.

Now, take me *higher.*

Take me where the Big Bang banged, where stars sing falsetto light, where stardust turns into DNA, where the galaxies dance slow and tight, where love seduces miracles.

Then grab a piece of the sun's bleeding heart and sculpt me into a lusty funk of fire, rhythm, and blues and let my perfect tears and songs of dust caress, and cover, your, our, sinful, sacred, streets.

Then watch me burn, *mi reina de los ángeles.*

And as you stoke the fires of hope and despair, I'll kiss the flames of acceptance, redemption, salvation as I recreate myself in the fiery crucible of your soul—to rise again. And again. And again.

Watch me burn, *mi reina.*

Watch me burn.

Stoke the fire.

Kiss the flames.

c/s

INDEX

activism and benefit concerts, 12–13, 269nn1–2; in 1966 Sunset Strip Riots, 12, 62–63; *¡Angelin@s Presente!,* 325–26, 332; Arts 4 City Youth, 8, 174, 180–81, 262–63; for Boyle Heights, 323; against Columbus Day, 13, 158, 230; "Communities under Siege, Keeping the Faith" panel, 241–42; forums on L.A. muralism and Graff art, 262–63; against Iraq War, 13, 236–43; Manzanar Pilgrimage, 246–50; MEChA, 71, 100; *Mexamérica por la Paz* concert, 236; *Rock 'n' Rights for the Mentally Disabled* concert, 260–61; *Rushing Waters, Rising Dreams* film, 269n2; on Toypurina Monument removal, 257–59; *Who Are the People?,* 12, 73 *fig.,* 74, 79; against Wounded Knee, 253. *See also* protests; riots

Acuña, Rodolfo, 107, 168–69

Adler, Lou, 117, 218, 225

Alaniz, Steve, 292, 301 *fig.*

Algerian Graff art in France, 162–63

Almaraz, Carlos, xii, 142, 159, 174, 325, 332

"Altar de Luz / Altar of Light" (Guevara), 282–83

Altoon, John, 65

Alurista, 154, 162, 297

Álvarez, Gloria Enedina, 178

Amarillas, Pablo, 46–47. *See also* Apollo Brothers

American Indian Dance Theater, 187

"America the Beautiful" (recorded by Guevara), 116–17, 117 *fig.,* 149

América Tropical (film by Treviño), 263

América Tropical (mural by Siqueiros), 200–201, 262

"Amor" (song), 18, 25, 32

Anáhuac, 223n1, 224

Anawalt, Sasha, 218

Las Angelinas, 133, 133 *fig.,* 135

An Angelino Gathering for Ramadan, 241–42

¡Angelin@s Presente!, 325–26

anxiety. *See* depression; panic attacks

Apollo Brothers, 2, 13, 46–48, 50, 52, 81–82, 303

Apollos car club, 12, 44, 46

Apostrophe (Zappa), 103

Arce, Elia, 152

Arellano, Javier, 155

Armendáriz, Alice "Bag", 171, 230

Arte Fronterizo Conceptual, 152

Artists Revitalizing the Eastside (ARTES), 322

Arts 4 City Youth, 8, 174, 180–81, 262–63

Arvizu, Lazaro, 154

Asco, 120, 129, 132, 136

Ask the Dust (Fante), 334, 335–36

"As Long as There's Love" (Guevara), 254–56

Avila, John, 301 *fig.*

¡Ay Califas! Raza Rock: The '70s & '80s, 186

Ayubbi, Asiyah, 326

Azteca (band), 100

Aztec/Mexika culture, 109, 130–34, 130n1, 154

Aztec Watts, Guevara as, 2, 54

Urista, Arturo, 154, 155
US-Mexico Fund for Culture program, 223

Valadez, John, 7, 174–79, 178 *fig.*, 292, 315
Valdez, Patssi, 7, 155, 160 *fig.*, 166
Valens, Ritchie, 45, 56, 218
Van Gogh, Vincent, 163, 164
Van Teers (vocal group), 46
Variety, 102
Vega, Carla, 326
Vegas, Pat and Lolly (né Vázquez), 60
Veracruz, Mexico, 108
the Vibrations (vocal group), 12, 45, 46
"View From the Sixth Street Bridge: A
    History of Chicano Rock" (Guevara),
    228
Village Voice, 128
Villahermosa, Mexico, 109–10
"La Virgencita de Boyle Heights" (Guevara),
    232–33, 294, 302
Viva! (Guevara, Sr.), 23
Volk, Tommy "Flash," 46–47, 81–82. *See
    also* Apollo Brothers
El Vuh, 225

war protests: against Iraq War, 13, 236–43;
    against Vietnam War, 12, 73 *fig.*,
    74, 79
Warren, Robbie "Rodent," 46
Watada, Ehren "Erin," 242–43
Watts 103rd Street Rhythm Band, 269
Watts Riots (1965), 12
West, Bruce, and Laing, 101
"When I Was Young" (Guevara), 283,
    285–86, 292
Whisky a Go Go, 59, 85, 102, 119, 121–22
Whittier Narrows earthquake (1987), 145
Who Are the People? (Guevara), 12, 73 *fig.*,
    74, 79
Wild, Bill, 52, 56, 82, 91
Wild Cards, 133
Williams, Henry, 11, 41, 46
Winterland, 97–98
women in Guevara's life, 3–6, 313–14; Binnie,
    36–37; Enchantress, 196–99; La Gatita,

38, 40–42; Guevara as celibate funk
    monk, 5, 221–22, 283–84, 313–14; L.A.
    poet, 121; Magdalena, 109, 114, 118; Miss
    Altar in the Sky, 276–84, 290; Miss
    Aztlán, 124, 125; Miss Beijing, 306–8;
    Miss Blue Eyes, 95–96; Miss Chino,
    89–90; Miss Claremont, 87–88; Miss
    Mongolia, 203–5; Miss Pamela, 85–86;
    Miss Santa Barbara, 76–79; Miss Tokyo,
    220–21; Southern Belle, 64–65, 66–67,
    103; Xia, 309–11. *See also* marriages of
    Guevara
Wong, Kristina, 7, 267, 269n1, 317
Woodruff, Jeff, 65
Word Up!, 267–69
Wounded Knee protests (1973), 253
Wright, Charles, 269

Xela, 262, 268
X Festival Ibéroamericano del Teatro de
    Bogotá, 264–66
Xia, 309–11
Xicano, 222n1
Xikano, 222, 224, 225, 226, 228, 244, 289,
    292, 294
Xipetotec Danza Azteca, 131, 135

Yanagita, Mike, 246, 315
"Yangna (From the Yangna Hotel)"
    (Guevara), 176–77
Yellow Pearl Remix, 253–54
Yoshida, George, 229–30
"Yuriko and Carlos" (Guevara), 250–52

Zamora, Bobby, 83
Zappa, Frank, 296n1; albums of, 66, 103,
    296n1; connection with Guevara, 8–9,
    80–81; death of, 103; fictitious band by,
    52n1, 66, 296n1; mottos of, 129, 296n1,
    304; partying with, 60; shows with
    Ruben And The Jets, 85, 87, 89, 97–98,
    101. *See also* Frank Zappa and the Moth-
    ers of Invention
Zoot-Suit Riots (1943), 113, 280
Zyanya Records, 128, 186

Made in the USA
Las Vegas, NV
29 September 2021